European Identi
Policy Discourse

This book examines the relationship between national identity construction and current foreign policy discourses on Russia in selected European Union member states in 2014–2018.

It shows that divergent national discourses on Russia derive from the different ways in which the country was constructed in national identity. The book develops an interpretive theoretical framework and argues that policy makers' agency can profoundly influence the contestation between different identity narratives. It includes case studies in policy areas that are of primary importance for EU–Russia relations, such as energy security (the Nord Stream 2 controversy), the Ukraine crisis and Russia's military intervention in Syria. Focusing on EU member states that have traditionally taken different stances vis-à-vis Russia (Germany, Poland and Finland), it shows that at the peak of the Ukraine crisis national discourses converged towards a pragmatic, but critical narrative. As the Ukraine crisis subsided and new events took centre stage in foreign policy discussions (i.e. the Syrian civil war, international terrorism), long-standing and identity-based divergences partly re-emerged in the discourses of policy makers. This became particularly evident during the Nord Stream 2 controversy. Deep-rooted and different perceptions of the Russian Other in EU member states are still influential and lead to divergent national agendas for foreign policy towards Russia.

This book will be of interest to students and scholars working in European and EU politics, Russian and Soviet politics, and International Relations.

Marco Siddi is Senior Research Fellow in the European Union Programme at the Finnish Institute of International Affairs (FIIA), Finland.

Routledge Studies in European Foreign Policy

Series Editors:
Richard Whitman
University of Kent, UK
and
Richard Youngs
University of Warwick, UK

This series addresses the standard range of conceptual and theoretical questions related to European foreign policy. At the same time, in response to the intensity of new policy developments, it endeavours to ensure that it also has a topical flavour, addressing the most important and evolving challenges to European foreign policy, in a way that will be relevant to the policy-making and think-tank communities.

The European Union's Evolving External Engagement
Towards New Sectoral Diplomacies?
Edited by Chad Damro, Sieglinde Gstöhl and Simon Schunz

EU Induced Institutional Change in Post-Soviet Space
Promoting Reforms in Moldova and Ukraine
Ryhor Nizhnikau

The European Union's Approach to Conflict Resolution
Transformation or Regulation in the Western Balkans?
Laurence Cooley

The Proliferation of Privileged Partnerships between the European Union and its Neighbours
Edited by Sieglinde Gstöhl and David Phinnemore

EU–Turkey Relations
Civil Society and Depoliticization
Özge Zihnioğlu

The Politics of the European Neighbourhood Policy
Agnieszka K. Cianciara

European Identities and Foreign Policy Discourses on Russia
From the Ukraine to the Syrian Crisis
Marco Siddi

European Identities and Foreign Policy Discourses on Russia

From the Ukraine to the Syrian Crisis

Marco Siddi

Routledge
Taylor & Francis Group

LONDON AND NEW YORK

First published 2020
by Routledge
2 Park Square, Milton Park, Abingdon, Oxon OX14 4RN

and by Routledge
52 Vanderbilt Avenue, New York, NY 10017

Routledge is an imprint of the Taylor & Francis Group, an informa business

© 2020 Marco Siddi

British Library Cataloguing in Publication Data
A catalogue record for this book is available from the British Library

Library of Congress Cataloging in Publication Data
Names: Siddi, Marco, author.
Title: European identities and foreign policy discourses on Russia : from the Ukraine to the Syrian crisis / Marco Siddi.
Description: Abingdon, Oxon ; New York, NY : Routledge, 2020. | Series: Routledge studies in european foreign policy | Includes bibliographical references and index.
Identifiers: LCCN 2020006744 (print) | LCCN 2020006745 (ebook) | ISBN 9781138231528 (hardback) | ISBN 9781315315164 (ebook)
Subjects: LCSH: Russia (Federation)–Foreign relations–European Union countries. | European Union countries–Foreign relations–Russia (Federation) | National characteristics, European–Political aspects. | Russia (Federation)–Foreign public opinion, European. | Ukraine Conflict, 2014- | Syria–History–Civil War, 2011–Participation, Russian. | Natural gas pipelines–Europe. | Natural gas pipelines–Russia (Federation)
Classification: LCC JZ1616.A54 S53 2020 (print) | LCC JZ1616.A54 (ebook) | DDC 327.4704–dc23
LC record available at https://lccn.loc.gov/2020006744
LC ebook record available at https://lccn.loc.gov/2020006745

ISBN: 978-1-138-23152-8 (hbk)
ISBN: 978-0-367-50610-0 (pbk)
ISBN: 978-1-315-31516-4 (ebk)

Typeset in Times New Roman
by Wearset Ltd, Boldon, Tyne and Wear

Contents

Preface   vi
List of abbreviations   viii

1   Identity, memory and the Russian Other   1

2   Identity and foreign policy: a discourse-historical
    approach   17

3   The historic construction of German, Polish and
    Finnish identities and their Russian Other   34

4   Confronting the Russian Other – the Ukraine crisis   56

5   The EU's discursive strife on Nord Stream 2   82

6   The Russian Other in the Syrian crisis and
    MENA geopolitics   101

    Conclusion: (dis)united we stand? National
    discourses and the Russian Other, 2014–2018   118

Bibliography   130
Index   163

Preface

This book explores the relationship between national identity and political discourses on Russia in Germany, Poland and Finland between 2014 and 2018, in the context of the Ukraine crisis, the Nord Stream 2 project and the Syrian conflict. The book is the outcome of the research that I have conducted during both my doctoral (2010–2014) and postdoctoral (2015–2019) studies. I am particularly thankful to the Finnish Institute of International Affairs, the European Commission, the University of Edinburgh and the University of Cologne for providing me with the means to do the research and write the book. I am also thankful to my partner, Barbara, for her patience during the numerous evenings that I spent writing and editing this book.

The theoretical, methodological and conceptual framework of the book draws largely on the approach I have used in my PhD dissertation and my first book publication, M. Siddi, *National Identities and Foreign Policy in the European Union* (2017b). While my first book focused on the years 2005–2014 – taking the first Nord Stream project, the 2008 Russian–Georgian War, the protests in Russian cities in 2011–2012 and the outbreak of the Ukraine crisis as case studies – this book analyses more recent empirical material. Since 2015, the security debate in EU–Russia relations has extended to other contexts beyond Ukraine, most notably the Syrian conflict, Middle Eastern and Mediterranean geopolitics. Sanctions and disagreements over Ukraine have become the 'new normal' but attempts to mediate the conflict have continued. Moreover, confrontation in the Ukraine crisis has spilled over to aspects of domestic security in EU member states, as highlighted by allegations of Russian interference in European electoral processes. I have analysed these issues also in my FIIA Report, M. Siddi, *EU Member States and Russia: National debates in an evolving international environment* (2018a).

At the same time, some European member states have maintained and even reinforced economic cooperation with Russia in strategic fields, most notably energy trade. The Nord Stream 2 project exemplifies this cooperation, in defiance of contemporary political tensions. This was also the subject of my article 'Theorising conflict and cooperation in EU–Russia energy relations: ideas, identities and material factors in the Nord Stream 2 debate', published in the journal *East European Politics* (2019). Chapter 5 of this book expands on this work, with more specific analysis on German, Polish and Finnish debates. Russia continues to be an essential provider of energy to the European Union. After 2015, it has showed that it can play a decisive role in numerous and important contexts, ranging from the Middle East to the Iranian nuclear deal and economic and security relations with China. Hence, for the European Union and its member states, Russia remains an inescapable interlocutor. This book investigates how the interaction of identity-based narratives on Russia with current international events shapes different European discourses and policy responses towards the Kremlin.

Helsinki, February 2020

Abbreviations

AA	Association Agreement
DHA	Discourse-Historical Analysis
EEU	Eurasian Economic Union
EU	European Union
FSA	Free Syrian Army
LNG	liquefied natural gas
MENA	Middle East and North Africa
NATO	North Atlantic Treaty Organisation
OPEC	Organisation of the Petroleum Exporting Countries
OSCE	Organisation for Security and Co-operation in Europe
UN	United Nations

1 Identity, memory and the Russian Other

Since the beginning of the Ukraine crisis and the annexation of Crimea in March 2014, Russia has returned to the centre stage of European political debates. Analysts and politicians have argued that in 2014 'the European security system established in the wake of the Cold War collapsed in a spectacular manner' (Sakwa 2017: 1), and described the ensuing confrontation between Russia and the West as 'the most profound menace to European security for many decades' (Youngs 2017: 1). While some scholars have described the Ukraine conflict as the culmination of a long-term crisis in relations between the European Union (EU) and Russia (Forsberg and Haukkala 2016), most observers were surprised by its timing and intensity. In the EU, Russia was increasingly seen as a revisionist actor, and no longer as a strategic partner. In Russia, the EU was portrayed as a deceptive and declining power that irresponsibly supported a coup d'état in Ukraine as part of a hegemonic geopolitical agenda (DeBardeleben 2018).

What is more, after 2014, tensions between the EU and Russia extended beyond the Ukraine crisis to other fields and theatres. Russia's military intervention in the Syrian crisis in September 2015 heightened European concerns about the tumultuous developments in the Middle East, at a time when a growing number of people from this region sought asylum in the EU. While the EU plunged in an internal crisis due to the reluctance of many member states to host asylum seekers, Russian officials stated that Western and EU support of the Arab Spring contributed to destabilising the Middle East and North Africa, and thus to the intensification of the humanitarian crisis (Dannreuther 2019). On the other hand, some analysts argued that the humanitarian crisis provided an opportunity for Russia to put pressure on European leaders. The alleged Russian support of European far right parties (cf. Shekhovtsov 2018), which used the crisis to challenge the political establishment, was seen as part of this scheme. As populist forces won elections in the US and Europe, Russia was also accused of interfering in Western democratic processes as part of a multifaceted 'hybrid war' (Siddi 2018a).

At the same time, and despite the mutual imposition of sanctions, the path dependencies forged between Russia and the EU during previous decades prevented a complete breakdown in relations. In fact, EU–Russia energy trade continued almost unhindered and even grew in volume during the Ukraine crisis

(Siddi 2018b). In the EU, Russia continued to be seen as an important interlocutor for the resolution of crises such as the one in Syria, and even as a like-minded partner in the international negotiations concerning the Iranian nuclear programme. Most significantly for this book, different views persisted in EU member states regarding the best way to approach to Russia. While political leaders in Poland and the Baltic States framed Russia as a geopolitical threat, their colleagues in Italy, Germany and France considered dialogue with Moscow as an essential precondition for a stable security system. The deep crisis and quick succession of political developments in which Russia was involved (or was considered to be involved) since 2014 reawakened constructions of the Russian Other that had become part of national identity narratives in European countries over the previous decades, or even centuries (Siddi 2017b). In turn, these constructions contributed to shaping the response of European states towards Russia in the post-2014 crises.

The book explores the relationship between national identities and foreign policy discourses concerning Russia in selected member states of the European Union. In doing so, it builds on previous studies that focused on European and national identities and the role of external factors in the process of identity construction. An increasingly large body of European Studies literature has explored the emergence of a shared European identity (cf. Bayley and Williams 2012, Checkel and Katzenstein 2009, Herrmann *et al.* 2004, Kuhn 2015, Risse 2010). These works generally argue that European identity is, at best, still developing next to national identities. Following Willfried Spohn's (2005: 2) categorisation, three main perspectives can be identified in the literature. The first sees European identity as a weak addendum to strong national identities. The second one assumes that European identity will unfold in the long run and restructure national identities through the gradual Europeanisation of the latter. The third one hypothesises the future emergence of a variable mix of European and national identities. Some scholars have highlighted that the attachment to a European identity is stronger among particular social groups within each country, and that European and national identities are not necessarily mutually exclusive (Kuhn 2015). Broadly speaking, however, most scholarship converges on the argument that national identities remain more influential than constructions of a shared European identity.

As these initial observations suggest, national identities play an important role in Europe and may provide a key to understanding European politics. Scholars studying nationalism have argued that we are unlikely to see the transcendence of national identities by a strong European identity during our lifetime (Smith 1996a: 363). The recent revival of nationalist and Eurosceptic parties in many European countries seems to corroborate this argument. Researchers working on memory politics, a discipline that partly overlaps with identity studies, have come to similar conclusions in their assessments of the prospects for a common European memory: national discourses are pervasive in collective memory and can hardly be reconciled into a shared European discourse (Bell 2006: 16, Jarausch and Lindenberger 2007: 1, Pakier and Stråth 2010,

Siddi 2017a). This is not surprising, as nation-states have a much longer history than European institutions. Linguistic, historical and cultural differences contribute to the endurance of national identities and of political constructions that draw their legitimacy from national communities.

The focus on the national level in this book should not lead to the assumption that the concept of European identity can simply be dismissed. A feeling of attachment to Europe and to the political structures of the European Union is observable both among European elites and citizens, however weak and inconsistent it might be (cf. Standard Eurobarometer 83 2015: 112, 123). The creation of a common European market, the removal of barriers to the free movement of citizens and numerous transnational schemes have contributed to its emergence. However, as most of the relevant scholarly literature argues, in Europe national identities and memories are still stronger than transnational ones. Studying national identities is thus important to understand both the dilemmas surrounding European identity and, most importantly, current European politics.

Social constructivist literature has highlighted the strong relationship between national identity and foreign policy discourses.[1] The book applies a social constructivist theoretical model to examine this relationship in three European states – Germany, Poland and Finland – and assess the prospects for a shared European foreign policy discourse concerning Russia. The key argument is that divergent national foreign policy approaches to Russia are due to the different ways in which the country was constructed in national identity. However, the analysis also shows that national identity is malleable, and a country's leaders can reformulate dominant narratives in order to achieve particular foreign policy goals. Under certain circumstances, for instance in response to major international crises, national discourses on Russia can be reconciled if divisive identity narratives are marginalised and common foreign policy goals are pursued.

Relations with Russia have been chosen as a litmus test for a shared European foreign policy discourse because they have proven to be one of the most dividing issues among European Union countries (Cadier 2014, Casier 2011, David and Romanova 2015, David *et al.*, 2011 and 2013, Gromyko 2015, Haukkala 2015 and 2010a, Korosteleva 2016, Nitoiu 2016, Romanova 2016). In 2007, former EU trade commissioner Peter Mandelson stated that 'no other country reveals our differences as does Russia' (cited in Kagan 2008: 14). Over a decade later, such divisions continue to exist and are reflected in the different stances of EU member states concerning the future of relations with Russia after the Ukraine crisis (Emmott 2016, Romanova 2016). Russia is the EU's largest neighbour, a key energy supplier and an essential, though often very controversial factor in the European security architecture. As highlighted by the profound crisis that erupted in Ukraine in the fall of 2013, the European Union and its member states cannot guarantee the stability of their Eastern neighbours without taking into account Russia as a geopolitical factor. Furthermore, the political system built by post-Soviet Russian leaders arguably challenges some of the European Union's founding values, particularly in the field of democracy and human rights (Shiraev 2013).[2]

Relations with Russia are a test for the very idea of a united EU foreign policy because they have traditionally been based on a bilateral, national dimension. The most frequent explanations for this bilateralism refer to the different economic interests and security concerns of EU member states, as well as to Russia's preference for dealing with European countries separately (cf. David *et al.* 2011: 183–184). This book proposes an alternative understanding of the EU's and its member states' relations with Russia that is based on national identity. The focus on national identity provides a useful research angle because, in contrast with predominant analyses focusing on power politics and economics, it seeks to explain relations with Russia through an investigation of historical and cultural factors.

The conceptualisation of identity as a key element in international relations provides a much-needed alternative to realist and liberal institutionalist models framed around the notions of anarchy, balance of power and institutional cooperation. The book analyses international relations as a social construction, of which national identities are essential constituents. Drawing on constructivist literature, a theoretical model is developed highlighting the mutually constitutive relationship among national identity, interests and foreign policy discourses. In particular, the historical dimension of national identity formation is explored in order to examine its relevance in current foreign policy discourses. Hence, the book adopts a historicist approach, which assigns key importance to cultural and historical context. Foreign policy discourses are studied through discourse-historical analysis (DHA), a variant of critical discourse analysis developed by Ruth Wodak (2002a). DHA was previously used by scholars to study debates about immigration and identity politics in the media, in EU institutions and among the wider public (Krzyzanowski 2010 and 2009, Oberhuber *et al.* 2005, Reisigl and Wodak 2001, Wodak 2009). This book constitutes one of the first applications of the methodology to the analysis of national foreign policy elites' public discourses.

Empirically, the book also contributes to the understanding of the European Union's and its member states' current foreign policy towards the Eastern neighbourhood. It constitutes an attempt to strengthen the strand of research focusing on the role of nationalism, identity and memory politics in EU–Russia relations. The surge of nationalist sentiment and widespread political use of history during the current Ukrainian crisis has exposed that these are powerful factors in EU–Russia relations (Klymenko 2019, Luhn 2014, Siddi 2017a). The book shows that national identity and memory politics played an important role in this relationship well before the beginning of turmoil in Ukraine. The empirical chapters highlight the significance of identity and memory politics in events that took place during the last decade in fields of extreme importance for the EU, such as energy security, the stability of the neighbourhood and Russia's role in the European security system. Through an interdisciplinary approach combining social constructivist theory, discourse theory and historical analysis, the book sheds light on the deep identity and cultural roots of relevant foreign policy discourses.

The focus of the empirical analysis is restricted to key foreign policy leaders (heads of state or government and foreign ministers) for reasons of feasibility and relevance. Covering thoroughly three national discursive arenas, each having thousands of participants, would not be possible within the scope of this book. However, in countries such as those under analysis, key foreign policy decisions are ultimately made by a restricted group of leaders who received a mandate from a parliamentary majority or a majority of electors. These leaders also represent the country internationally and, thanks to their political prominence, they have the discursive power to steer the country's main foreign policy debates. Most important for this analysis, their behaviours and decisions are influenced by the national identities in which they are embedded.[3] Furthermore, the discourses of state officials enjoy a powerful position in constructing national identity due to their access to information from the state, their constitutional legitimacy, and privileged access to the media (Aydın-Düzgit 2018).

National identity is a very useful concept to understand the domestic construction of international politics because it encompasses and is forged by the defining cultural, historical and political constituents of a state. Its relationship with foreign policy discourses is complex. It is mutually constitutive, because national identity and foreign policy discourses influence each other. It is also malleable, because the two concepts are in constant flux and change over time. Moreover, as Aydın-Düzgit (2018) has noted, foreign policy is a key area through which state officials' role in the discursive construction of a state's identity becomes possible and visible. For some scholars, the notion of national identity might be elusive (cf. Malesevic 2011). However, it is exactly the complexity of the concept and its changing and multifaceted nature that make it a fascinating research topic. National identities are not the only element in the complex scenario of international politics, but certainly one that scholars cannot ignore in a comprehensive analysis.

Nations, national identity and collective memory

Constructivist scholars argue that grasping the relationship between national identity and foreign policy is essential in order to understand international relations. Before exploring why this might be so, it is fundamental to define and explore the concepts of nation and national identity. Due to their diverse uses and confusion with concepts such as nationalism, the terms are highly ambiguous and have generated a lively discussion among academics. The most relevant debates took place among historians and sociologists who, especially from the 1980s onwards, attempted to assess the role played by nations and nationalism in international politics during modern and contemporary times.

Prominent scholars such as Ernest Gellner, Eric Hobsbawm, Benedict Anderson and Anthony D. Smith used different parameters to define nation and national identity, alternatively emphasising concrete elements (for instance territory, economy), psychological and abstract factors (memories, myths) or both. Some considered the terms too ambiguous for a precise classification and adopted only working definitions (Hobsbawm 1990), others rejected them altogether as explanatory variables (Malesevic 2011). Most treated national identity as a corollary of the nation, a collective belief in belonging to a national community and to its defining elements. Although the relationship between nation and national identity is in fact more complex, a close link exists between the two concepts. To understand national identity, we thus have to grasp the concept of nation first (cf. Guibernau 2004: 134, Smith 1991: 9).

One of the most widely debated definitions of nation is the one provided by Anthony D. Smith (1996a: 359): 'A named human population sharing a historic territory, common myths and memories, a mass public culture, a single economy and common rights and duties for all members'. Smith's definition provides an apparently easy way out of terminological issues: it includes both the concrete and the abstract factors highlighted in previous definitions of nations. However, Smith broadens the scope of the definition at the expense of clarity: does a nation need to satisfy all these characteristics to be classified as such? Which elements are more important? Furthermore, additional terminological problems arise: what is 'a mass public culture' and what is meant by 'historic territory'? Cannot diasporas constitute or be part of a nation because they do not share a historic territory?

Smith's definition reveals one of the main confusions that occur in debates on the nature of nations: by listing 'common rights and duties for all members' as one of their key elements, it conflates the concepts of nation and state. As Montserrat Guibernau (2004: 127) argues, judicial functions pertain to the state and are not inherent in the nation. While most nations have their own states, and thus also their own judicial systems, some do not. Furthermore, due to immigration and globalisation, many states are no longer nation-states: they include sizeable minorities that are bound by the same rights and duties and yet do not lose their distinctive identity. To avoid confusion, states and nations have to be classified differently. Borrowing from Max Weber's conceptual framework, a state can be defined on the basis of its coercive powers, namely as a body that successfully claims monopoly of legitimate force in a particular territory (cited in Miller 1997: 19–20). A state has the means to enforce its rules and a legal system to discipline those who do not comply with them.

In contrast, a nation is defined more by feelings of attachment to both concrete and abstract elements, rather than in terms of powers and prerogatives. Ernest Gellner (1983: 7), a pioneer in the study of nationalism, identified two essential components of the nation, namely a shared culture – broadly meant as a system of ideas, signs, associations and ways of behaving and communicating – and its members' mutual recognition of belonging to the same nation. Gellner stressed that nations are human artefacts, social constructions deriving from people's convictions and loyalties. Benedict Anderson (1991: 6) also focused on the constructed nature of nations and defined them as 'imagined political communities'. According to him, nations are imagined because the members of even the smallest nations will never meet most of their fellow members, but the image of belonging to a single community lives in all their minds.

Anderson argued that nations are political communities because they emerged simultaneously to concepts such as popular sovereignty (namely the idea that political power rests in the hands of the people), at the time of the Enlightenment and of the French Revolution. The argument that nations originated with the advent of the modern age connects them closely with nationalism, namely the political principle which holds that the political and national unit should be congruent (Gellner 1983: 1). This connection generated a lively debate among academics. According to modernists such as Ernest Gellner, Eric Hobsbawm, Montserrat Guibernau and Benedict Anderson, nations emerged in modern times because they were the product of nationalism. Conversely, ethno-symbolists such as Anthony D. Smith and John Hutchinson argued that the constitutive elements of many nations, notably their foundation myths and their ethnic and cultural heritage, predated the French Revolution and the modern age (Guibernau and Hutchinson 2004, Smith 1996a).

The academic dispute between modernists and ethno-symbolists was arguably the longest and liveliest in the field of nationalism studies so far. It is relevant to this analysis because it highlights different ways of conceptualising the nation and national identity. Modernists claim that, from the early nineteenth century on, nationalists were successful in disseminating the concept of nation thanks to mass schooling and the standardisation of national languages (Hobsbawm 1990: 10). Nationalists carefully selected pre-existing cultural elements and branded them as defining components of the nation (Gellner 1983: 55). Hence, according to modernists, nations are constructed entities and national identity is a fabrication of the modern state, which attempts to gain the support of citizens by uniting them in a single national community (Guibernau 2004: 140).

Ethno-symbolists concur that creating national identities was one of the objectives of the nationalist movement during the nineteenth century. However, they maintain that collective memories, cultural heritage and traditions developed before the age of nationalism played the key role in the formation of nations. According to ethno-symbolists, modern nations are not simply political constructions or imagined communities, but are founded on concrete cultural elements and tend to have strong ties to pre-modern ethnic identities. Ethnic groups are considered as the precursors of nations, having 'shared ancestry myths and memories or "ethno-history", with a strong association [...] to a historic territory or homeland' (Smith 1994: 382). The emphasis on ethnicity highlights the major weakness of the ethno-symbolist approach: in order to define the nation, it introduces other concepts that are equally ambiguous. The same criticism applies to modernist definitions, which refer to the complex phenomenon of nationalism to explain the emergence of nations and national identity. Although all these concepts are interrelated, cross-references in their classification are confusing. A clear and comprehensive definition of nation and national identity should take into account the most insightful observations of ethno-symbolists and modernists, without relying on equivocal terms.

David Miller's (1997: 18, 22–27) definition of a nation provides a good starting point. According to Miller, a nation is a community with shared beliefs and mutual commitment, extended in history and connected to a particular territory. It is marked off from other nations by a distinct public culture, including political principles, social norms and cultural ideals. Like Gellner, Miller argues that members' mutual commitment and recognition of one another as compatriots is an essential precondition for the emergence of a nation. This reciprocal sense of obligation is extended over time, in the past, present and future, and ensures the historical continuity of the nation. Collective memories play an important role in this respect, as they remind the members of a nation of their forebears' presumed achievements and cultural heritage.

Collective memories are instrumental to the formation of national identities. National identity can be defined as the psychological attachment of a collective to the nation and its defining elements. Shared memories and culture are the main sustaining factors of this attachment, as they constitute the core of narratives stimulating identification with the nation (Anderson 1991: 205). As Anthony D. Smith (1996b: 383) argues, 'only by remembering the past can a collective identity come into being'. Collective memories provide the 'cognitive maps and mobilising moralities of nations as they struggle to win and maintain recognition' (Smith 1988: 14). According to Smith (1996b: 384–385), vital elements of the nation such as its drive for regeneration, the sense of national authenticity, collective mission and national destiny depend on collective memory. Similarly, Eric Hobsbawm and David Kertzer (1992: 3) argue that 'nations without a past are contradictions in terms. What makes a nation *is* the past; what justifies one nation against others is the past'.

The politics of memory and national identity

While Hobsbawm and Smith are right to emphasise the importance of the past for national identity, the way in which a nation remembers its past is more complex and ambiguous than their statements may suggest. In fact, the collective memory and the past of a nation are fundamentally different concepts. The term 'collective memory' refers to the shared memories held by a community about the past (Hunt 2010: 97), an image of the past constructed by a subjectivity in the present (Megill 2011: 196). Collective memory is a discourse about historical events and how to interpret them based on a community's current social and historical necessities (Arnold-de Simine 2005: 10, Pakier and Stråth 2010: 7). It is neither a mere or accurate reflection of the past, nor the product of historical research. As Maurice Halbwachs (1992) argues, collective memories are socially framed: they form when people come together to remember and enter a domain that transcends individual memory. According to Andreas Huyssen (2003: 6), collective memory is also essential to imagine the future and give a strong temporal and spatial grounding to life.

The study of collective memory is of particular relevance at institutional level (Lebow 2006: 13–14). Political elites formulate or adopt selective discourses of past events in order to forge national identities that strengthen social cohesion. In particular, politicians try to forge national memories, a particular type of collective memory where the collective coincides with the nation (Gillis 1994: 7). National memory is disseminated primarily via political leaders' official discourses and commemorations in realms of memory (*lieux de mémoire*), namely historical or pseudo-historical sites that are reminiscent of selected events in national memory (Nora 1992: 7). This does not preclude the role of other, unofficial actors in the forging of national memory. Individual or other group memories coexist side by side with official national memories and often influence them. However, political leaders play a decisive role in the construction and diffusion of national memory because they have easier access to mass media, which makes them highly influential. Richard Ned Lebow, Wulf Kansteiner and Claudio Fogu (2006) call the selection and dissemination of discourses on a country's past 'the politics of memory'. It involves actors who use their public prominence to propagate narratives about the past which are functional to their political goals (Lebow 2006: 26–28).

Memory matters politically because it can be used by the political establishment as a source of legitimacy for its power. For instance, policy makers can make reference to events that play an important role in national memory and construct plausible historical analogies to obtain support for their policies (Bell 2006: 20, Gildea 2002a: 59, Koczanowicz 1997: 260, König 2008: 27–34, Olick 2007: 122). The inherent ambiguity of collective memories, which are in constant flux, facilitates their manipulation and mobilisation in the service of national identity formation (Berger 2002: 81, Müller 2002: 21–22, Ray 2006: 144). As Emmanuel Sivan and Jay Winter (1999: 6) have noted, political elites manipulated the past on a massive scale during the twentieth century. Manipulations of national history took place in particular after wars and regime changes, when states and new political elites attempted to restore social cohesion. Following major social dislocations, political elites tend to formulate and propagate official narratives that reflect their view of history and exclude all events and elements that do not fit therein (Hunt 2010: 110). They construct national histories as triumphant narratives, a selective retelling of the past based on accounts that stimulate strong identification with the nation (Eder 2005: 214–215).

Due to the constant influence of a multiplicity of political, historical and social factors, collective memories are not fixed; they undergo a process of gradual change and adaptation. As Pierre Nora (1989: 8) argues, national memories are constantly constructed and reconstructed in a selective way; they are 'in permanent evolution, a perpetually present phenomenon'. During the last 20–30 years, this process has been fuelled by a dramatic upsurge of public memory debates in North American and European societies (Huyssen 2003: 12–15). Politicians have attempted to intervene and guide these debates in a way that suited and served both their political aspirations and their conception of national identity (Gillis 1994: 3, Müller 2002: 23, Smith 2011: 235).

A widespread use of the politics of memory to forge national identities took place in almost all European countries immediately after the Second World War and again after 1989 in most East-Central European countries, following the collapse of the Soviet bloc (Assmann 2006: 260, Evans 2003: 5, Judt 1992: 96).[4]

Both in 1945 and 1989, the new political elites that emerged from the ordeal of war and from regime change needed founding myths to strengthen social cohesion at a time of economic dislocation and transformation from authoritarian to democratic forms of government (Müller 2002: 7–9). This political necessity led new leaders to search for a 'usable past' in national history and reframe it in narratives that propped present political goals (Moeller 2003a).

The national memories that were constructed in Western Europe after 1945 and in East-Central Europe after 1989 constitute the core of current national memory discourses. This is due to the fact that many of the founding myths of today's national political systems in Europe date back from these two historical moments. In countries such as the ones under analysis in this work, the images of Russia that crystallised in national memories during these periods, partly in continuity with pre-existing perceptions and partly based on new elements, influenced the process of national identity construction. Thus, particular perceptions of Russia as a foreign policy actor have become enshrined in national consciousness and still affect attitudes to Moscow.[5]

National memory can be conceptualised as an essential component and driving factor of national identity. Unsurprisingly, the two concepts share many of their essential features. Like national memories, national identities are multiple, malleable, contested and provide a powerful instrument for the political elites that have enough power to manipulate them. Their multiplicity derives from different conceptions of national identity across the large and diverse national community. However, states tend to propagate one particular narrative of national identity, which becomes dominant in official discourses. Individual and other group identities coexist and interact with officially endorsed versions of national identity, thereby creating alternative and competing variants that can become dominant within new historical and institutional contexts.[6]

National identities are malleable because they are influenced by domestic and external events and can change over time (Rumelili and Todd 2018, Siddi 2018c). Changes usually take place gradually; core constituents such as the founding myths and cultural frameworks of reference of the nation (notably in literature, the arts and music) are relatively stable. However, sudden changes in national identity discourses may also occur, particularly when historical events force upon the nation a reconsideration of its values and interests.[7] Moreover, national identities are contested because they are subject to manipulations by social groups vying for dominance and because they compete for people's allegiance with class, religious, local and supranational identities (Miller 1997: 45–46). Narratives of national identity tend to be used as political instruments because they are generally formulated and propagated by the state in order to strengthen and legitimate the existing political system (Guibernau 2004: 140). Political leaders are both the main advocates and beneficiaries of national identity construction. National identity promotes homogeneity in a community because it cuts across class and local differences and transcends divisions of rank, descent, region and profession. It is therefore functional to the creation of a strong bond between political leaders and ordinary citizens, as well as among different sections of the population (Benner 2001: 162, Greenfeld 1990: 550).

Since national identity provides a very useful tool for the unity and cohesiveness of a state, governments employ several strategies to promote it. They disseminate a specific image of the nation that usually relates to the dominant ethnic group. In addition, they confer citizenship and advance numerous symbols and rituals that serve the purpose of reinforcing the sense of community among citizens, as well as their loyalty towards the state. National identity is constructed also through the steering of public education and the mass media. This phenomenon is particularly marked in authoritarian states but also exists in democratic countries.

Furthermore, states often attempt to strengthen national identity by creating external enemies (Guibernau 2004: 140). For instance, France and Germany constructed each other as external threats for nearly a century (from the 1860s to the 1940s) and used the image of the menacing neighbour to foster national unity in moments of crisis. Past rivalries in Franco–German relations left a trace in national identity that influenced the political debate at a later stage, as shown by the French reservations about German reunification in 1989–1990 (Gildea 2002b). Similar patterns of national identity formation against an external Other, namely an actor that tends to be perceived as alien and antithetical, can be detected *inter alia* in Soviet–US, US–Chinese and Europe–Russia relations.[8]

Russia as Europe's Other

As Iver Neumann (1998: 67–112) has shown, numerous primary sources suggest that Russia has played the role of Europe's Other for more than four centuries. This is not to say that Russia was the only or the main Other for Europe throughout this long historical phase. For instance, Turkey was also a significant external actor against which European and national identities were constructed. Moreover, discourses on Russia were not homogeneous all over the continent and differed depending *inter alia* on the social milieu, political orientation and personal experiences of observers. Nevertheless, numerous and significant patterns consistently pointing at Russia as Europe's Other can be detected throughout this period. Studying these patterns is essential and of current relevance because Russia is still central to national identity discourses and to the debate on European identity. As Morozov (2018: 32) has put it, Russia has become an 'indispensable Other for the EU'. Analysing dominant perceptions of Russia also helps to understand present political discussions, such as the one concerning the European security order (Webber 2009).

Furthermore, Russia has often played an active role in European identity politics by negotiating and contesting dominant discursive constructions (Rumelili and Morozov 2012). Russia has consistently defined its own identity in relation to Europe. This continued to be true also at times of reciprocal tensions. The often-quoted dispute between Russian 'Westernisers' and 'Slavophiles' concerned the question of whether Western Europe should serve as a role model for Russia or if Russia itself should become the leader of European (and world) civilisation. None of the sides in this controversy questioned Russia's European nature, even if some Slavophiles placed it within a broader Eurasian framework and attributed to it a global civilising mission (Tsygankov 2008: 766–770). Even during the current crisis in Ukraine, Russia took the EU as a model for the institutional setup of its own regional integration project, the Eurasian Economic Union (Samokhvalov 2017: 212). The Eurasian Union was conceptualised as complementing, rather than competing with the EU; it was an articulation of the Russian vision of a 'Greater Europe' from Lisbon to Vladivostok (Sakwa 2017: 147). Hence, as Morozov (2018: 31) has claimed, Russia's identity is 'undoubtedly European', but its 'Europeanness is fundamentally conditioned by its subaltern position in the European international society and the global capitalist system'. Western representations have contributed to consolidating (self-)perceptions of Russia's subalternity and marginality vis-à-vis the European 'centre'.

European depictions of Russia show a tendency to portray it as a liminal case of European identity. Russians were often depicted as barbarous and deficient in terms of civility, form of government and religion (Poe 2003: 21). The first depictions of Russia as 'the barbarian at the gates', a recurrent theme in European discourses of the powerful Eastern neighbour, emerged in the descriptions of Russian soldiers during the Northern War against Sweden in the early eighteenth century. Around the same time, geographical handbooks argued that Russians were constructed as 'body and nature', whereas Europeans were constructed as 'mind and civilization'. The metaphor of the Russian *ursa major*, which associated Russia with wild nature, originated in this context. Its endurance over time is demonstrated by the fact that it is still used today in modern variants, most notably the depiction of Russia as a threatening and irascible bear (Naarden 1992: 7–27, Neumann 1998: 67–80).

During the Napoleonic wars, Russian soldiers advanced as far as Paris and, after Napoleon's defeat, Russia was accepted as a legitimate player in the Concert of Europe. However, this acceptance was relativised by the enduring perception of Russia as 'the barbarian at the gates', a country that lacked the rationality which had become a defining element of European civilisation during the Enlightenment. European liberals, democrats and socialists were particularly keen on describing Russia as a socially and economically backward power. Conversely, conservative forces saw it as a bulwark of legitimism and of the European *ancien régime* (Neumann 1998: 66–93, 96–97). The Bolshevik revolution inverted radical and conservative views of Russia. The Bolsheviks' radical political programme made the Soviet Union a threat to conservative political elites in the rest of Europe throughout the interwar period. The threat was substantiated by the fact that the Soviet Union could count on the extraterritorial presence of faithful allies, organised in European communist parties. On the other hand, numerous European radicals praised the political and economic system of the USSR, as well as the allegedly higher morality of the Soviet model (Naarden 1992: 28–39, Neumann 1998: 99–102, Service 2007: 85–96).

During the Second World War, the idea of the Russians as a barbarous civilisation was pushed to the extreme by the Nazi racial discourse, which depicted them and all other Slavic peoples as sub-humans (*Untermenschen*). The idea that Russians should be excluded from humankind, and not just from Europe, was radically new (Müller and Ueberschär 2009: 209–252). However, there was continuity between some themes used by Nazi propaganda and pre-existing discourses about Russians, such as the claim that they were a barbarous and uncivilised Asiatic people. Some of these themes also characterised discourses about the Soviet Union in the post-war period; Konrad Adenauer's 1946 statement that 'Asia stands on the Elbe' (cited in Rupnik 1994: 94) provides an excellent example in this respect. Adenauer referred to the presence of the Red Army in Eastern and Central Europe, which became one of the main determinants of European perceptions of the Soviet Union during the Cold War. While in the inter-war period the Soviet Union had been mostly perceived as a political threat, during the Cold War it primarily constituted a military threat in the mindsets of most West Europeans. The perception of a political threat persisted in the immediate post-war period, but gradually decreased as communist parties in Western Europe lost their support or became critical of the Soviet Union (Neumann 1998: 99–100, Service 2007: 261–271, 379–390).

The Cold War played an important role in the construction of European perceptions of Russia also because it became the setting in which a distinct East-Central European narrative developed. This discourse, fiercely critical of both the Soviet Union and of its perceived Russian core, emerged in East-Central European countries that were located within the Soviet sphere of influence and was reflected in the writings of dissident intellectuals from the region. Milan Kundera's (1984) article *The Tragedy of Central Europe* is the most representative of these writings. Kundera, a Czech writer living in exile in France, argued that Central Europe (in which he included the nations of the former Austro-Hungarian Empire and Poland) was a part of the West that had been 'kidnapped, displaced and brainwashed [by the] totalitarian Russian civilisation'. According to Kundera, Central Europe was the cultural heart of Europe and its separation from Western Europe meant that the latter was losing its cultural identity. On the other hand, Central Europe kept defending its identity and 'preserving its Westerness' despite the Soviet domination. The main difference between Central Europe and Russia, Kundera argued, was above all cultural, as demonstrated by the fact that the anti-Soviet revolts of 1956 and 1968 were led by local students and intellectuals. One of the key objectives in Kundera's article was that of drawing the attention of the Western world towards the oppression of East-Central European countries under Soviet influence. In order to show that these countries culturally belonged to Europe while Soviet Russia did not, he described the former as the 'vital centre of gravity of Western culture' and the latter as 'the radical negation of the modern West'.

Kundera's views on Russia were echoed by other intellectuals from East-Central Europe. Different epithets, such as 'Second World', 'authoritarian' and 'totalitarian' (as opposed to 'First World', 'democratic' and 'free'), were associated with Soviet Russia in order to differentiate it from Europe and the West. Some extreme voices in the intellectual world used racial arguments against Russia. For instance, Hungarian philosopher Mihaly Vajda (1989: 170–173) argued that Russia had made the choice to become non-European and that Russians were 'incapable of tolerating another civilization, another form of life'. Vajda also spoke of 'the Russian beast' and Russian practices of 'holocaust, imprisonment, banishment, exile', forgetting that the Holocaust was actually a page of European history, rather than a Russian crime, and that its perpetrators had spoken of Russia in a way very similar to his own.

In 1989, when the Soviet Union left its satellites free to choose their political future and the incumbent leaders were ousted from their posts, new East-Central European political leaders such as Vaclav Havel started to speak of a 'return to Europe' (Powers 1990). However, it soon became clear that the Central Europe to which Kundera had referred to in his 1984 essay had not emerged from the Cold War as a united political or cultural entity. East-Central European countries had only managed to pass themselves off as a united entity vis-à-vis third parties by using the image of the Soviet Union as a common Other. After 1989, the new East-Central European leaders emphasised cultural differences between their countries and Russia, with the objective of creating a Self compatible with Western Europe and strenuously opposed to Russia. This strategy was meant to create the cultural preconditions, both at home and abroad, for the integration of East-Central European countries into the EU and NATO (Neumann 1998: 144, 158).

When East-Central European states joined the European Union, they brought along the legacy of four decades of resentment and confrontation with Soviet Russia. In some cases, notably those of Poland and the three Baltic States, anti-Russian feelings dated back from much earlier than the Cold War period. Anti-Russian discourses and attitudes in these countries did not vanish once their 'return to Europe' had been accomplished. Historical conflicts, the enduring fear of a resurgent Russian military might and economic issues, aggravated by the energy dependence of East-Central Europe on Russia, continued to characterise the relations of the former Soviet satellites with Moscow. Furthermore, conflicts between the new East-Central European EU member states and Russia were transferred to the EU level and risked paralysing EU–Russia relations. Poland's decision to veto negotiations on a new partnership agreement between the EU and Russia in 2006, following a quarrel over a Russian import ban on Polish meat, was the clearest manifestation of this.

The persistence of European perceptions of Russia as a liminal case of European identity was not only the result of East-Central European countries joining the EU and gaining discursive power within its institutions. As argued, constructions of Russia as Europe's Other were widespread also in Western Europe and did not vanish with the end of the Cold War. With regard to Russia, Western thinking continued to display features typical of Orientalism, such as the exaggeration of difference, assumptions of Western superiority and resort to clichéd analytical models (Brown 2010). These ideational constructs played a role also in the period under investigation in this book.

Structure of the book

This introductory chapter presented the main research themes, highlighted the significance of the topic under analysis and the intended theoretical and empirical contribution of the book. It defined key concepts, namely those of nation, national identity and collective memory. It also introduced the European context of the topic and showed that Russia was traditionally perceived as Other by the rest of Europe. Furthermore, the chapter argued for the necessity to explore identities and discourses on Russia at the national level due to the fragmented nature of European history, politics and identity construction. The next chapter examines in greater detail the significance of the Other in identity construction. It provides a survey of relevant debates in International Relations theory and a theoretical framework for the ensuing empirical analysis. The focus is on social constructivist scholarship, which emphasises the importance of concepts such as identity, the construction of Others and collective memory to understand international relations. The chapter also outlines the features of discourse-historical analysis, the methodology adopted in this study. Subsequently, it explains and justifies the selection of case studies and of the sources for the analysis of discourses on Russia.

Chapter 3 examines national identity construction in Germany, Poland and Finland, with a special focus on Russia's role as Other. It takes a *longue durée* perspective that follows the construction of national identity in the three countries approximately from the nineteenth century until the present. This perspective allows an investigation of how Russia was internalised in national identity starting from the emergence of modern national identities, with a focus on the historical events that mark key fractures in the selected countries' process of identity formation and relations with Russia. The *longue durée* approach best fits the study of national identity construction, which took place slowly, over a long time span. Dominant themes in identity discourses and discourses on Russia over time are identified and provide an interpretive key for the subsequent analysis of policy makers' discourses on Russia from 2014 to 2018. Chapters 4 to 6 analyse policy makers' discourses on Russia in the selected countries in response to three major events in which Russia was a prominent actor: the Ukraine crisis, which began in the fall of 2013 and led to the most serious post-Cold War crisis in EU–Russia relations; the Nord Stream 2 pipeline project and the related European controversy; and Russia's intervention in the Syrian civil war and its growing assertiveness in the Middle East since 2015.

The analysis of the relationship between these discourses and national identity constitutes the main empirical contribution of the book. It sheds light on how conceptions of Russia framed within national identity relate to contemporary foreign policy discourses, and how the latter in turn contribute to the consolidation or change of the images of Russia enshrined in national identity and memory. Due to Russia's assertiveness and partly confrontational stance vis-à-vis the EU in the period under consideration, we can expect historical constructions of the Russian Other to (re)acquire a prominent role in European foreign policy discourses. Furthermore, the book explores the interaction of German, Polish and Finnish leaders' discourses on Russia in the European discursive arena, and thus offers insights into the deeper, national identity roots of European foreign policy discourse. The empirical chapters also include a comparative analysis of the findings and discuss avenues for further research. Drawing on the comparative analysis, the concluding chapter assesses the prospects for the emergence of a shared foreign policy discourse on Russia in the European Union.

Notes

1 See Chapter 2 in this book for a detailed discussion.
2 All references to the Treaty on European Union concern the treaty version as amended by the Treaty of Lisbon.
3 See Chapters 2 and 3 in this book.
4 Following the classification adopted by Konrad Jarausch (2010: 310–311), in this work East-Central Europe includes EU member states that were located in the Soviet sphere of influence during the Cold War (Poland, Czech Republic, Slovakia, Hungary, Romania, Bulgaria) or were part of the Soviet Union (Lithuania, Latvia and Estonia).
5 The analysis of different national perceptions of Russia is beyond the scope of this chapter. However, Chapter 3 provides a thorough discussion of Russia's role in German, Polish and Finnish collective memory and identity.
6 For instance, as shown in Chapter 3, unofficial narratives of national identity in pre-1989 Poland became part of official discourses following the fall of communism.
7 Germany after the Second World War provides a good example in this respect.
8 See Chapter 2 in this book for a theoretical discussion of 'othering' and of the construction of the Other.

2 Identity and foreign policy

A discourse-historical approach

This chapter outlines the theoretical and methodological framework of the book. It first explores the conceptualisation of identity in the three main grand theories of International Relations, namely neorealism, neoliberalism and social constructivism. Drawing on social constructivist literature, it presents an interpretive theoretical model that conceptualises the relationship between identity, interests and foreign policy as mutually constitutive. The chapter discusses how this relationship is studied at the discursive level, through discourse-historical analysis (DHA).[1] Finally, it illustrates the selection of three national discursive arenas and three case studies for the investigation of official narratives concerning Russia.

Identity and International Relations Theory

Russia is arguably one of the most divisive issues in European foreign policy. Divergent views often emerge when EU member states are required to formulate a foreign policy response to a major event that sees Russia as a protagonist. Different opinions have frequently resulted in the prevalence of bilateral approaches over a united EU position. The response of EU member states to the 2008 Russian–Georgian war and to Moscow's energy projects provide prime examples of diverging European approaches to Russia (David *et al.* 2013, Siddi 2017b). Despite belonging to a single economic and defence community, EU member states perceive Russia differently, particularly with regard to their security interests. The reasons for these differences go beyond neoliberal and neorealist theorisations of institutional cooperation or interstate relations in an anarchic and hostile environment. They must be investigated at the domestic level, where national identities and interests are constructed and discourses on Russia are formulated.

The constructivist school of thought defines the politics of identity as one of the keys to understanding how a country's domestic dynamics interact with and affect global politics (Hopf 1998: 192). Constructivists treat identities and interests as endogenous to interaction, whereas neoliberals and neorealists consider them as exogenously given and constant. For neoliberals and neorealists, states have uncomplicated and unchanging identities and interests, which neither affect nor are influenced by agents and structures (Laffey and Weldes 1997: 193–237;

Waltz 1979). Neoliberals investigated the significance of norms and ideas in international relations, but did not explain whether and how they play a role in identity construction. Neoliberal studies tend to consider ideas and norms only as intervening factors between states seeking self-help in the anarchic international system and their subsequent actions (Waever 2002: 21). They largely neglect the domestic level of analysis and the function that the domestic constituency plays in the formulation of foreign policy preferences. Hence, neoliberalism does not provide solid theoretical foundations to analyse the domestic construction of national identity and its interaction with international politics.

Neorealism also focuses on structures and treats states as monoliths, unproblematic units that follow the logic of self-help and power-balancing in an anarchic international environment (cf. Waltz 1979: 102–128). The neorealist approach to international relations does not attribute any role to domestic and social factors such as national identity in foreign policy making. Due to the lack of attention to these factors, neorealism offers a static view of international politics and is unable to explain change, particularly peaceful change (Ruggie 1998: 874–875). This deficiency is due also to the neorealists' inability to articulate a convincing framework to understand the formulation of state interests. State interests cannot be derived from the condition of anarchy, as neorealists claim, because anarchy is an ambiguous concept. In fact, neorealism handles interest formation by assumption (Ruggie 1998: 862–869).

Moreover, neorealism oversimplifies the process of preference formation and decision making. Decision makers are not always rational, as neorealists tend to assume (Legro and Moravcsik 1999: 53). They may rely on heuristic, the logic of appropriateness (Müller 2004) and the logic of practice (Pouliot 2008), in which the decision-making process is deeply influenced by the social embeddedness of actors, their identity and other cultural elements. Thus, decision-making processes are best studied within a constructivist framework that analyses the multifaceted, malleable and complex nature of identities, as well as their mutually constitutive relationship with agents and structures (Checkel 2008: 72).

According to social constructivists, national identity tends to be defined in relation to one or more significant Others, namely actors in the international environment that are perceived as different or antithetical by the nation (or Self). It operates as a cognitive device that provides a state with an understanding of other countries, their motives, interests, probable actions and attitudes (Hopf 2002: 5). Language and discourses play an essential role in the construction of national identity and its significant Others. Dominant identity discourses are the cognitive structures through which policy makers formulate national interests and take foreign policy decisions. A country's leaders, particularly its political and intellectual elites, are the primary agents and interpreters of national identity construction, as they shape and are influenced by the dominant discourses of the national environments in which they are embedded. These discourses also enable and legitimate their policy decisions (Checkel 2006: 63, Lebow 2008a: 556–564).

Identity, interests and foreign policy
in constructivist research

The concept of identity has been discussed widely in constructivist scholarship. The term originates from social psychology, where it describes the individuality and distinctiveness of an actor (the Self) in its evolving relations with significant Others (Jepperson *et al.* 1996: 59). Alexander Wendt transposed the concept to international relations theory and argued that identities are relatively stable (albeit subject to change in the long run) role-specific understandings and expectations about an actor that are constructed in interactions with other actors. The type of social structure that prevails in the international system depends on how actors construct their identity in relation to others. Relatively stable identities and expectations about each other develop as a result of continuous interaction (Wendt 1994: 384–396).

According to Wendt (1999), national identity formation happens at state level, but it is also influenced by international structures. In the international arena, countries define the boundaries of their Selves and those of their respective Others so as to consolidate their distinctive national traits. National interests are rooted in national identity because an actor 'cannot know what it wants until it knows who it is' (Wendt 1999: 231).[2] In particular, national identity determines the interests of a state based on how other actors are perceived (Wendt 1999; cf. Adler 1997, Hopf 1998). Such perceptions are profoundly influenced by historical interaction between the state and its Others. An actor that has played the role of Other over a protracted historical period becomes internalised as such in a country's national memory (Barnett 1996: 446, Lebow 2006: 3, Smith 1992: 58). In the national memory of several European states, Russia has been internalised as a significant Other (Lebow 2008a: 10, Neumann and Medvedev 2012: 13). Together with Turkey, Russia constituted the main Other against which identities were constructed in early modern and modern Europe (Neumann 1998, Rumelili and Morozov 2012). The concept of otherness is thus fundamental to understand Russia's role in national identity construction in European states.

The antithesis between Self and Other is a central theme in modern philosophy, social anthropology, psychology and literary theory (Neumann 1996: 141–154). In the early nineteenth century, Hegel (1999: 15–20) argued that the citizens of a state develop a collective identity as a result of conflicts with other states. In the second half of the century, Nietzsche elaborated on Hegel's thinking and stated that Self and Other are not fixed elements, but perceive each other from changing perspectives (cited in Neumann 1998: 148). Following the same line of argument, a century later Carl Schmitt (1976) claimed that political identities can best be formed in struggles against others. During the last 20 years, the dichotomy between Self and Other became a pivotal topic in International Relations theory. David Campbell (1998: 191–205) attempted to explain US foreign policy as a continuous search for new collectives to treat as Others in order to consolidate national identity and rally domestic support. Campbell argued that, following the demise of the Soviet Union, Washington identified new Others in Saddam Hussein's Iraq and China. Writing a decade later, Richard Ned Lebow (2008a: 11) asserted that American domestic and foreign policy after the terrorist attacks of 9 September 2001 showed how easy it was for political leaders to exploit the fear of Others to create solidarity at home. Popular arguments focusing on a supposed 'clash of civilisations' (Huntington 1997) can also be seen as an articulation of the Self/Other dichotomy.

Ole Waever (2002) analysed the relationship between Self and Other from an interpretive constructivist perspective focusing on the role of discourses. According to Waever, a collective Self is predicated on some essential political ideas, such as what constitutes a state or a nation. The Self attempts to make these ideas the core of institutionalisation in political cooperation, which produces discursive clashes with the Other. Waever argued that these conflicts can be studied as the substance of world politics in an alternative, identity-based approach to foreign policy analysis. Further studies investigated specific aspects of the Self/Other dichotomy. Erik Ringmar (1996: 80) highlighted the active participation of the Other in an actor's identity construction. He claimed that Others are the main recipients of the Self's narratives and determine whether such narratives are a valid description of the Self through interaction. Jennifer Mitzen (2006: 341–370) studied the use of Others in the framework of ontological security. She contended that states become dependent on security dilemmas – a condition in which one state's gain in security decreases the security of other actors (Jervis 1978: 169–170) – due to their reliance on routines that help consolidate their identities in relation to significant Others.

Elaborating on Wendt's theoretical framework, the essays in Peter Katzenstein's (1996) edited volume *The Culture of National Security* further investigated the dichotomy between Self and Other. Most importantly, they offer crucial insights for the study of the relationship between identity and foreign policy. In an introductory essay, Katzenstein, Wendt and Ronald Jepperson argued that cultural and institutional elements of states' domestic and global environments shape national identity. Variations in national identity determine the security interests and policies of a state and in turn affect normative structures, namely culture and institutions (Jepperson *et al.* 1996: 53–65).

The case studies in Katzenstein's volume provide convincing empirical evidence for these theoretical claims. Among these, Thomas Berger's work (1996: 318) argued that, due to historical experiences and how these are interpreted by domestic political actors, Germany and Japan have developed national identities which make them reluctant to resort to the use of military force.[3] Berger showed that German and Japanese post-1945 identity politics, notably the decision to construct an antimilitaristic national identity, had a direct impact both on policy making and on the domestic institutional context where defence policy is formulated. Bjola and Kornprobst (2007) corroborated this argument by highlighting the identity-based narratives that motivated Germany's refusal to support the Iraq war in 2003.

Robert Herman's (1996) essay on Soviet foreign policy in the late 1980s showed the interrelation between identity construction, the formation of interests and the formulation of foreign policy. Herman argued that the end of the Cold War was a consequence of Gorbachev's new thinking, which caused a radical reconceptualisation of state interests. This redefinition was determined by the emergence of a new identity in some post-Brezhnev Soviet elites, who thought that Soviet interests could best be served by overcoming the East–West division and by cooperating with the United States to achieve peace and stability. The new Soviet thinking allowed progress in arms control, produced a peaceful response to the revolutions in Central and Eastern Europe and led to a democratic shift in Soviet political culture and institutions. Thus, Herman's work illustrated the effects that changes in identity can have on normative structures.

Michael Barnett's analysis of alliances in the Middle East showed that often the politics of identity offers a better explanation than the realist logic of anarchy of the mechanisms that lead a state to identify partners and threats to its security. Most notably, Barnett (1996: 401) claimed that there is a correlation between an actor's identity and its strategic behaviour. Furthermore, Thomas Risse-Kappen's essay (1996: 397) argued that collective identities based on shared democratic values ensure the longevity of institutions and applied this logic to explain the endurance of NATO after the end of the Cold War. According to Risse-Kappen, the longevity of NATO could hardly be understood following the realist logic of balancing, as the fall of the Soviet Union meant the disappearance of the superpower which the Atlantic Alliance was supposed to balance.

Other scholars elaborated on the theoretical framework developed in Katzenstein's edited volume. Richard Ned Lebow (2008a) showed that identity construction can explain events which have traditionally been analysed in terms of power and rational choice, such as the Cuban missile crisis (Allison and Zelikow 1999). Lebow argued that individuals, armies and political elites are committed to asserting and maintaining their identities. To achieve this purpose, they use all available means and power, which Lebow conceived not simply as material power, but also as immaterial capabilities. Lebow (2008a: 552–557) also claimed that actors are reluctant to behave in ways and take decisions that do not conform to their identities, even when such behaviours and decisions appear more rational. Policies that are at odds with national identity create domestic conflict and weaken decision makers' legitimacy at home.

As Ted Hopf (2002) argued, decision makers are embedded in social cognitive structures that are shaped by national identity. National identity and political elites (the decision makers *par excellence*) are mutually constitutive: the latter are influenced by, contribute to create and act based on the former (cf. Jepperson *et al.* 1996: 51). Hence, determining dominant identity discourses is an essential component of national politics. At the domestic level, political elites vie for control over the discursive power that is necessary to produce meaning and acquire legitimacy in a national group. However, their behaviour is also influenced by supranational structures. In particular, their foreign policy decisions are constrained and empowered by prevailing social practices both at home and abroad (Checkel 1998: 343–344, Hopf 1998: 179–196).

On the other hand, the Wendtian conceptualisation of identity was criticised for its lack of complexity and for not taking into consideration its domestic construction. According to Zehfuss (2001), Wendt focused more on the boundaries of the Self than on its internal construction. He neglected identity construction at the domestic level to focus on social identities at the systemic level (cf. Checkel 1998: 341). As Ted Hopf (1998: 196) argued, any state identity in world politics reflects the social practices that constitute identity at home. Identity politics in the domestic arena enables and constrains identity, interests and actions abroad. Moreover, critics argued that Wendt's positivist approach be applied to studying the relationship between identity and foreign policy. Identities are continuously rearticulated and contested, they can be complex and multiple, which makes it difficult to use them as variables or as explanatory categories. Due to the nature and complexity of national identities, tracing direct causal links between them and foreign policy is not possible. The interaction and mutually constitutive relationship between national identities and foreign policy is best analysed as a fluid, multifaceted phenomenon.

Wendtian constructivists were also critiqued for exaggerating the role of threatening Others in identity construction. Richard Ned Lebow (2008a) has shown that identity is not always constructed against or to exclude others. It can also form prior to the construction of the Other. In addition, the Other is not necessarily associated with negative stereotypes; positive interaction also occurs. As Ted Hopf (2002: 7) contended, identities are always relational (we understand them only by relating them to other identities) but only sometimes oppositional. Furthermore, Lebow (2008b: 473–492) convincingly argued that cultural and other differences can be overcome through assimilation and allegiance to a common humanity, which allows transcending the dichotomy between Self and Other. For instance, prominent German intellectuals such as Kant and Hegel constructed the German Self by incorporating crucial elements of the French Other (Lebow 2008a: 12). Ancient Roman identity was also built by assimilating numerous cultural elements from the Greeks and other civilisations.

Positive othering also occurred in European discursive constructions of Russia. Empirical studies have shown that Russia's role as a negative Other for Europe has often been exaggerated. Iver Neumann (1998: 67–80) has documented that Russia was portrayed as a liminal case of European identity: while it was often perceived as a threatening Other, at times many Europeans considered it as a full member of the European family of nations and even as a political and civilisational model.[4] Both when Russia was constructed as a threatening Other and as part of the European Self, its considerable power in the international scene constituted an essential determinant of these constructions. Hence, both ideational and material factors must be taken into account in the analysis of the Russian Other (cf. Waever 2002). The relationship between ideas and material factors is dialectical. Material power acquires significance only in particular discursive constructions that define it as, for instance, threatening or not.

The discursive relationship between identity and foreign policy

This book explores how foreign policy discourses interact with national identity construction in both the national and European discursive arenas. In order to do this, it elaborates on the theoretical framework developed by Katzenstein, Wendt and Jepperson and discussed above. The relationship between national identities and foreign policy discourses on Russia is studied as the interaction of discursive formations, rather than as a causal concatenation of variables. The association between national identity and foreign policy discourses is conceptualised as complex, dialectical and mutually constitutive (cf. Prizel 1998: 12–37). In the model, foreign policy discourses reflect and in turn constitute the essence of national identity. National identity provides the cultural context for national interest formation and for a country's behaviour in the international arena. It is in turn influenced by international structures and by the pursuit of national interests therein. Hence, the model for this analysis looks as follows in Figure 2.1:

The arrows in the model represent mutually constitutive discursive relationships. Numerous identity and foreign policy discourses exist in each national context. This work focuses on dominant official discourses formulated by heads of state or government and foreign ministers, as these actors are the main decision makers in the realm of foreign policy. Their discourses matter most because they are formulated in institutional settings that are authoritative and conducive to persuasion (Checkel 2004: 240). Dominant media discourses are occasionally referred to in order to contextualise policy makers' statements and reconstruct the main Russia-related themes in public debates. These debates influence the social cognitive structure in which policy makers are embedded and help understand the domestic roots of their discourses about Russia (cf. Hopf 2002: 20).

Decision makers' agency, namely their capacity to act and influence dominant discourses and policies, is central to the model adopted for this analysis. As argued, national identity guides and constrains decision makers' choices. However, national leaders can also make selective and instrumental use of particular identity discourses in order to achieve specific foreign policy goals. For instance, decision makers who intend to strengthen economic relations with Russia will emphasise narratives portraying it as a good and reliable partner. Conversely, politicians who oppose the partnership with Russia, or who attempt to strengthen domestic consensus by constructing negative external Others, will rather stress identity discourses portraying it as threatening and unreliable.

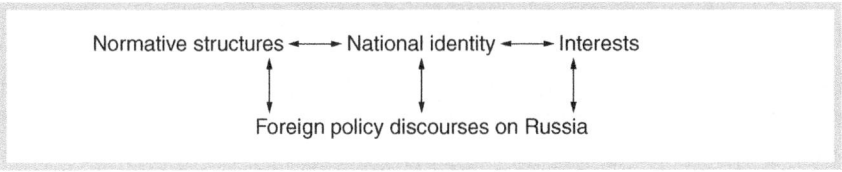

Figure 2.1 Interaction between national identity and foreign policy discourses.

National identity and foreign policy narratives are studied both at the domestic level, in their process of national formation and contestation, and in their interaction with international structures. In this latter regard, the focus is on interaction with Russia and its construction as an Other in national identity. Russia is not considered *a priori* as a negative Other against which national identity is constructed. The investigation of the historical construction of national identities shows that, occasionally, positive interaction between Russia and the three countries under analysis occurred in the past.[5] Furthermore, the boundaries between Self and Other are treated as blurred and not as sharply delimited. For instance, in spite of their historical rivalry, post-1945 Poland and Russia followed parallel paths of social and economic development, which are reflected in some similar national identity narratives today (for example, those expressing a rejection of communism as a political model or emphasising the role of religion in society).

While Russia is a significant Other for the three countries under investigation, it is by no means the only one. For a long historical period, France and Sweden were at least equally important Others for Germany and Finland respectively. Today, due to its double role as Other in the international arena and as the country of origin of millions of immigrants, Turkey may be an even more critical Other for Germany. Furthermore, Polish identity construction was affected by interaction with several significant Others, including Germans, Ukrainians, Lithuanians and Jews (Prizel 1998: 38–152). Following 9/11 and the refugee crisis, migrants (Muslim ones in particular) have been essentialised as the main Other in mainstream European discourses. Hence, the analysis of Russia's role as Other in national identities and foreign policy discourses has to take into consideration this tangled web and the fact that additional Others may often influence and even feature more prominently in these discourses.

The theoretical model adopted in this work investigates both the cultural and the material factors constituting national discourses on Russia within a constructivist framework. Material power is seen as acquiring significance only within particular discursive constructions. For instance, Polish leaders have considered Russia's energy power both as a positive factor, as after the Polish–Russian agreement to build the Yamal–Europe pipeline in the early 1990s, and as a national threat, as shown by Warsaw's overt hostility to the German–Russian Nord Stream pipeline (Castle 2006, Prizel 1998: 132). Polish national identity, notably the construction of the Russian and German Other therein, provides the key to understanding radically different perceptions of the same material power.

Discourse-historical analysis

In this work, 'discourse' is defined as a form of social practice, a specific type of language use in social interaction, both in speech and in writing. Discourses are socially constructed and have a mutually constitutive relationship with social structures. Discursive practices contribute to sustaining, reproducing and transforming social structures. They reflect and affect power relations through their representation of the world. No discourse can be fully understood without taking into account the context in which it was produced; it is meaningful only in its cultural, historical and ideological embedding (Wodak 1996: 14–19).

Most important for the purpose of this study, discourses on a country's identity and external Others are of essential relevance to the formulation of foreign policy (Waever 2005: 35). As Ruth Wodak (2002b: 66) has noted, a dialectical relationship exists between discursive practices and the field of action in which they are embedded. Accordingly, policy makers' discourses on Russia affect their country's foreign policy towards Russia. Discursive practices are constructed domestically in hegemonic struggles for political and moral-intellectual leadership. They are instrumental in perpetuating, justifying or transforming national identities. They also involve the formation of social antagonism, most notably the exclusion of threatening Others. Discourses about external Others – like all discourses – are fluid and should be studied as flexible, historically-bound constructs. Hegemonic discourses become dislocated when they prove unable to explain new events (de Cilla *et al.* 1999: 157, Torfing 2005: 15–16).

Critical discourse analysis, particularly its discourse-historical approach, offers a suitable methodology to study national discourses on Russia and their relationship to foreign policy in their evolving, historical dimension. Discourse historical analysis (DHA) is an interpretive and explanatory methodology that systematically reduces the number of possible readings of a text by identifying its cultural and historical embedding. It deconstructs texts and relates them to their social and ideological background (Wodak 1996: 19). It is applicable to different genres of text, including political speeches and newspaper interviews, which are the main primary sources for this work. Texts and discourses are not studied in isolation; relationships with other texts (intertextuality) and discourses (interdiscursivity) are also investigated (Wodak 2002b: 69–70).

DHA has a contextual and historicist view of discourses. It seeks to place them against their historical background in order to understand how they evolve and to investigate political attempts at restructuring them (Torfing 2005: 14). By integrating knowledge about the historical sources and the background in which discursive events are embedded, DHA provides a comprehensive interpretation. Accordingly, the analysis of Russia's role in German, Polish and Finnish national identity formation in the next chapter serves the purpose of delineating the historical framework of current discourses on Russia. Furthermore, DHA explores how discourses are subject to diachronic change. Hence, the historical background is studied as a factor affecting the development of discourses over time (Wodak 2002b: 65; cf. de Cilla *et al.* 1999: 156).

Most of the textual analysis involves tracing the development of key concepts and themes, including their historical origins and relationship to other subjects (cf. Waever 2005: 36). Key concepts and themes identify semantic macrostructures that play a fundamental role in communication and interaction. They reflect what a discourse is about globally speaking and exemplify its most important information; they epitomise the gist of a discourse, namely the essence that an audience retains from it (van Dijk 2002: 101–102). Language users are unable to memorise and process all meanings in a discourse; they reorganise them into a few global meanings. Key themes are often explicit in titles, headlines or summaries of a text. Sometimes they are not observable directly, but can be inferred through a careful analysis of the text (van Dijk 2002: 102, Wodak 2002b: 66).

Undoubtedly, there is no single reading of texts and diverging selections of key themes are possible also if the number of primary sources under analysis is large. However, the deconstruction of numerous and authoritative texts will at the very least offer sufficient data for a plausible interpretation of key themes. In this work, the plausibility of the interpretation is augmented by the fact that it is guided by and can be confronted with the findings of existing scholarly literature on national identity and discourses on Russia. As Teun van Dijk has noted, no complete discourse analysis is possible, as a thorough examination of even a short passage may require months and hundreds of pages of explanation. However, a satisfactory investigation of key themes in discourses can be performed if specific structures are selected for closer analysis (van Dijk 2002: 99). Accordingly, in this work the focus will be restricted to the textual extracts concerning descriptions and interpretations of Russia's domestic and foreign policy.

The analysis of national identity construction and of historical discourses on Russia is based mostly on secondary literature. The investigation of secondary literature serves the purpose of identifying dominant discourses on Russia over time, which helps situate current discourses within a broader historical framework. Most importantly, it provides in-depth background information and hence a solid foundation for the ensuing interpretive textual analysis. As Lene Hansen (2006: 83) argues, 'the writing of good discourse analysis of primary texts requires knowledge of the case in question, and knowledge comes, in part, from reading standard works on the history, processes, events and debates constituting a foreign policy phenomenon'. The analysis of secondary literature complements the interpretive theoretical framework outlined earlier in this chapter, which requires thorough historical and contextual grounding.

After examining the secondary literature, I analysed primary sources, with a focus on the presence of historically constructed images of Russia in foreign policy discourses. For each text under investigation, information concerning its immediate context was sampled: who is the author? When was the text produced? Which contemporary events does it make reference to? What is the target audience? Relevant political, historical and sociological background is incorporated in the analysis. The text genre was examined too, as it may provide important indications on how the text should be read. For instance, a speech delivered by a foreign minister in front of an audience of diplomats is likely to be much more cautious in terms of wording and judgements than a pre-election speech or a newspaper interview. Following Hansen (2006: 86), both highly formal texts and texts with more clear articulations of identity are included in the analysis, reflecting the broad spectrum of genres in foreign policy discourse.

Once this preliminary and background information on the text was acquired, I identified dominant discourses. In order to detect dominant discourses, their essential constituents were traced in texts: recurrent arguments, the corresponding semantic structures (the use of specific verbs, nouns and adjectives to construct meaning) and the logical outcome of an argument in terms of policy making. I also explored interdiscursivity and intertextuality. Based on the dominant discourses, I investigated linguistic constructions (adjectives, images, metaphors, other figures of speech) focusing on how Russia was defined and presented as an actor.

Furthermore, I examined discursive strategies and specific linguistic markers that constitute dominant themes and discourses. Discursive strategies are systematic ways of using language in order to achieve a particular social, political, psychological or linguistic aim (Wodak 2002b: 73). Membership categorisations in order to construct in-groups and out-groups are examples of discursive strategies. For instance, peoples are categorised as Europeans and non-Europeans with cultural or geographic arguments, with the use of figures of speech such as metaphors (asserting that something is the same as an otherwise unrelated object) or synecdoches (when a term for a part of something is used to refer to the whole or vice versa; for instance, calling Russia 'Asia'). Other discursive strategies such as predication (defining the action, state or quality of the subject) are used to label social actors in positive or negative ways. For instance, the previously mentioned category of non-Europeans can be labelled with stereotypical attributions of positive or negative traits. In the texts under analysis, Russia was labelled alternatively as 'a reliable energy partner', 'an existential threat for Europe', 'an aggressive neighbour' and 'an important neighbour'.

Argumentation and perspectivation are other frequently used discursive strategies. Argumentation is used to justify positive or negative attributions and to bolster the main message or purpose of a text. It is based on the use of *topoi*, namely content-related parts of a discourse that connect the arguments with their logical conclusion (Wodak 2002b: 74). Perspectivation aims at expressing involvement and positioning the speaker's point of view. For instance, this is done by reporting an event that the speaker witnessed and on which he or she claims to have inside knowledge.

Once dominant discourses and themes, discursive strategies and linguistic markers were identified, I interpreted the meanings resulting from the analysis and, with reference to my theoretical model, I addressed the research questions. After comparing across texts and discourses, I made an extensive interpretation concerning the role of national identity and of historically constructed images of Russia, thereby assessing their relevance to current foreign policy discourses.

Selection of national discursive arenas and case studies

The selection of case studies for this analysis involves two aspects. First, due to the impossibility of investigating national identity construction and discourses on Russia in all EU member states within the scope of this work, a few national discursive arenas have been selected for in-depth study. Second, specific policy areas and events have been chosen for the analysis and comparison of national discourses on Russia.

The discussion of distinct East-Central European narratives concerning Russia in Chapter 1 highlighted the dangers of assuming the existence of a homogenous EU discursive arena. As Iver Neumann (1998) has shown, occasionally it is possible to identify similar discourses on Russia across European countries, particularly in intellectual circles, which constitute the main subject of Neumann's analysis. However, a thorough investigation must take into account the national level. The history of the European continent is profoundly divided along national lines and European countries had remarkably different relations with Russia, which presupposes different national discourses.

Geography and history, particularly the nature of political relations in the past, are the main discriminants when examining the interaction between European countries and Russia. These two factors are closely interlinked. States that are closer to Russia's borders also tend to have deeper and more complex historical relations with Russia than those that are located further away. There are exceptions to this observation: despite its considerable distance from Russia, Britain had intense and controversial relations with it from the early nineteenth century until the present, mostly due to the two countries' great power status and geopolitical competition (cf. Ewans 2004, Keith 2006). However, this exception does not apply to most other West and South European countries. Their historical involvement with Russia was much more limited than that of Central and East European states.

Since the focus of this book is on the relationship between national identity and discourses on Russia, it is logical to focus on countries where Russia is likely to have played a role in national identity construction, hence those geographically close to and with deep historical interactions with Russia. Furthermore, as we want to compare different foreign policy discourses within the European Union, it is fundamental to focus on member states which traditionally have a different foreign policy stance towards Russia. The analysis can thus explore how national identity constructions where Russia played a role are related to different national foreign policy discourses. Conversely, if the investigation focused on countries chosen for their geographical spread within the EU, it would risk coming to the tautological conclusion that national identity is an important factor in foreign policy discourses on Russia only or mostly in states that are closer to it. Geography, and not national identity, would likely be the main or the only determining factor.

This explains why large and influential EU member states such as France, Italy or Spain were not included in the analysis. A preliminary consultation of secondary sources confirmed that Russia did not play an important role in their national identity construction (cf. Bedani and Haddock 2000, Boyd 1997, Gildea 2002a and 2002b, Isnenghi 2010, Kamen 2008, Nora 1992). Their cooperative, largely unproblematic relations with Moscow are mostly the result of commercial interests, rather than of deeply engrained identity narratives (cf. Leonard and Popescu 2007: 31–36). Investigating foreign policy discourses in one of these countries could be useful to highlight how, by contrast with EU member states that are closer and had deeper historical interactions with Russia, national identity and memory do not hamper current relations. However, this analysis is beyond the scope of this book, which focuses on how different constructions of Russia in national identity influence foreign policy discourses. Furthermore, examining more than three national discursive arenas in some depth is not possible within the constraints of this work.

Germany, Poland and Finland have been selected as focus for this analysis because they best satisfy the analytical criteria outlined above. Tsarist and Soviet Russia was a neighbouring power for most of their modern history, which is still true of Poland and Finland today. Russia and Germany shared a border from 1871 (1815, if we consider Prussia as Wilhelmine Germany's predecessor) until 1918 and again in 1939–1941. Although there was no shared border during the Cold War, the presence of Soviet troops and political advisors throughout East-Central Europe and in East Germany practically meant that Soviet Russia was for Germans both a neighbouring and an occupying power from 1945 until the early 1990s. The three countries under consideration had deep and contro-versial historical relations with Russia during their modern history, including several armed clashes and the occupation of part of their territory by Russian or Soviet troops. We can thus assume that Russia played a role in national identity construction. This assumption is verified through a review of secondary liter-ature in Chapter 3.

Furthermore, the countries selected for analysis are particularly active in current relations with Russia, both at bilateral level and within the European Union. Their actorness vis-à-vis Russia contributes to making them interesting and relevant case studies. Within the EU, Germany has had a leading role in shaping energy and economic policies towards Russia (Högselius 2013, Makarychev and Meister 2015, Siddi 2016a and 2018d, Timmins 2011). Poland has been one of the most active member states in advocating policies concerning the EU's and Russia's shared neighbourhood in Eastern Europe. For instance, it was one of the main supporters of the Eastern Partnership, a policy that aims to intensify the EU's relations with post-Soviet countries in Europe (excluding Russia) (Cichocki 2013, Copsey and Pomorska 2014, Cadier 2018). Finland has been the main promoter of the EU's Northern Dimension, a framework to address environ-mental and health issues in border areas between Russia and North European EU member states (Etzold and Haukkala 2011, Haukkala 2010a: 152–156).

Although all countries under analysis had controversial relations with Russia in the past, their current foreign policy stances towards Moscow differ consider-ably. German foreign policy makers tend to be less critical and more positive about Russia, whereas Polish leaders often have overtly hostile overtones (Krumm 2012, Reeves 2010, Siddi 2016a and 2018c). Within the European Union, Germany and Poland epitomise the member states' two main and con-trasting approaches to Russia (Stewart 2012: 165). The German approach tends towards accommodating Russia and is followed by West and Central European member states such as France, Italy, Spain and Austria. The Polish approach is much more sceptical towards Russia and is generally followed by East-Central European member states (particularly the Baltic States), occasionally joined by the United Kingdom and Sweden. The Finnish position is somewhere in between and reflects an apparently neutral pragmatism (Etzold and Haukkala 2011: 253–254, Stewart 2012: 187). These divergences may be due to dissimilar ways of internalising historical experiences in national identities and to the different nuances of past and current bilateral relations with Russia. Hence, a detailed analysis of Russia's role in national identity construction and of the broader picture of bilateral relations is a precondition for the study of current discourses on Russia.

In order to have a common basis for analysis, the book focuses on national policy makers' discourses concerning four major international events in which Russia was directly involved between 2014 and 2018. These include the Ukraine crisis, the Nord Stream 2 pipeline project and the Syrian crisis. This selection of events allows studying discourses on Russia in three areas that are of utmost relevance to the relationship between the European Union and Russia, namely energy trade and the stability of their shared neighbourhood in Eastern Europe and the southern shore of the Mediterranean Sea. The events under investigation were among the most controversial issues in EU foreign policy. In the three countries selected for analysis, they caused intense debates on the nature of Russia's foreign policies. These debates offer an ideal context to identify dominant national narratives on Russia.

State leaders' public statements as primary sources

The book analyses public texts, mostly speeches and interviews of top state officials (heads of state or government and foreign ministers) recorded in electronic archives of national foreign ministries and in prominent national newspapers. The choice of focusing on public texts, as opposed to private or internal documents, is motivated primarily by the theoretical foundations of this work. The contestation among different national identity discourses and narratives on Russia takes place in the public sphere, where their advocates compete for dominance. Hence, the analysis attempts to identify official discourses that are dominant there. Discourse analysis is the best methodology for this investigation because it focuses on public texts (Waever 2002). Focusing on public texts and discourses that are easily accessible involves an important methodological advantage. Easy access to sources ensures the transparency of the research, as it allows a quick verification of the plausibility of interpretations and the cogency of arguments (Blaikie 2010: 217, Bryman 2008: 380).

Focusing exclusively on discourses of top state officials may result in an analysis that does not reflect all the complexities involved in identity construction and the formulation of foreign policy. Other actors at lower levels in the power chain or civil society also play a role in shaping identity and foreign policy discourses. Business and other advocacy groups (such as religious, environmental and pacifist organisations) lobby governments to take foreign policy decisions that conform with their economic or social objectives. Scholarly literature has highlighted the role of epistemic communities in influencing decision makers (Adler 1992, Davis Cross 2013, Haas 1992 and 2004, Sebenius 1992, Zito 2001). Epistemic communities are networks of professionals with recognised expertise and policy-relevant knowledge in a specific area. Prominent think tanks, regulatory agencies and governmental policy research bodies provide ideal locations for members of an epistemic community to gain leverage over policy choices. Former political leaders, diplomats, judges, high-ranking military officials, bankers and international lawyers often become part of these expert groups and use their prestige and expertise to influence decision makers (Davis Cross 2013: 155–159, Haas 1992: 2–4).

In order to have a more complete picture of all national identity and foreign policy narratives, the discourses of epistemic communities, advocacy groups and civil society organisations would have to be investigated. However, covering three whole national discursive spaces is practically impossible and a bias towards a selected category of actors is inevitable. Within these constraints, the choice of focusing on discourses of leading state officials is motivated by the fact that they are the main foreign policy actors and steer relevant public debates (Waever 2002: 42). Their discourses have practical relevance, as they condition possible policies. Policy is strongly related to discursive structures because decision makers need to be able to justify policy choices in public and reconcile them with the self-image of the state (Waever 2002: 27).

The sources selected for this analysis are essentially excerpts of public debates. They are policy makers' interviews targeted to a broad audience or transcripts of policy makers' speeches held in meetings with other state officials and with civil society. All of them were publicly and freely accessible at the time when the empirical research was performed. They can be thought of as snapshots of dominant discursive constructions concerning national identity, foreign policy and relations with Russia. The electronic archives of the Finnish, German and Polish foreign ministries proved essential to retrieve foreign ministers' speeches. Additional sources were investigated for transcripts of speeches and interviews given by other top state officials who were particularly active in foreign policy making in the case studies under consideration. For Finland, the Eilen Archive and Chronology of Finnish Foreign Policy (curated by the Finnish Institute of International Affairs) was used to retrieve speeches by Finnish prime ministers and presidents of the republic. For Germany and Poland, the official online archives of the speeches, interviews and press conferences held by the German federal chancellor, the Polish prime minister and the Polish president of the republic were consulted. Furthermore, several interviews and statements made by top German, Polish and Finnish officials were retrieved from prominent European and North American mass media.

In order to identify relevant texts in large databases such as the online archives of the German and Finnish foreign ministries, search functions on the websites were used. Texts (articles, interviews, speeches, press releases and travel reports) dating from the period 2014–2018 and including the terms

'Russia', 'Ukraine', 'Syria' and 'Nord Stream 2' were preselected for further analysis. This data collection procedure allowed retrieving material from similar databases (institutional websites) for the three countries under consideration. The texts under investigation date from 2014 to 2018. More specifically, the analysis of texts concerning the Ukraine crisis starts from early 2014, when the crisis escalated and Russia annexed Crimea. The analysis of speeches concerning the Nord Stream 2 project begins in the summer of 2015, when the project was officially announced. Finally, the chapter on Syria investigates debates following Russia's military intervention in Syria in September 2015.

Conclusion

This chapter has argued that social constructivism provides the best theoretical approach to examine the relationship between national identity and foreign policy discourses. Following social constructivist theory, national identity reflects historical relations with Russia and influences foreign policy narratives in the countries under analysis. Conversely, neorealist and neoliberal approaches largely ignore the importance of identity and interaction with the Other in the formulation of foreign policy discourses. After an overview of positivist constructivist scholarship from the 1990s and 2000s, the chapter developed an interpretive constructivist model for the ensuing empirical analysis. In the model, identity is conceptualised as a multifaceted and fluctuating construct. Its relationship with foreign policy is best studied as the interaction of discourses, both at the domestic level and in the international arena. This relationship is complex and mutually constitutive. Concretely, this means that national identity narratives both influence and are shaped by interaction with Russia.

The relationship between national identity and top national leaders, the primary agents in foreign policy making, is also mutually constitutive. The leaders of a country are embedded in social cognitive structures shaped by national identity. Hence, they are reluctant to enact policies that do not conform to it. However, as they are also the main agents in the construction of national identity, they sometimes develop new narratives that complement and further develop dominant identity discourses, thereby contributing to identity change. The chapter also highlighted the relevance of a discursive approach to the study of national identity, foreign policy and the construction of a country's Others. It argued that the discourse-historical approach, a variant of critical discourse analysis, provides an appropriate methodology because it focuses on the historical dimension of discourse. It is therefore functional to the investigation of the relationship between deep-rooted national identity narratives and foreign policy discourses about Russia. In addition, its focus on discursive strategies allows for a systematic analysis of the linguistic and rhetorical tools that are used in the construction of Russia as the Other.

Three national discursive arenas within the EU (Germany, Poland and Finland) were chosen for closer inspection. This selection was based on the depth of the countries' historical interactions with Russia, actorness in current relations and representativeness of the main national positions towards Russia within the EU. As the selected countries play an important role in EU–Russia relations and epitomise the member states' main stances towards Russia, the analysis also offers insights about influential discourses on Russia at the EU level. Furthermore, three case studies in which Russia played a major role between 2014 and 2018 were selected in order to provide a common basis for the analysis of discourses in each national arena. These events concern key policy areas in EU–Russia relations, namely energy trade, European security and the stability of the EU's Eastern and Southern neighbourhood.

Notes

1 I have used the same theoretical and methodological approach in Siddi (2017b). The practical steps in its application are explained in greater detail in this earlier book.
2 To emphasise the tight correlation between identity and interests, Wendt (1999: 231–232) also claims that 'interests are needs or functional imperatives which must be fulfilled if an identity is to be reproduced'.
3 Events with enduring significance for a country, such as the Second World War for Germany and Japan, create dominant collective memories that allow the mobilisation of national identities in particular directions (Liu and Hilton 2005: 545).
4 See Chapter 1 in this book.
5 See Chapter 3 in this book.

3 The historic construction of German, Polish and Finnish identities and their Russian Other

This chapter analyses the historic construction of German, Polish and Finnish identity, with a focus on discourses that are most relevant to national foreign policy towards Russia. Drawing on extensive scholarly literature, it shows that perceptions of Russia played an important role in national identity formation and that Russia was a prominent Other in national foreign policy discourses. The focus is on the period starting from the nineteenth century, when modern national identities began to be constructed. This *longue durée* approach highlights the historical roots of current national identities and foreign policy behaviours, as well as their mutually constitutive relationship. For each of the three countries under analysis, the dominant themes and historical trends of national identity construction are investigated alongside their relationship with contemporary foreign policy. The role of Russia as Other in identity formation and the evolution of national discourses on Russia are analysed in greater depth in specific sub-sections. The chapter provides a historically grounded interpretive framework for the discourse analysis in the following chapters.

The historic construction of German identity

Scholars have argued that the economic and political crises of the first half of the twentieth century, culminating in the Third Reich's genocidal experience, have influenced deeply German national identity and foreign policy after 1945 (cf. Banchoff 1999, Berger 1997, Bjola and Kornprobst 2007, Risse 2007, Siddi 2018c, Wittlinger 2011). These events have led post-war (West) German leaders to formulate a pacific security culture, which prioritises multilateral frameworks and tends to reject the use of force as a means to solve international disputes. Support for European integration, the transatlantic alliance and the quest for cooperation with Eastern European neighbours, most notably Russia, have become central tenets of German foreign policy. Moreover, democracy, economic stability and the respect of human rights have become essential constituents of national identity. These values permeate Germany's approach to international affairs.

The dominant identity discourses that constitute current German foreign policy have been constructed as a rejection of the national experience between 1871 and 1945 and of the East German regime (Jarausch and Geyer 2003: 235–240).

In 1945, the German nation had no 'usable past' (Moeller 2003a) to reconstruct its political identity.[1] The record of united Germany between 1871 and 1945 was widely considered as catastrophic, as it was associated with two world wars, economic instability, dictatorship and genocide. Militaristic and chauvinistic Imperial Germany (1871–1918), the economically and politically unstable Weimar Republic (1919–1933), let alone the racist and genocidal experience of the Third Reich (1933–1945), could provide no positive reference.

Foreign occupation and the existence of two radically different German states after 1949 further complicated the emergence of a new sense of national identity. In the first post-war decade, West Germany focused on material and economic reconstruction. The swift achievements in these fields, including the so-called economic miracle (*Wirtschaftswunder*), created a feeling of identity based on collective working ethics and the resolve to rebuild a country that lay in ruins (James 1989: 177–195). In foreign policy, West German leaders considered alignment with the United States and support of European integration as absolute priorities in order to be accepted as a full member of the Western community.

From the 1960s onwards, the memory of the Holocaust became a dominant public and institutional discourse, as well as a crucial constitutive element of West German identity and foreign policy (Herf 1997: 334–372). The sense of responsibility for genocide prevented the redefinition of (West) German identity in nationalistic terms. In foreign policy, the rejection of unilateralism and the support of European and Western integration appeared even more as the only possible course of action to re-establish the country's reputation (Banchoff 1999: 273–274). West German attitudes to national identity and foreign policy choices led many intellectuals to argue that, by the 1970s, the country had become a post-national democracy. According to this view, West Germans had learnt from the past and moved beyond the ideas of nation and nationalism (Berger 1997: 77–108, Jarausch and Geyer 2003: 240, Winkler 1996).

Meanwhile, in the German Democratic Republic (GDR), the political leadership drew a thick line between the Third Reich and the newly-founded state. Official rhetoric urged GDR citizens to identify with Communist heroes and victims of the Nazi regime (Fulbrook 1999: 55–59, Naimark 1995). It attempted to construct a new East German identity based on anti-fascism and the rejection of Western capitalism. However, the sense of belonging to a broader German nation never disappeared. In fact, the GDR authorities' focus on defining their country in opposition to West Germany acted as a constant reminder of all-German commonalities among East German citizens (Fulbrook 1999: 198). The fall of the Berlin Wall showed that a German nation had survived Cold War divisions.

The experience of the East German state was a controversial issue that the reunified Germany had to come to terms with in order to forge a shared national identity. The social problems and the economic difficulties resulting from reunification ensured that the East German past was present in public debates in both the 1990s and the 2000s (Ahonen 2011, Gellner and Douglas 2003). Undeniably, the existence of two German states with different political and economic systems left material and cultural traces in post-1990 united Germany (cf. Arnold-de Simine 2005, Herf 1997, Kocka 1996, Weidenfeld 2001). Although elements of a distinct GDR identity survived among its former citizens and sometimes resurfaced in nostalgic filmic and cultural representations, they did not overshadow dominant identity discourses and were contested by competing narratives highlighting the authoritarian and repressive nature of the East German regime (Arnold-de Simine 2005, Sabrow 2009). This contributed to reinforcing the stress on democracy and human rights and the rejection of any form of authoritarianism in post-1989 German identity discourses.

While reunification revived the feeling of a German national identity, it neither reawakened the extreme nationalism that had characterised the history of Germany in 1871–1945, nor did it mark a sudden departure from pre-1989 West German identity and foreign policy discourses. The latter became dominant also in reunified Germany. Memory of the Holocaust and the suffering inflicted upon other nations during the Second World War play a central role in the collective identity of united Germany (Langenbacher 2010: 43–49, Wilds 2000, Wittlinger 2011: 139–140). If anything, debates on these issues have become deeper and more prominent since the 1990s, including social groups that had been neglected earlier (such as Soviet prisoners of war and forced labourers, Roma and Sinti, homosexuals). The erection of numerous monuments commemorating the victims of National Socialism in reunified Berlin has led some authors to label it as 'the capital city of remorse' (in German, *Hauptstadt der Reue*; cf. Reichel 2005).

Since the late 1990s, the German public debate has also addressed the issue of German suffering during and in the aftermath of the Second World War. This concerned in particular the expulsion of approximately 12 million ethnic Germans from East-Central Europe between 1945 and 1950, the rape of thousands of German women in the last months of the war by Allied soldiers, the carpet bombing of all main German cities and the internment of millions of Wehrmacht soldiers in Soviet camps (Langenbacher 2010: 49–54, Moeller 2003b). These debates have been received with suspicion or hostility in some of Germany's Eastern neighbours, Poland and the Czech Republic in particular, where many feared that they could pave the way for a broader reinterpretation of history and German compensation claims. However, the public debate on the suffering of German civilians has not significantly altered the nature of dominant German identity and foreign policy discourses. If anything, it strengthened their pacifist and anti-totalitarian components by emphasising the pernicious consequences of aggressive and unlawful policies (cf. Langenbacher 2010: 50). As we shall see in Chapter 6, the memory of German suffering during the Second World War led many Germans to empathise with civilians fleeing from the Syrian civil war in the 2010s.

International Relations scholars have attempted to define the nature of post-reunification German foreign policy by developing the concept of civilian power (Harnisch and Maull 2001). Civilian powers are defined as states that actively promote the 'civilising' of international relations through efforts to constrain the use of force, strengthen the rule of law and promote international cooperation. The endorsement of participatory forms of decision-making, social equity, sustainable development and interdependence are also important features of civilian powers (Harnisch and Maull 2001: 3–4). The leaders of reunified Germany pursued or claimed to pursue these goals. The idea of civilian power is therefore useful to conceptualise Germany's foreign policy identity.

The contested nature of the Russian Other in German discourses

During the nineteenth and twentieth centuries, Russia was a significant Other in German identity construction. German perceptions of Russia were predominantly negative, emphasising its presumed social and economic backwardness and threatening military power. However, a counter-narrative that relativised these negative views existed, notably in particular social *milieux* and historical periods. A significant strand of German official discourses emphasised the necessity of a cooperative approach to Russia that took into account its strategic importance for Germany and in the international arena. From the late 1960s onwards, these discourses, together with the quest for better relations with the GDR and the pursuit of reconciliation with Germany's Eastern neighbours, drove a cooperative West German foreign policy towards the Soviet Union that has become enshrined in the concept of *Ostpolitik*. The term literally means 'Eastern policy' and generally refers to Germany's foreign policy towards its Eastern neighbours. It acquired a more specific meaning in the context of Cold War detente, when West German *Ostpolitik* established a tradition of cordial bilateral contacts that has remained an important element of reunified Germany's policy towards Russia.

The *Ostpolitik* approach coexisted with negative perceptions of Russia that had become rooted in German identity over the centuries. Negative perceptions of Russia became dominant in the nineteenth century and were fuelled by popular publications such as Astolphe de Custine's *Empire of the Czar*. Published in 1839, it portrayed the Tsarist Empire as a corrupt, inefficient and despotic police state (de Custine 1989). Contemporary German liberals were particularly critical of Russian autocracy and the overall backwardness of the Tsarist Empire. For them, Russia was a threat to German and European liberal values (Schröder 2012: 99). Conservatives tended to be less contemptuous of the Tsarist political system. Between 1847 and 1852, Prussian agricultural expert August von Haxthausen published a report on his trips to Russia, describing it as a well-ordered patriarchal monarchy. Von Haxthausen's (1972) publication promoted a competing, more positive discourse on Russia and was particularly popular among German aristocracy, which considered the Tsarist Empire as a bulwark against revolution and democracy. However, even pro-Tsarist conservatives were convinced of Germany's cultural superiority (cf. Schröder 2012: 99–100).

After the Bolshevik revolution, racial discourses became intertwined with political ones. The German elites and middle class associated the 'Bolshevik threat' with Jewish commissars and savage Slavs that were keen to commit atrocious crimes and enslave Europe. On the other hand, a sizeable minority (mostly radicals and communists) viewed the Soviet Union as an economic and social model. From the opposite side of the political spectrum, some conservatives remained sympathetic to Russia, in spite of its communist regime, because they saw it as a partner in their fight against the Versailles system (cf. Schröder 2012: 100–103). However, following Hitler's rise to power, racist and anti-Bolshevik discourses became omnipresent; the Nazis silenced all competing views. From the start of the war with the Soviet Union (June 1941), the Nazi regime incessantly disseminated propaganda that described Russians and other peoples of the Soviet Union as 'sub-humans' (*Untermenschen*).

Elements of these narratives outlasted the Third Reich. The image of Russians as uncivilised Asians, threatening German and European values, persisted in post-war West German discourses (Schildt 2003: 158). Even West German chancellor Konrad Adenauer believed that the Soviet Union represented the 'culture of the most backward part of Asia' (cited in Moeller 2003a: 102–103). The post-war division of Germany and Berlin and the presence of Soviet troops on German soil contributed to West German constructions of the Soviet Union as a threat. As West Germany left behind the historical enmity with France and the United Kingdom, the Soviet Union and its satellites became the only neighbouring foes. Hence, in the 1950s and 1960s, the Soviet Union was the main Other against which West German identity was constructed.

As argued, a strong competing narrative began to emerge in the late 1960s, when Nazi crimes became the focus of an intense public debate in West Germany (Moeller 2003a: 176–177). German collective identity was redefined in opposition to the country's genocidal past, which thus became the main Other in national identity. A large proportion of Nazi crimes had been committed in Eastern Europe and the Soviet Union. The increasing awareness of this drove West German leaders to seek reconciliation with their Eastern neighbours. The agency of Social Democratic Chancellor Willy Brandt contributed to the reconceptualisation of the Russian Other in German identity and foreign policy. His genuflection in the former Warsaw ghetto in 1970 and his cooperative *Ostpolitik* with the Soviet Union epitomise the shift in official West German identity narratives and policies towards the Soviet bloc (cf. Ash 1993: 298–300).

Brandt combined the pursuit of historical reconciliation with that of economic and strategic goals. His *Ostpolitik* enhanced trade exchanges between West Germany and the Eastern bloc and resulted in a series of treaties, signed between 1970 and 1973, that improved diplomatic relations. Negative discourses on Russia did not disappear among West German political elites (Hildermeier 2003: 41; cf. Satjukow 2008). However, the Soviets were no longer perceived as uncompromising enemies. The image of a peaceful neighbour that could become an economic partner gained momentum (Schildt 2003: 169–171; cf. Albert 1995, Thumann 1997). *Ostpolitik* created a new, powerful discourse showing that cooperation was possible and beneficial to both Moscow and Bonn. Brandt's *Ostpolitik* was eventually endorsed by all the main political parties.

Leaders of the conservative opposition did not change course when they won elections and became the ruling majority in the 1980s.

A further positive turn in German discourses on the Soviet Union took place in the late 1980s, when Mikhail Gorbachev played an important role in ending the Cold War and consented to German reunification. The collapse of state socialism in Russia and East Germany brought the end of ideological controver sies. West German leaders took pride in arguing that peaceful transformation in Eastern Europe had taken place also as a result of their cooperative *Ostpolitik* with the Soviet Union. Furthermore, chancellor Helmut Kohl developed a personal friendship with Gorbachev, thereby establishing a tradition of cordial relationships between Russian and German leaders that lasted for nearly two decades. In the euphoria of reunification, the narrative of Russia as a threatening Other lost dominance (Ahrens and Weiss 2012: 149–150, Krumm 2012: 115–117). Official narratives constructed Russia as a democratising country and as an economic and security partner.

In the post-Cold War years, this view was challenged by Russia's domestic developments, most notably the bombing of the Russian parliament in 1993, the wars in Chechnya and the deterioration of human rights and of the rule of law. Crony capitalism and the 1998 financial crisis also undermined positive perceptions of post-Soviet Russia (Ahrens and Weiss 2012: 153, Krumm 2012: 118–119, Siddi 2017b). Nonetheless, the country's economic recovery in the 2000s gave ground to new hopes in German official circles. Russian president Vladimir Putin enjoyed the support and personal friendship of chancellor Gerhard Schröder. German policy makers perpetuated the traditional *Ostpolitik* approach, arguing that political cooperation and economic partnership would be beneficial for both countries.

However, Russia has remained a divisive topic in German politics and society, and the debate has become more contentious after the Ukraine crisis (Siddi 2018c). The main fault line is the one between *Russland-Kritiker* and *Russland-Versteher*. *Russland-Kritiker* take a more critical stance vis-à-vis Russia's authoritarian developments and foreign policy. They include especially some members of the Green and Christian Democratic parties, advocates of Germany's transatlantic orientation and some intellectuals. To a certain extent, their stance resembles that of German liberals towards the Tsarist empire in the nineteenth century. *Russland-Versteher* are arguably a more diverse group. They include the Social Democratic heirs of Willy Brandt, who have tried to apply his *Ostpolitik* concept to relations with post-Soviet Russia, large business groups (notably the *Ost-Ausschuss der Deutschen Wirtschaft*) and other intellectuals. Among their ranks there are also politicians who are critical of US and Western policies towards Russia (mostly from the Left Party), or who sympathise with the Russian establishment and the conservative values that it advocates (mostly from the right-wing Alternative for Germany and the Christian Social Union) (Forsberg 2016). While all these actors have contributed to the debate on Russia in the following case studies, Christian Democratic and Social Democratic leaders have been the most influential in foreign policy making, as they held the posts of chancellor and foreign minister from 2014 until 2018.

The historic construction of Polish identity

The construction of Polish national identity has been influenced deeply by Poland's partitioning and foreign occupation until 1918 and its devastation during the Second World War. Today, Polish politicians generally argue that the country recovered its full independence only after 1989, with the dissolution of the Eastern bloc and the Warsaw Pact. Since then, the country has pursued a West-oriented foreign policy that led it to join NATO and the European Union (in 1999 and 2004 respectively). However, the long periods of foreign occupation and tutelage have left a profound impact on the construction of Polish identity. Post-1989 identity and memory politics has emphasised the suffering and heroic resistance of the Polish nation (Orla-Bukowska 2006). Narratives constructed during the nineteenth and twentieth centuries frequently re-emerge in current public discussions and interact with debates concerning Poland's foreign policy.

In national identity narratives, the partitioning of Poland by Germany, Russia and Austria in the late eighteenth century marks the beginning of the country's suffering and heroic resistance. Symptomatically, in 1990 post-Communist Poland restored 3 May as a national holiday, thereby establishing an ideal link with the Polish–Lithuanian Commonwealth of the eighteenth century. On 3 May 1791 the Commonwealth had adopted its first democratic constitution, only four years before ceasing to exist as an independent state (Davies 1996: 699). It took until 1918 before an independent Polish state re-emerged. During this period, many debates that still characterise Poland's self-image as an international actor were initiated (Porter 2000). At the same time, the conception of the Polish nation evolved from one that allowed for some cultural, religious and ethnic diversity to a more ethnonationalist understanding.

In the early nineteenth century, Polish intellectuals conceptualised the nation as an inclusive and diverse community. While the feeling of national belonging was still limited mostly to the educated few, this definition theoretically allowed the inclusion of other Christian ethnic groups. Catholic Poland was also considered as a Christian rampart (*antemurale christianitatis*). Tyranny, rather than a specific country or nation, was identified as the main Other, and the Polish nation was said to be ready to sacrifice itself for the freedom of nations ('for your freedom and ours', as a contemporary Polish romantic motto emphasised). These ideas provided the foundations for the 1830 uprising in the part of Poland occupied by the Russian empire, while Russia came to be seen as an embodiment of tyranny (Porter 2000: 16–22, Prizel 1998: 40–41).

Polish intellectuals perceived the crushing of the 1830 uprising as a betrayal of these values by other European nations, which did not join the battle against the Tsarist Empire. The commitment that Polish volunteers had shown in the fight for the freedom of other nations (for instance, during the American Revolution and the Napoleonic wars) remained unreciprocated. The theme of unrequited commitment to the freedom of nations became a dominant theme in Polish identity discourses and was later rearticulated and radicalised into accusations of outright betrayal addressed to the West (Prizel 1998: 41–42, 72–73). Polish elites started to see their nation as the 'Christ of nations', an image propagated in particular by the national poet Adam Mickiewicz after the 1830 uprising (cf. Mickiewicz 1833). According to this interpretation, the Polish nation sacrificed itself for the sake of all other nations, but one day it would resurrect. Mickiewicz's metaphor appealed to the Poles' deep religious sentiment and aptly combined political and religious imagery to foster faith in national rebirth.

The hopes of romantic nationalists suffered a fatal blow in 1863, when another major uprising was crushed in Russian Poland and the Tsar launched policies of cultural and linguistic Russification (Stauter-Halsted 2001: 244–246, Porter 2000: 15).[2] After 1863, the ideals of Polish romantics were gradually displaced by those of positivists. With the advent of Positivism, the definition of nation became more focused on Polish culture and language. Positivists believed that national minorities in the former territories of the Commonwealth (notably Lithuanians, Ukrainians, Jews and Belarusians) would converge towards Polish culture and language due to Poland's cultural superiority. The positivist reconceptualisation of the nation paved the way for ethnonationalism, an aggressive and more exclusive form of nationalism (Prizel 1998: 40–50). Ethnonationalism was advanced by political organisations that originated in the 1880s, most notably the National League of Roman Dmowski. Its nationalist discourse was authoritarian, xenophobic and anti-Semitic. Thanks to its diffusion among the peasantry at the end of the nineteenth century, ethnonationalism became a mass movement (Porter 2000: 125–126, 136–155).

Ethnonationalism influenced dramatically the relationship between ethnic Poles, internal minorities and neighbouring nations. It portrayed Jews, who numbered several million in the former territory of the Commonwealth, as an alien body that had to be either expelled or polonised. Ethnonationalists became convinced that a Polish state had to be rebuilt within the Commonwealth boundaries (stretching over most of today's Lithuania, Belarus and Ukraine), but with the Poles as a dominant ethnic group. Poles were also seen as having the messianic task of educating ethnic Ukrainians, Belarusians and Lithuanians, with the ultimate objective of polonising them (Porter 2000: 158–177, Prizel 1998: 52–67). Between 1918 and 1939, when Poland temporarily regained its independence, ethnonationalist leaders were appointed to leading state positions and their narratives became dominant in official discourses. Although national minorities constituted one third of Poland's interwar population, they were marginalised and had hardly any representation in political institutions (Prizel 1998: 62–67, Snyder 2003; cf. Brubaker 1996: 416–430).

The interwar Polish state was dismantled abruptly in 1939, when Nazi Germany and the Soviet Union partitioned the country. The brutal Nazi and Soviet war occupations strengthened and radicalised Polish perceptions of Germany and Russia as hostile Others. As the Second World War is the key episode in current national memory, resentment towards both Germany and Russia has been perpetuated in dominant discourses until today (Ruchniewicz 2007, Siddi and Gaweda 2019). Polish characterisations of their Second World War experiences can be clustered around the themes of suffering and heroism.

Discourses on suffering stress that Poland was the first country to be attacked by Nazi Germany (and simultaneously by the Soviet Union), experienced the longest foreign occupation in the war and endured enormous human and material losses. This discourse was influenced by and perpetuated nineteenth century narratives on national martyrdom that portrayed Poland as the 'Christ of nations'.

The discourse on Polish heroism is closely linked to that of suffering and stresses that the nation strenuously opposed the Nazis (Ruchniewicz 2007: 19). The opening of the Warsaw Rising Museum, which was inaugurated in the Polish capital in 2004 and immediately drew thousands of visitors every month, highlights the enduring relevance of the discourse on heroism (Żychlińska and Fontana 2016). The historical event has been turned into a founding myth of post-1989 Poland, regardless of its disappointing outcome, the large number of civilian casualties and the ensuing destruction of Warsaw. Poland's wartime experience also led to a revival of the discourse on Western betrayal and the unreciprocated support to the cause of freedom. Poles felt betrayed in 1939, when the United Kingdom and France provided no military assistance during the German invasion, and particularly at the Yalta conference in 1945, when the Western Allies agreed to leave Poland in the Soviet sphere of influence (Prizel 1998: 73–74).

The outcome of the Yalta conference and Poland's swift Sovietisation after the Second World War led Polish intellectuals and political opposition to reassess the country's role in the international scenario (Prizel 1998: 75–87). Poland's communist leaders attempted to develop a socialist, pro-Soviet identity, but were unable to dispel the perception that they were ruling Poland at the behest of a foreign power. Next to the official communist discourse, prominent oppositional discourses originated in the underground and in *émigrés* communities. The literary-political *émigré* magazine *Kultura* was one of the leading forums for the discussion of Polish identity and the future role of Poland in the international arena. In a fundamental break with Poland's interwar foreign policy, *Kultura* advocated the acceptance of existing borders and the recognition of Ukraine, Lithuania and Belarus as equal nations (Fedorowicz 2007). By the late 1980s, *Kultura*'s foreign policy ideas had become widely accepted among the Polish underground opposition (Snyder 2003: 220–225).

The support of the Polish Catholic Church and the Vatican facilitated the success of *Kultura*'s ideas. This endorsement was fundamental to promote the new international self-image of Poland among the masses, as the Church enjoyed widespread support in civil society. Due to the protracted lack of independent state structures, the Polish Catholic Church was able to profile itself as the main repository of the country's national identity. In popular perceptions, the Polish Catholic Church was one of the main factors leading to the end of communist rule in Poland. With the support of the Vatican, where Polish cardinal Karol Wojtyła became Pope in 1978, the Catholic trade union Solidarity became a mass movement and challenged the regime, eventually leading to its demise in

1989. After the collapse of state socialism, the Church acquired a dominant role in Poland's political and societal life, including identity politics (Gaweda 2017 and 2019, McManus-Czubinska and Miller 2008, Prizel 1998: 90–91, 229–230).

After 1989 the theme of the 'return to Europe', meant as joining the achievements of post-war Western Europe (Snyder 2003: 291), became dominant. Polish governments made EU and NATO integration their primary foreign policy goals. In order to achieve these aims, Warsaw adopted the policy of reconciliation with its neighbours conceptualised by *Kultura* and embraced a rhetoric that stressed so-called European standards (Snyder 2003: 256–258, cf. Curry 2008: 186–187). The ethnonationalist, xenophobic and anti-Semitic discourses of the interwar period lost dominance, but they did not disappear and remained widespread in important sections of the Catholic Church, right-wing political parties and public opinion in general (Bikont 2012). The fact that by 1990 Poland was almost a mono-ethnic state, having lost most of its interwar national minorities, made previous ethnonationalist discourses about threatening internal Others anachronistic. However, deep-seated perceptions of Western Europe as a treacherous ally and of Germany and Russia as Poland's historical enemies survived (Orla-Bukowska 181–187). Between 2005 and 2007 and again after 2015, when the right-wing party Law and Justice was in power, these perceptions constituted the backbone of official discourse (Reeves 2010, Siddi and Gaweda 2019). Its strong anti-German and especially anti-Russian rhetoric shows that, for a considerable part of its leadership, Poland still lives in an insecure international environment, where it is threatened by its historical Others.

Poland's nemesis: the Russian Other

Throughout Poland's modern history, Polish identity discourses constructed Russia and Germany as aggressive and threatening Others. Poland's post-1990 rapprochement to Germany and European integration have not cancelled negative images of the Western neighbour, which are strongly rooted in national memory. However, they have contributed to reconciliation and to the belief that a new era in Polish–German relations has begun (cf. Langenbacher 2008: 74–75). In this context, Russia has become the dominant Other in official Polish discourses. Russian domination over Poland was the longest the country ever experienced, stretching from 1795 to 1918 and then again (under the Soviet banner) from 1939 to 1941 and – according to a widespread Polish perception of the Cold War period – from 1945 to 1989. Soviet tutelage during the Cold War tends to be seen as the continuation of Tsarist domination and the terms 'Russia' and 'Russians' are used as metonymies for 'Soviet Union' and 'Soviets' (Orla-Bukowska 2006: 203).

Russia plays a key role in the narratives about Polish heroism and martyrdom. The discourse on Polish heroism was constructed mostly in the context of wars and uprisings against Russian domination. The 1830 and 1863 uprisings against the Tsarist Empire, the Polish–Soviet war of 1920 and the uprisings of 1956, 1968, 1970 and 1980 are considered as a *continuum* in a two century-long tradition of anti-Russian struggle (Loew 2008: 87–95, Ruchniewicz 2007: 11–12). Particular importance is attributed to the 1920 Polish–Soviet war. The decisive battle of the war, fought at the gates of Warsaw, is commonly referred to as 'the miracle at the Vistula', as it averted a Bolshevik victory that had seemed inevitable (cf. Orla-Bukowska 2006: 204).

Within the martyrdom discourse, Russia plays a key role as the oppressor that crushed nearly all Polish attempts to regain freedom. Most notably, it is portrayed as the brutal, dictatorial power that partitioned Poland with the Nazis in 1939 and exterminated nearly 22,000 Polish officers in the Katyn massacre in April 1940. The massacre and the Nazi–Soviet Pact have been widely discussed in public only in post-1989 Poland, as both topics were taboo under state socialism (Levintova 2010, Paul 2010). Post-Soviet Russia, however, has refused to take responsibility for Stalinist crimes. In 2010 Russian president Dmitri Medvedev suggested that Warsaw lacked moral grounds to demand an apology for Katyn, as interwar Poland had been responsible for comparable crimes against the Soviet Union, such as the death of 16,000–20,000 Soviet prisoners of war in Polish detention camps (cited in Feklyunina 2012: 444). Polish narratives reject such comparisons and the dispute concerning responsibility for Katyn has not ended. In fact, the death of former Polish president Lech Kaczynski in a plane crash in April 2010, while he was going to commemorate the seventieth anniversary of the Katyn massacre, contributed to the continued prominence of the topic in public discourse. The ensuing debate on responsibilities for the plane crash showed that mutual distrust and hostility are still important factors in Polish–Russian relations (Shuster 2011, Sus 2018).

Russia's enduring role as Poland's threatening Other has turned the country into a negative reference point for the construction of the Polish Self and for Poland's understanding of its role in the international arena. In Polish discourses, Russia fulfils the function of relativising Poland's distance from the West. Russia is perceived as inherently undemocratic and as an inferior imitator of European civilisation (Zarycki 2004, cf. Prizel 1998: 82–85). Polish discourses orientalise Russia; they describe it as a less civilised and backward country, with a tradition of despotism linked to strong Asiatic influences. The ensuing feeling of cultural superiority allows Poles to strengthen their European identity, construct themselves as Central Europe and feel closer to Western European civilisation (cf. Said 1978). Polish identity narratives portray Russia as inherently imperialistic. Post-communist Russia's use of energy politics to achieve political objectives is constructed as a continuation of Tsarist and Soviet expansionist policies by different means. Arguably, the image of Russia as a potential threat has been the backbone of Polish foreign policy after 1989 and the main reason for Poland's pursuit of EU and NATO membership (Zarycki 2004: 607–614).

After the collapse of state socialism, relations between Moscow and Warsaw improved briefly when Red Army soldiers left their bases in Poland and Russian president Boris Yeltsin initially agreed to Polish NATO membership (Snyder 2003: 245–246). For the rest of the 1990s, Polish–Russian diplomatic relations were restricted to the bare minimum. In 2002 Vladimir Putin finally travelled to Poland, nine years after the last official visit of a Russian president (Feklyunina 2012: 438). However, the renewed activism of Russia's foreign policy under Putin, combined with its rapid economic growth in the years 2000–2008, reawakened deep-seated Polish fears of the powerful Eastern neighbour. In 2004, Poland and Russia got involved in the political crisis that followed the presidential election in Ukraine. Warsaw and Moscow resented each other's attempts to influence political developments in a neighbouring state. The following year was marred by a series of bilateral crises, culminating in a Russian ban on the import of Polish meat and dairy products. In response, Poland (an EU member since 2004) vetoed the start of EU–Russia negotiations on a new Partnership and Cooperation Agreement (Feklyunina 2012: 439). Furthermore, Putin's invitation of his Polish counterpart Aleksander Kwasniewski to the May 2005 celebrations of the Soviet victory in the Second World War revived the Polish public debate on Soviet crimes in Poland during the war (Onken 2007).

Polish official discourses about Russia became further radicalised due to the 2005 electoral victory of the profoundly anti-Russian party Law and Justice of Lech and Jaroslaw Kaczynski. The Law and Justice governments made constant use of historical analogies to address foreign policy issues with Germany and Russia. In 2006 Polish defence minister Radoslaw Sikorski dubbed the Nord Stream gas pipeline connecting Russia to Germany via the Baltic Sea (thereby circumventing Poland) a 'new Molotov–Ribbentrop pact' (cited in Castle 2006). A year later, Law and Justice foreign minister Anna Fotyga publicly called Russia and Germany Poland's 'historic enemies' (cited in Reeves 2010: 522). The government's decision to host elements of the US anti-missile shield on Polish territory, describing them as an anti-Russian guarantee, further spoiled relations with Moscow (Ozbay and Aras 2008).

In October 2007, when centre-right candidate Donald Tusk won the elections and became prime minister, Polish–Russian relations started to improve. The Tusk government sought partial reconciliation with Russia by adopting a pragmatic approach on economic issues and by fostering dialogue on sensitive topics such as the Katyn massacre. Anti-Russian discourses did not disappear but were toned down, at least at the official level. Bilateral visits took place and Poland partially softened its stance on Russia at EU level. Some progress was made also in discussions regarding historical controversies. In 2009, Putin attended the commemorations for the start of the Second World War in Gdansk and argued that the Molotov–Ribbentrop Pact had been immoral. In 2010 a forum of prominent Russian and Polish experts appointed by their respective governments produced a joint publication addressing sensitive issues, including the Katyn massacre and the origins of the Second World War (Feklyunina 2012: 438–441).[3] For the first time in the history of Polish–Russian relations, in April 2010 the Russian and Polish prime ministers jointly commemorated the Katyn massacre (Schwirtz 2010).

However, the atmosphere of reconciliation generated by the joint commemoration was marred by the aftermath of the plane crash in which Polish president

Lech Kaczynski died. The Polish right overtly blamed Russia for the plane crash and constructed a discourse juxtaposing Russian past and (alleged) present crimes, which swiftly became dominant. This discourse became more virulent in 2011, when a Russian enquiry commission published a report exculpating the Russian authorities from responsibility for the accident. Russia also refused to return the plane wreck to Poland. Conspiracy theories blaming Russia and Tusk for a 'new Katyn' became omnipresent in Polish media (Davies 2016, Shuster 2011). Hence, Poland's reconciliation with Russia under Tusk was only partial and has proven to be fragile. Profoundly anti-Russian discourses have remained prominent both at official and unofficial level and are often voiced by Law and Justice, which has regained the political control of the country following its victory in the 2015 parliamentary and presidential elections. Furthermore, relations with Moscow have become extremely tense following Russia's annexation of Crimea and destabilisation of Ukraine in 2014.

The historic construction of Finnish identity

Finnish national identity has been constructed around the concepts of marginality (and being a small country), Nordicity and the historical necessity to locate the country along an East–West continuum. These conceptualisations have profound cultural and political significance and have shaped the way Finns perceive their country and its role in the international arena. They were constructed during the last two centuries within historical frameworks that allowed Finland to become first an autonomous entity within the Russian empire, then a fully independent country.

The year 1809 marks an important date in the construction of Finnish national identity. After nearly six centuries of Swedish control, the Grand Duchy of Finland was created as part of the Tsarist Empire, with autonomous institutions and a distinct legal and administrative system (Tiilikainen 1998: 120–122). Within this political structure, Finns could develop for the first time a feeling of national belonging based on a common language and the rediscovery of their cultural heritage.[4] Finland was portrayed as a young nation in the process of maturation. Within this discourse, the autonomy acquired under Russian tutelage was seen as a considerable step forward from the period of Swedish domination. Central figures of the Finnish national movement such as Yrjö Sakari Yrjö-Koskinen and Johan Vilhelm Snellman argued that the nation could be constructed also within Russian imperial structures by focusing on the cultural sphere and temporarily renouncing ambitions of independence (Browning and Lehti 2007: 697, Joenniemi 2002).

In the nineteenth century, the emphasis on cultural identity was part of a discourse portraying Finland as a small nation that needed the protection of a stronger, benevolent Other while it developed a distinct identity. Simultaneously, Finnish nationalists used the peripheral location of the Grand Duchy in the Tsarist Empire and its administrative autonomy to relativise Finland's political dependence on Russia. Being marginal meant being distinct from the rest of the empire.

Marginality and the notion of being a small country amidst neighbouring great powers became dominant traits of Finnish identity and of Finland's self-image in the international arena (Browning and Lehti 2007, Tiilikainen 2006).

Towards the end of the nineteenth century, the Russification campaigns and increasing repressiveness of the Tsarist government led to a gradual rethinking of Finnish national identity and its relationship with Russia. While the Finnish leadership attempted to accommodate Russian requests and retain political autonomy, a new conception of national identity based on ethnicity and exclusive boundaries became widespread (Joenniemi 2002: 198). According to this view, national identity could not be constructed simply on cultural distinctiveness and political autonomy; Finns had to strive for full independence and the creation of a nation-state. The Russian revolution provided the opportunity to disentangle the country from the crumbling Tsarist Empire. In December 1917 Finland proclaimed its independence.

The newly-born Finnish state immediately experienced a bloody civil war between the political right and the left, which led to the radicalisation of national identity discourses. The victory of the right in Finland and the success of the Bolsheviks in the Russian civil war brought about fundamental changes in Finnish self-images and perceptions of the international role of Finland. The Soviet Union was orientalised and constructed as the main national threat, while Finland was portrayed as an outpost of Western civilisation (Joenniemi 2002: 199). From this time, locating Finland somewhere along a continuum between East and West became a permanent feature of national identity discourses (Browning and Lehti 2007: 691). In the following decades, the country was alternatively depicted as a Western, anti-Soviet bastion or as a bridge between East and West, with the function of bringing Russia closer to the latter.

In the interwar period, ethnonationalism dominated Finnish political discourses. It entailed the formulation of expansionist foreign policy ideas, such as the creation of a Greater Finland extending to Eastern Karelia and Siberia. Finns' confidence in the ability to stand on their own and confront larger neighbours was temporarily bolstered by the successful defensive campaigns of the Winter War against the Soviet Union (1939–1940). Eventually, however, such confidence was shattered by the entanglement in the broader geopolitical struggle between Nazi Germany and the USSR and, most importantly, by the defeat in the Second World War (Vehviläinen 2002). The conditions imposed by the Soviets at the end of the war, including the loss of considerable portions of national territory and a large indemnity, led Finnish leaders to reject the political course of the interwar years and reformulate the foreign policy of the country (Browning 2008: 169–178).

Dominant post-war discourses stressed that the involvement in great power politics had catastrophic consequences for Finland. Hence, the idea of Finland as a small nation that should adopt a pragmatic policy and stay aloof from geopolitical struggles remained central in foreign policy making throughout the Cold War. Pragmatism in foreign policy meant primarily accommodating the requests of the Soviet Union, the powerful neighbour with which Finland shared a border of over 1,000 kilometres. In 1948 a Treaty of Friendship, Cooperation and Mutual Assistance with the Soviet Union was signed. While maintaining good relations with the USSR, Finland became a neutral state. This pragmatic foreign policy doctrine became known as Paasikivi–Kekkonen line, from the names of Juho Paasikivi, who became president in 1946 and is credited with having started it, and his successor Urho Kekkonen, who was in office from 1956 until 1981 (Browning 2008: 169–171; Tiilikainen 1998: 146–151). The key objective of the Paasikivi–Kekkonen line was the preservation of independence and territorial integrity, which appeared seriously threatened at the end of the Second World War. This conception also constituted the pragmatic essence of 'Finlandisation', a termed coined in the German scholarly debate during the Cold War that referred to the policy of securing sovereignty by making political concessions to the Soviet Union (Forsberg and Pesu 2016, Jokela 2010: 56).[5] Following this policy line, Finland would accommodate Soviet requests and obtain in return Soviet acceptance of its independence, political system and free market economy (Browning 2008: 176).

The choice of neutrality in the East–West confrontation was also pragmatic and functional to Finnish foreign policy interests. It sent a positive message to both Cold War camps. For the communist world, it meant that Finland would stay neutral in international crises, despite its adherence to Western values. For the West, neutrality was a message of belonging: it could be read as evidence that Finland had to accommodate Soviet security interests, but while doing so it kept Western political and economic structures. As the Cold War unfolded, Finnish neutrality evolved from a defensive policy for the preservation of sovereignty to an opportunity to acquire an active role in mediating the East–West conflict. Finland was constructed as a successful bridge builder within the framework of detente between the two blocs. The signature of the Helsinki Final Act at the 1975 summit of the Conference on Security and Co-operation in Europe, held in the Finnish capital, was arguably the greatest success of the Finnish policy of bridge building between East and West (Tiilikainen 1998: 153–156).

The policy of neutrality allowed Finland to become active and construct a distinct identity also in other fields of world politics where some room for manoeuvre existed outside the East–West conflict. Most notably, the country became a prominent supporter of 'internationalist solidarism' (Browning 2007: 33), namely the efforts to bridge the economic gap between rich and poor states. Finland was a fervent advocate of the United Nations (UN) and, together with the other Nordic countries (Sweden, Norway and Denmark), provided 25 per cent of the military personnel deployed in UN operations during the Cold War (Browning 2007: 35). Alongside the focus on international solidarity, Finland shared with its Nordic neighbours the domestic model of egalitarian social democracy (portrayed as a third way between communism and capitalism) and the international image of being a peaceful and highly modern society. These three elements became the foundations of a Nordic identity through which Finland constructed its international role during the Cold War (Browning 2007: 32–35).

When the Cold War ended, the main tenets of Nordic identity and of Finland's self-image were challenged by the new geopolitical reality and the economic recession that hit the country in the early 1990s. Defining the Nordic social democratic model as a middle way between Western European capitalism and state socialism no longer seemed appropriate, as the latter no longer existed. Even so, the Nordic model retained its appeal domestically and abroad. In foreign policy, Finland had to face the fact that it no longer appeared useful to define its identity in terms of an East–West continuum (Browning 2007: 36–43, Tiilikainen 1998: 159; cf. Waever 1992).

This conundrum was solved through the combination of a new identity discourse and the adaptation of pre-existing discourses. The new narrative argued that Finland could finally return to the West and to Europe, after being forced to stay at their margins in order to retain its sovereignty during the Cold War (Browning and Lehti 2007: 704). This was exemplified by the first Finnish foreign policy moves after the end of the Cold War. The 1948 treaty with the Soviet Union expired in 1992 and Finland applied for membership in the European Union, which was granted after nearly 57 per cent of Finns voted in favour in a referendum held in October 1994 (Joenniemi 2002: 186). The shift in Finland's foreign policy identity brought about by accession to the EU could be reconciled with pre-existing identity discourses. The EU was conceptualised as a democratic community that did not intrude on the Finnish social model, national security policy and Nordic identity (Joenniemi 2002: 204). Within the European Union, Finland also attempted to keep its Cold War role as a bridge builder to Russia. The Northern Dimension, a Finnish initiative launched in 1998 to coordinate the cross-border policies of the EU with Norway, Iceland and particularly Russia, provides the best example of these attempts (cf. Haukkala and Ojanen 2011: 159–161).

By stressing interdependence and the need for cooperation among the countries involved, the Northern Dimension sought to blur the boundaries between the European (and Finnish) Self and the Russian Other. In particular, it endeavoured to harmonise the EU's views and policies with those of its partners (Haukkala 2005: 287–288). Despite the EU's declared objective of creating a common foreign, defence and security policy for its members, Finland did not fully relinquish its neutrality. The Finnish security discourse was partially reframed in terms of alignment. Helsinki conceded that it had aligned with the West and the EU politically and economically, but continued to adhere to military non-alignment (Jokela 2010: 61). This position has constantly enjoyed the support of the majority of Finns, which highlights how strongly the country's public opinion has internalised military neutrality as part of national identity (Möller and Bjereld 2010: 371). Even after the Ukraine crisis and the perception of a growing threat from Russia, a clear majority of Finns opposed NATO membership (Yle 2016).

The awareness of being a small nation with limited room for independent manoeuvre in foreign policy has continued to be a key characteristic of Finnish political identity (Tiilikainen 2006, cf. Forsberg and Pesu 2016).

Accession to the EU was also seen as a way of compensating for Finland's political marginality, as well as a statement of belonging to democratic Western Europe. However, Finnish policy makers have framed Finland's small-state identity also in more positive terms. A discourse on Finland as a young, future-oriented nation that quickly adapts itself to the challenges of the modern world has emerged, somewhat in continuation with the country's early nineteenth century depictions (cf. Joenniemi 2010: 56). Locating Finland at the economic centre of the globalised world, in spite of its small size and geographic marginality, is the main aim of the current discourse (Browning and Lehti 2007: 708).

Russia in Finnish discourses: economic partner and security deficit

The discussion of Finnish national identity construction has highlighted the prominent role of Russia and the Soviet Union in Finnish history and foreign policy choices. By contrast with dominant Polish narratives, Russia has not always been portrayed as a threat in Finnish discourses. In fact, for most of the nineteenth century most Finns considered the Tsarist Empire as a benevolent Other that allowed Finnish culture and national identity to blossom (Joenniemi 2010: 48). Russia's relative benevolence was contrasted with the previous period of Swedish government, during which Finns had enjoyed less autonomy and cultural independence. This experience constituted an important precedent for later Finnish leaders who made the case for peaceful coexistence and close cooperation with Russia (Browning 2003: 53).

The positive memory of the early Tsarist period is however counter-balanced by that of the conflicts that characterised bilateral history in the first half of the twentieth century. The Russian Revolution allowed Finland to break off the Tsarist Empire and acquire full political independence, but it also created an ideological and military adversary east of the newly-born Finnish state. With the rise of Finnish ethnonationalism in the 1920s and 1930s, a new narrative depicting Russians in overtly racist terms (as evil, treacherous and culturally inferior) became prominent. The border with the Soviet Union was considered a civilisational demarcation between European and Asian culture (Browning 2007: 700). The radicalisation of negative discourses about the Soviet Union reached a peak during the Winter War (1939–1940), when Stalin's regime attempted a full-scale invasion of Finland. The unexpected and strenuous Finnish defence saved the country's independence and became one of the key national myths. In this narrative, the Russians play the role of brutal aggressors against whom the whole country united. The loss of the region of Karelia to the Soviet Union and the resettlement of its inhabitants to other areas of Finland were constant reminders of the suffering inflicted by the Soviets (cf. Forsberg 1995, Vehviläinen 2002). The desire to avenge Soviet aggression led Finland to the disastrous decision of participating in the German attack against the Soviet Union in 1941.

Military defeat eventually stimulated a reconsideration of Finland's stance towards its powerful Eastern neighbour. The virulent anti-Soviet discourses of the interwar years were considered responsible for the outbreak of a war that Finland could not win. They had also legitimised Soviet security concerns and subsequent military action. Finland's post-war leaders concluded that criticism of the USSR had to be curtailed in order to avoid a new confrontation (Browning and Lehti 2007: 700–701). Since the Soviet victory and the geopolitical realities left no alternative, the majority of Finns supported this policy line. Finland's economic success, the development of an alternative social model and its global role as a peace-maker translated into constant support for a neutral, Soviet-friendly foreign policy throughout the Cold War (Forsberg and Pesu 2016). Criticism of the Soviet Union was self-censored and the country was publicly described as an important partner for Finland (cf. Vihavainen 2006: 31). Threat perceptions did not disappear, but they were not voiced at official level.

The collapse of the Soviet Union and the expiry of the 1948 treaty have changed the nature of Finland's relations with its Eastern neighbour. Finnish media and public opinion have often criticised Russia openly in the post-Cold War period. The post-war policy of political concessions to Moscow no longer provides a model for Finnish foreign policy and has been retrospectively criticised by some politicians. However, at official level rhetoric has not changed dramatically. There are no prominent bilateral controversies left unsolved from the past. After the crises and instability of the 1990s, Russia has become again an important trade partner for Finland. When Finnish politicians refer to their country's historical relationship with Russia in public, they tend to emphasise positive moments, such as the development of Finnish national identity under Russian rule in the nineteenth century and the special Finnish–Soviet relationship during the Cold War (Vihavainen 2006).

However, Finnish perceptions of a security threat emanating from Russia still exist. Evidence for this is provided by Finland's continued reliance on territorial defence and a relatively large army of reservists. Finnish political and military leaders do not openly mention Russia as a menace, but they refer to it indirectly, often speaking in code and with euphemisms such as 'Finland's security deficit' (Forsberg 2006: 143). The Ukraine crisis has rekindled threat perceptions. Some scholars argue that the image of a Russian threat is still present in Finnish psyche and is an essential component of the grand national narrative (cf. Medvedev 1999: 104). However, a majority of Finns and the Finnish political establishment has been in favour of non-confrontational relations with Moscow, including energy trade and cooperation on the Arctic and environmental issues. Within the European Union, Finland is one of the main advocates of a policy of pragmatic engagement with Russia. Finns consider maintaining a positive dialogue with Moscow essential in order to avoid confrontation at their country's borders (Etzold and Haukkala 2011: 253–254).

Furthermore, Helsinki has retained positive bilateral relations with Moscow, which guarantee a safe channel of communication whenever the European Union proves unable to formulate a shared policy towards Russia (Haukkala and Ojanen 2011: 165; cf. Vihavainen 2006: 45). The Finnish public opinion and numerous politicians tend to believe that Finland's accession to NATO would alienate Russia, thereby producing more security drawbacks than benefits. Russian leaders have confirmed this belief and argued that Russia would take countermeasures if Finland were to join NATO. Hence, Finland has upheld its pragmatic policy towards Moscow and has reconciled EU membership with its traditional role as bridge builder between the West and Russia.

Conclusion: national identities and historical discourses as interpretive frameworks

This chapter showed that current German, Polish and Finnish national identities are the result of a *longue durée* process of construction that extends well into the nineteenth and twentieth centuries. The analysis emphasised that, following the experience of National Socialism (as well as of state socialism in the GDR), German identity has been constructed around the rejection of authoritarianism and war. Economic prosperity, political stability, democracy and multilateralism in international politics (notably the advocacy of policies agreed upon at EU level) have become key tenets of German identity. In Poland, national identity narratives have focused on the themes of martyrdom and heroism. The martyrdom narrative focuses on the country's foreign occupation from 1795 until 1918 and during the Second World War, as well as on its constrained independence during the Cold War. The heroism narrative stresses that Poland never accepted its loss of independence and consistently fought for its freedom, in spite of overwhelming hostile forces and the indifference of Western democracies. During the periods of foreign occupation and tutelage, the Catholic Church and Catholicism acquired fundamental importance as key constituents of Polish identity, providing ideological and institutional support for the political forces fighting for independence. On the other hand, Finnish identity construction was profoundly influenced by the country's geographical location and its geopolitical implications. Narratives of marginality and Nordicity played an essential role, with the latter acquiring particular importance during the Cold War. In this historical phase, Finland closely identified with the Nordic model, including an egalitarian society, support for international solidarity and multilateralism as a way to address international disputes. Most importantly, Finland was conceptualised as a country moving along an East–West continuum, belonging to the West ideologically but simultaneously acting as a bridge builder towards the East, namely Russia and the Soviet Union. This self-perception as mediator between East and West also contributed to turning neutrality into a key factor of the country's post-1945 identity.

Russia emerged as an important Other in national identity narratives in the three countries under investigation. However, constructions of Russia varied significantly from country to country and over time. In the nineteenth and twentieth centuries through to the Cold War, most German discourses dismissed Russia as authoritarian, corrupt and backward. While these narratives still played a role in post-reunification Germany, new discourses have emerged, portraying Russia as an economic partner and a key international actor that Germany must engage. The *Ostpolitik* discourse, advocating dialogue and partnership with Russia, has been particularly influential from the 1970s onwards. By contrast, Russia was constructed as the main negative Other in Polish identity throughout Poland's modern and contemporary history (sharing this role with Germany until 1945 and occasionally later). Dominant Polish narratives have portrayed Russia as imperialist, aggressive, undemocratic, oriental and therefore unaware of the Western values that Poles claim to cherish. Only in recent years, during the tenure of Donald Tusk as prime minister (2007–2014), a more positive discourse on Russia has emerged highlighting its role as potential partner in a pragmatic foreign policy. However, the conflict in Ukraine has undermined the tentative Polish–Russian rapprochement. Dominant Finnish narratives alternated positive and deeply negative representations of Russia. In the early nineteenth century, Russia was considered mostly as a benevolent Other that emancipated Finland from Swedish oppression and allowed it to become autonomous. As a result of the policies of Russification in the latter part of the century and the Bolshevik revolution, dominant discourses changed radically. Soviet Russia was seen as the most formidable threat to Finnish independence, a perception that was strengthened after the Soviet aggression in 1939. Both positive and negative discourses survived after the Second World War, but were reformulated in more moderate terms. Russia was portrayed both as an essential economic partner and, due to its military might, as the chief source of Finland's security deficit.

Hence, the analysis of national identity and historical narratives on Russia revealed considerable differences across the three countries under investigation. Table 3.1 summarises the dominant discourses as they emerged from the analysis in this chapter. In the following chapters, these findings are used as an interpretive framework to examine foreign policy makers' speeches and statements on Russia between 2014 and 2018. It is possible that some of the identity constituents and narratives listed in Table 3.1 may have a stronger reflection than others in the foreign policy speeches under analysis. With the passage of time, some identity discourses that played a role in foreign policy making in the past may have lost importance, while others may have emerged in a slightly different form, adapted to present circumstances. While allowing for these eventualities, the analysis refers to key elements in *longue durée* national identity formation and historical discourses on Russia to deconstruct and provide one way of understanding foreign policy makers' speeches.

Table 3.1 Main themes and the Russian Other in German, Polish and Finnish identity discourses

	German discourses	*Polish discourses*	*Finnish discourses*
Discourses on Russia	Ostpolitik	Imperialist and aggressive	Benevolent Other
	Authoritarian, corrupt, socially and economically backward	Brutal occupying power for most of Poland's modern history	Economic partner
	Economic partner	Oriental, undemocratic and corrupt	Finland's security deficit
	Key actor in international arena	Relativising Poland's distance from the West	
		Partner in pragmatic foreign policy	
National identity discourses	Democracy and human rights	National martyrdom (Christ of nations)	Moving along an East–West continuum (bridge builder to East/ Western outpost)
	Economic prosperity and stability	National heroism	Marginality
	Rejection of war as means to solve disputes	Catholicism	Nordicity (egalitarian model, international solidarity, multilateralism), Europeanism
	Pro-European Union and multilateralism	Euro-Atlanticism	Neutrality/military non-alignment
		Unreciprocated commitment to the West	Finland as a young and modern nation

Notes

1 While in 1945 Germany had no 'usable past' in political terms, a large part of German cultural and artistic heritage was not discredited by the catastrophic outcome of national unity until 1945 and – together with the shared language – continued to constitute a powerful unifying factor in the following decades.

2 In 1866–1867 Russian was established as mandatory language for the teaching of all subjects in all Polish secondary school, with the exception of religion (Porter 2000: 79–80).

3 The forum was named 'Group on difficult issues' and their work was published under the title *White Spots – Black Spots: Difficult Issues in Russian–Polish Relations* (Feklyunina 2012: 440).

4 In 1835 the *Kalevala* was published, a national epic of Finland and one of the main works in Finnish literature. It had a profound impact on virtually all aspects of Finnish cultural life.

5 In Finland the term 'Finlandisation' has acquired a negative meaning, indicating an excessive willingness to appease the Soviet Union (cf. Browning 2008: 207, Jokela 2010: 56).

4 Confronting the Russian Other – the Ukraine crisis

Introduction

This chapter investigates national leaders' discourses on Russia during the political and military crisis in Ukraine from 2014 until 2018. It shows that perceptions of a threatening Russian Other became prominent in German, Finnish and especially Polish narratives. This paved the way for the joint, EU-level condemnation of Russian policies in Ukraine and the imposition of sanctions. Debates became focused on legal and security issues, whereas narratives about economic cooperation receded from the foreground. In the period between Moscow's annexation of Crimea and the signature of the Minsk-2 agreement, the national narratives under investigation converged towards the unanimous denunciation of Russia's use of force and violations of international law. However, differences began to arise between the German and the Finnish narratives, on the one hand, and the Polish one, on the other, during the course of 2015. In the following years, these discursive differences reflected divergent ways of approaching Russia in certain important fields, such as energy security and other sectoral cooperation. Broadly speaking, German and Finnish leaders attempted to maintain a good working relationship with Moscow in a number of areas, whereas their Polish counterparts essentialised Russia as a security threat and left little room for cooperation or dialogue. The chapter contends that these divergences highlight the enduring relevance of conflicting national identities and constructions of Russia within the EU.

The Ukraine crisis and EU–Russia relations

The confrontation between the EU and Russia following Moscow's annexation of Crimea can be viewed as the culmination of a crisis that had been simmering for years (Forsberg and Haukkala 2016: 33). Since the late 2000s in particular, the Russian leadership felt increasingly excluded from Western security and institutional structures. This clearly emerged in Vladimir Putin's speech at the Munich Security Conference in February 2007, where he criticised US unipolarism and disregard of international law, NATO's Eastern enlargement and George W. Bush's plans to deploy ballistic missile defence in Eastern Europe (cf. Sakwa 2017: 112). Following a peak of tensions between Russia and the West during the Russian–Georgian War of August 2008, a temporary improvement in relations occurred after the election of Barack Obama to the US presidency and the launch of an EU–Russia 'modernisation partnership' (David and Romanova 2015). However, in late 2011 West–Russian relations began to deteriorate again due to Russia's domestic developments, different views on the Libyan and Syrian conflicts and, ultimately, competing plans for the economic and political integration of the post-Soviet space (Sakwa 2017: 112–115).

The flawed Duma election of December 2011 and the crackdown on ensuing civil society protests elicited criticism from the US (and, to a lesser extent, the EU, cf. Siddi 2017b: 117–136), which the Russian leadership perceived as meddling in Russia's domestic affairs. Moreover, Russian leaders attempted to strengthen their popularity by adopting a conservative-patriotic narrative and controversial legislation, including the 'foreign agent' law (targeting non-governmental organisations that received funds from abroad) and the 'anti-gay propaganda' law, which discriminated against sexual minorities (Gel'man 2016, Wilkinson 2014). However, it was on foreign policy issues that disagreements between the EU and Russia escalated into a full-blown crisis. Following his re-election to president of Russia in March 2012, Vladimir Putin accelerated plans to create a Eurasian Economic Union (EEU), a Russia-led effort at economic and political integration in the post-Soviet space (Roberts and Moshes 2016). Together with Russia, Belarus and Kazakhstan endorsed the EEU project since its inception; Armenia and Kyrgyzstan also joined the EEU in 2015. From the Russian perspective, Ukraine's membership was key to the success of the EEU. However, Kiev was simultaneously pursuing the path towards greater integration with the EU, which included the prospective conclusion of an Association Agreement (AA) at the EU's Eastern Partnership summit in Vilnius in November 2013. Prior to the Vilnius summit, Putin convinced Ukrainian president Viktor Yanukovych to postpone the signing of the AA with the EU (for a full account, see Forsberg and Haukkala 2016: 35–36 and Sakwa 2017: 50–80).

Yanukovych's decision led to large-scale popular protests in Ukraine. The demonstrators assembled in the central square of Maidan Nezalezhnosti in Kiev and their movement became known as 'Euromaidan'. Several EU leaders expressed sympathy with the demonstrators and some, including German foreign minister Guido Westerwelle, demonstrated with them in Maidan Square. Nevertheless, Yanukovych attempted to dislodge and silence the protestors. In January and February 2014, the confrontation between demonstrators and the government became violent. Following several days of intense clashes and a failed attempt of the foreign ministers of Germany, France and Poland to mediate the crisis, the Yanukovych regime dissolved on 21 February (Yanukovych himself left Kiev and fled to Russia) and the demonstrators claimed control of governmental buildings. A new government was formed under the leadership of opposition politicians. One of the first parliamentary acts of the new majority was the repeal of a law that allowed the use of minority languages in courts, schools and other government institutions in areas where national minorities exceed 10 per cent of the population. This led to protests and demonstrations in several predominantly Russian-speaking parts of Ukraine. The situation in the country remained unstable, and on 1 March thousands of people in the Eastern and Southern regions protested against the new political order in Kiev (cf. Sakwa 2015: 81–99, Wilson 2014: 86–98).

Beginning on 27 February, within few days, Russian special forces without insignia took over government buildings in Crimea and cut off the peninsula from the rest of Ukraine, while pro-Russian political forces took control of the Crimean parliament. Following a swiftly organised referendum that was not recognised internationally, the new local authorities declared the independence of Crimea on 17 March and requested the Russian government to incorporate the breakaway republic into the Russian Federation. The request was accepted by the Russian side and Crimea was annexed to Russia. The vast majority of the international community did not recognise Russia's annexation of Crimea. The European Council (2014) condemned Russian actions in Crimea in an extra-ordinary meeting on 6 March. From March 2014, the EU progressively imposed sanctions on Russia in response to the annexation of Crimea and the destabilisation of Ukraine. Initially, these included diplomatic measures (i.e. the cancellation of bilateral summits and the exclusion of Russia from the G8), asset freezes and travel restrictions against individuals that were considered responsible for Russian actions in Ukraine (excluding Putin) and restrictions on economic rela-tions with Crimea. The sanctions were expanded significantly in July and September 2014, targeting whole sectors of the Russian economy and limiting Russian access to EU capital markets, arms and energy-related technologies (European Council 2016; cf. Portela 2019). Russia responded by imposing sanc-tions on a number of Western politicians and a ban on the import of food and agricultural products from the EU, US, Norway, Canada and Australia.

In April 2014, the crisis escalated again in the Donbass region, resulting in the occupation of government buildings by pro-Russian militants and the proclamation of the Donetsk and Luhansk People's Republics. The uprising led to the military intervention of the Ukrainian armed forces and various militias, which were countered by local rebels, volunteers from Russia and, increasingly, members of the Russian armed forces (see also Matveeva 2016). The fighting in the Donetsk and Luhansk regions intensified throughout the spring and summer of 2014, causing thousands of casualties and hundreds of thousands of refugees (Sakwa 2015: 148–182, Wilson 2014: 118–143). Moreover, on 17 July 2014, the Malaysian Airlines flight 17 was shot down over the conflict zone, most prob-ably by pro-Russian insurgents, resulting in the death of 298 people. The tragedy had a strong impact in the EU (most passengers were of Dutch nationality) and led the Union to impose sectoral sanctions on Russia, which had presumably supplied the pro-Russian fighters with modern anti-aircraft missile systems.

A ceasefire was agreed at peace talks in Minsk on 5 September 2014 with the mediation of the OSCE, but it was breached repeatedly by both sides. After a period of relative calm in December 2014, the fighting escalated again in January and February 2015. After rejecting US proposals to supply arms to the

Ukrainian government, German chancellor Angela Merkel and French president Francois Hollande took the initiative to negotiate a peace plan in Minsk on 11–12 February (Gordon *et al.* 2015). The peace talks resulted in the Minsk-2 agreement, including a ceasefire, the pull-out of heavy weapons (both under OSCE monitoring), the holding of elections in the Donetsk and Luhansk regions according to Ukrainian law and a constitutional reform in Ukraine that would grant special status to both regions (*Telegraph* 2015). The fighting abated and, although violations and shelling continued to occur, the ceasefire mostly held in the following months. However, by the end of 2015 the conflict appeared to have been frozen, rather than resolved (Burridge 2016). Neither the elections in the Donbas and Luhansk regions, nor the Ukrainian constitutional reform had taken place as specified by the Minsk-2 agreement.

Thus, the conflict in Ukraine remained a major source of confrontation between the EU and Russia, with both sides extending the duration of the sanctions that were initially imposed in 2014. In late 2014 and early 2015, the Russian economy was hit severely by the combined effect of the sanctions and, most significantly, the fall in the oil price. Despite the crisis in EU–Russia relations, the German and French political leaders continued to support peace negotiations. Since June 2014, the negotiations have taken place in the 'Normandy format', including the leaders of Ukraine, Russia, France and Germany. Bilateral US–Russian negotiations have also taken place, particularly after Donald Trump succeeded to Obama as US President. On the other hand, after the February 2014 negotiations in Kiev, Polish leaders have been excluded and Poland ceased to play a role as a mediator in the crisis.

In the second half of 2015, some modest (and divisive) steps towards the resumption of economic and diplomatic cooperation between Russia and some EU member states took place. Arguably, this was made possible by the lack of large-scale fighting in the Donbass. Moreover, the simultaneous occurrence of other crises – notably the European refugee crisis, Brexit, the Syrian civil war and terrorist attacks in Europe – shifted Western attention away from Ukraine. While upholding the EU sanctions, Germany has been one of the staunchest advocates of dialogue with Moscow (Siddi 2016a). In 2015 and 2016, German leaders advocated US–Russia cooperation in the Syrian crisis and the fight against terrorism (see Chapter 6). Most notably, Berlin supported the construction of Nord Stream 2, an extension of the Nord Stream pipeline that would transport additional Russian gas to Germany via the Baltic Sea (see Chapter 5). However, the broader EU–Russia relationship continued to be marred by mistrust and crises, and the conflict in Ukraine remained the main driver of confrontation.

During 2016, Russia's bombing campaign in Syria increased tensions with the EU. Accusations of Russian interference in the US presidential elections in 2016 and in the German and French elections in 2017 extended the confrontation from international politics to Western domestic political arenas (Siddi 2018a). In March 2018, 16 EU member states expelled Russian diplomats and the EU imposed sanctions on members of the Russian intelligence following the poisoning of Sergei Skripal, a former Russian military officer and double agent for the UK's intelligence services, on British territory. Meanwhile, low-intensity and occasionally more serious clashes continued to occur in Donbass (however, the fighting never reached the intensity of 2014 and early 2015). Furthermore, in late November 2018 the Russian coast guard fired upon and captured three ships of the Ukrainian navy that were attempting to cross the Kerch strait, connecting the Black Sea and the Azov Sea. The incident highlighted the risk of new military clashes between Russia and Ukraine. The lack of progress in the implementation of the Minsk-2 agreement led the EU to uphold its policy of sanctions against Russia. Hence, the Ukraine conflict remained the main stumbling block in EU–Russia relations throughout the period under analysis. Some progress towards the resolution of the conflict was made only in the second half of 2019, following the election of Volodymyr Zelensky to the presidency of Ukraine (BBC 2019).

Germany: rethinking *Ostpolitik*?

Chancellor Angela Merkel and foreign minister Frank-Walter Steinmeier played a prominent role in the mediation of the Ukraine crisis. On 20 February 2014, Steinmeier flew to Kiev (together with his Polish and French counterparts, Radoslaw Sikorski and Laurent Fabius) to negotiate a deal that aimed at ending the clashes between the Ukrainian police and Euromaidan demonstrators. Angela Merkel coordinated the European response to Russia's annexation of Crimea. The EU's policy of condemning violations of international law, sanctioning Russia and calling for a diplomatic resolution of the crisis was largely shaped by the German chancellor. Together with French president Francois Hollande, Merkel negotiated the Minsk-2 agreement in February 2015 and has held several consultations with the representatives of both Russia and Ukraine ever since.

Throughout the crisis, Steinmeier endeavoured to keep communication channels with Russia open. In 2016, he proposed the so-called 'Steinmeier formula' in order to break the deadlock in the implementation of the Minsk-2 agreement. The proposal called for the holding of free and fair elections in the separatist-held territories under OSCE supervision, after which these territories would be reintegrated in Ukraine with a special self-governing status. The proposal influenced subsequent conflict resolution efforts, particularly following Zelensky's endorsement in 2019 (Miller 2019). Therefore, Merkel's and Steinmeier's statements were highly influential and analysing them is essential in order to understand both Germany's and the EU's stance vis-à-vis the conflict in Ukraine. Steinmeier's successors at the German foreign ministry, Sigmar Gabriel (from January 2017 to March 2018) and Heiko Maas (since March 2018), were fellow Social Democrats who maintained a similar stance on Russia and the Ukraine conflict.

The main German official discourse – endorsed by both Merkel and Steinmeier – focused on Russia's violations of international law resulting from the annexation of Crimea and the destabilisation of Eastern Ukraine. It emphasised the need of imposing sanctions on Russia and their link to Moscow's support of the implementation of conflict resolution efforts. Simultaneously, it argued for upholding negotiations with the Russian leadership in order to solve the conflict by peaceful means. This discourse was dominant throughout the period under investigation. A second narrative emerged progressively after the signing of the Minsk-2 agreement. While reiterating the criticism of Russian violations of international law and the support of sanctions, it put greater emphasis on the positive results of diplomatic negotiations and the prospect of the eventual resumption of cooperation between the EU and Russia. This narrative acquired increasing prominence in the latter part of 2015, when the military confrontation in the Donbass de-escalated and the focus of European political debates shifted towards other scenarios (the Iranian nuclear deal, the refugee crisis and the Syrian civil war) where Russia could be seen as a potential partner. Hopes for an improvement in EU–Russia relations were frustrated by developments in 2016–2018, particularly new tensions over the Syrian crisis, accusations of Russian interference in EU politics and the bloody stalemate in the Donbass. This was reflected in the contemporary speeches of German leaders. Nevertheless, they continued to advocate the peaceful resolution of the Ukraine conflict based on the Minsk-2 agreement and the relaxation of tensions between the EU and Russia.

Condemning Russia's violations of international law in Crimea and Donbass

German leaders' condemnations of Russian actions in Ukraine were based primarily on legal arguments, notably the unilateral redrawing of international borders and the violation of the 1994 Budapest memorandum guaranteeing Ukraine's territorial integrity. Legal arguments were accompanied by historical considerations highlighting that Russia's actions allegedly constituted the first change of European borders through force since the Second World War and reflected nineteenth and twentieth century geopolitical thinking. In this discourse, history and legality were the *topoi* linking the main argument (Russia's actions breached international law and were anachronistic) to its logical conclusion that Russia should return to the negotiating table and solve the crisis in accordance with international law. The discourse reflected several key tenets of German identity, namely the rejection of the use of force in international relations and the commitment to multilateralism and international norms (see Chapter 3). Germany's peaceful security culture led to both the condemnation of Russia's actions and the refusal of trying to solve the crisis by military means (i.e. by supplying Ukraine with weapons), as advocated by some members of the US Congress and some European politicians (cf. Gordon *et al.* 2015).

In German official statements, the normative component of German identity prevailed over the traditional *Ostpolitik* cooperative approach to Russia. As emerges from Merkel's and Steinmeier's declarations on the Ukraine crisis, the deep shock provoked by Russia's annexation of Crimea had a profound impact on the agency of German policy makers, who relinquished the long-standing discourse portraying Russia as a partner. However, *Ostpolitik* thinking continued to influence the declared long-term objectives of German policy, which emphasised the inclusion of Russia in the European security architecture, energy cooperation (see Chapter 5) and the creation of a common commercial area from Lisbon to Vladivostok (see also Siddi 2018c).

The dominant German discourse emerges clearly from Merkel's and Steinmeier's statements in March 2014. Speaking at the German parliament on 13 March, Merkel (2014a) argued that 'Russia's actions in Ukraine undoubtedly represent a violation of fundamental principles of international law [...] in the heart of Europe, and it is vital that we do not simply return to business as usual'. Merkel's wish not to return to 'business as usual' with Russia highlights the departure from the cooperative approach that preceded the annexation of Crimea. Merkel put Russian actions in Ukraine in historical perspective by commemorating the 'recurring rounds of horrendous bloodshed' that had haunted Europe throughout the twentieth century. Merkel's criticism was conveyed through the choice of emphatic vocabulary ('horrendous bloodshed') and perspectivation. Steinmeier's rhetoric largely echoed that of Merkel. In a speech at the German–Russian forum in Berlin, he criticised Russia for acting 'according to the geopolitical categories of the twentieth century' and the 'attempt to redraw borders seven decades after the end of the Second World War' (Steinmeier 2014a). Both German leaders argued that Russia should face EU sanctions until it changed its policies, which implied the abandonment of the trade-driven *Ostpolitik* approach (cf. Forsberg 2016, Siddi 2016a).

Nonetheless, *Ostpolitik* thinking was not rejected altogether, but continued to permeate the German strategy for the long term. While Merkel announced that further sanctions would be imposed if Russia escalated the crisis, she simultaneously advocated 'working together with Russia to find ways to resolve outstanding conflicts in countries which are neighbours to us both' and potentially 'talking with Russia about a new economic agreement' (Merkel 2014a). Moreover, Steinmeier (2014a) stated that he was:

> deeply convinced that security in and for Europe can only be achieved jointly with, and not against, Russia. This still holds true, despite the current crisis. The aim of a common space, from Lisbon to Vladivostok, remains the right one.

This stance could be reconciled with efforts to stop the escalation of the crisis and solve it through negotiations, which were vocally supported by both German leaders.

> I for one could never forgive myself if we did not seek out and use every diplomatic tool at our disposal, for as long as possible, with a view to finding a solution.
>
> (Steinmeier 2014a)

The conflict cannot be resolved by military means. I say to everyone who is worried and concerned: military action is not an option for us.

(Merkel 2014a)

German leaders upheld this discourse throughout the Ukraine crisis, often using an emotional tone that emphasised both the gravity of the crisis and their personal involvement in solving it. When the fighting escalated in the spring and summer of 2014, and particularly after the downing of the MH17 flight, their rhetoric became harsher (see Steinmeier's 2014b and 2014c). German leaders, who had previously been wary of imposing economic sanctions on Russia (cf. Steinmeier 2014d), argued that the situation had 'changed radically' (Steinmeier 2014e) and economic sanctions had become 'unavoidable' (Merkel 2014b). However, neither Merkel nor Steinmeier ever questioned the diplomatic approach to solving the crisis. Following the MH17 tragedy, Steinmeier (2014f) argued: 'There may be some who advocate a military response to Russia's policy […] I don't share this view, and neither, I believe, do the majority of people in Germany'. Similarly, in the tense weeks that preceded the signature of the Minsk-2 agreement, Merkel (2015b and 2015c) repeatedly stated that the crisis could not be resolved by military means. In the winter of 2014–2015, the German chancellor strived to uphold the dialogue with Moscow by arguing that she wanted 'security in Europe with Russia and not against Russia' (2014c) and 'political cooperation with Russia' (2015a).

Throughout the crisis, German policy-makers attempted to present their leading role in negotiations as consistent with the EU's position and stressed the need of having a united EU response to the crisis. Merkel (2014d) stated that 'Europe has decided that it will not let itself be divided, but that it will act together more strongly than ever before in order to defend its peace order and its values'. The pro-EU rhetoric was accompanied by frequent reassurances to Germany's Eastern European NATO allies. In March 2014, shortly after the annexation of Crimea, Steinmeier (2014g) argued that 'NATO members must be sure their allies will protect them. There is no reason to doubt this'. This rhetoric reflected the deep-rooted support for European integration and the transatlantic alliance in German foreign policy thinking. At the same time, drawing on Germany's *Ostpolitik* tradition, German leaders attempted to act as bridge builders and maintain dialogue with Moscow in order to seek a diplomatic solution to the crisis (cf. Steinmeier 2014h).

Return to Ostpolitik?

The signing of the Minsk-2 agreement in February 2015 and the de-escalation of the conflict in the subsequent months allowed German leaders to intensify their rhetoric advocating a diplomatic solution of the crisis and the future return to a more cooperative relationship with Russia. German official discourses highlighted the positive results of the Minsk negotiations and argued that both the sanctions and Russia's isolation would end if the agreement was implemented.

In the latter part of 2015, Russia was also portrayed as a potential partner in other contemporary crises (the Iranian nuclear programme, the Syrian civil war and the fight against international terrorism). Legality and multilateralism were the *topoi* in the German argumentative strategy, connecting it to its logical conclusion that relations with Russia would improve if Moscow worked towards the implementation of Minsk-2 and helped to solve other international crises. This discourse reflected the normative dimension of German foreign policy, as well as *Ostpolitik* thinking and deep-rooted constructions of Russia as a key actor in the international arena.

In the statement that followed the conclusion of the Minsk-2 agreement, Merkel (2015d) argued: 'There is a genuine chance of improvement. Germany and France, France and Germany have together demonstrated that we have made a contribution, also in alignment with Europe'. The defence of the Minsk-2 agreement (which was often criticised by Western advocates of a tougher stance towards Russia) became a constant feature of her subsequent speeches. She defined it as 'the way to achieve a peaceful solution' (Merkel 2015e) and 'a ray of hope' (Merkel 2015f). Merkel (2015g) clarified that 'there [was] a correlation between existing sanctions and the full implementation of the Minsk package'. In the following months, both Merkel (2015e) and Steinmeier (2015a) expressed their opposition to imposing new sanctions on Russia. Steinmeier (2015a) argued that sanctions were not 'an end in themselves' but were 'intended to generate readiness to negotiate and pave the way for military de-escalation and political settlement'. Hence, he concluded that 'Once this road has been chosen […] there will be no reason to keep the sanctions at the current levels'.

The endurance of the *Ostpolitik* approach to Russia can be inferred from Steinmeier's (2015b) interview with *Handelsblatt* on 5 March 2015, where he referred to Willy Brandt's foreign policy and argued that isolating Russia from the EU would not help solve the crisis. His interview with *Neue Westfälische* in November 2015 best illustrates the influence of *Ostpolitik* in Steinmeier's thinking.

> The policy of détente towards the Warsaw Pact functioned in the days of the inter-bloc confrontation […] Today we are living in a world largely without ordered structures […] But the basic idea of overcoming a lack of communication and maintaining ongoing contact, despite clashing views, is still apposite.
>
> (Steinmeier 2015d)

In the months after the Minsk-2 agreement, the quest for dialogue and reconciliation shaped Steinmeier's diplomacy and rhetoric. In May 2015, he attended the commemorations for the seventieth anniversary of the end of the Second World War in Volgograd together with his Russian counterpart Sergey Lavrov. At the commemoration, Steinmeier (2015c) praised the historical reconciliation between Russia and Germany and linked it to current events by arguing that 'the people of Stalingrad […] are also heroes because to this day they remind us to work for peace!'. Remarkably, Steinmeier endorsed the Russian memory discourse emphasising the heroism of Soviet soldiers (Siddi 2017a, Torbakov 2011). Merkel pursued a similar policy, as witnessed by her trip to Moscow to jointly commemorate the anniversary together with Putin. However, she maintained a more critical stance and, while calling for reconciliation, she reiterated her condemnation of Russian policies in Ukraine (Merkel 2015h).

Attempts at seeking reconciliation with Russia intensified in the summer months of 2015. At the G7 summit in Germany, Merkel (2015i) stated that Russia 'needed to be a partner' on stopping Iran's nuclear programme and ending the civil war in Syria. In an interview published in June 2015, while defending the EU's double-track policy of sanctions and negotiations with Russia, Steinmeier (2015a) argued that:

> there can be no interest on our part in the G8 remaining the G7 in the long term. On the contrary, we urgently need Russia to help resolve entrenched conflicts in our European neighbourhood, such as those plaguing Syria, Iraq and Libya, as well as Iran's nuclear programme.

As the focus of political debates increasingly shifted towards other crises in the latter part of 2015, cooperation with Russia in these scenarios was seen as desirable in order to achieve a comprehensive relaxation of tensions between the West and Moscow. In her government statement of 15 October 2015, Merkel (2015j) argued for 'a process of political dialogue which also embraces Russia and other international and regional actors' to end the Syrian conflict (see also Chapter 6). Reflecting the German long-standing commitment to both the transatlantic alliance and the policy of dialogue with Moscow, Steinmeier (2015e) considered US–Russian cooperation in solving these crises as an essential step towards the improvement of relations. Moreover, both German leaders supported energy cooperation with Russia and defended plans to build the Nord Stream 2 pipeline (see Chapter 5).

Managing a protracted crisis

In 2016–2018, German diplomacy supported efforts to uphold the ceasefire in the Donbass and break the deadlock in the implementation of the Minsk agreement. Steinmeier (2016d) addressed Russian–Ukrainian disagreements on which parts of Minsk-2 should be implemented first by arguing that 'security and the political process ultimately go hand in hand. We urgently need to make progress in both areas.' This was the reasoning behind the so-called 'Steinmeier formula' to solve the Donbass conflict. German leaders continued to see the Minsk agreement as the main conflict resolution instrument, and its implementation was tied to the lifting of the EU's sectoral sanctions. However, they also criticised the lack of progress and welcomed other diplomatic initiatives based on multilateralism, such as the proposal to deploy a UN peacekeeping force, which was consistent with Germany's peaceful security culture.

The respect of international law remained the main *topos* of German discourses on the Ukraine crisis, and Russia was frequently criticised for having violated it. At the same time, the logic of *Ostpolitik* continued to shape the German approach and drive its quest for dialogue with Russia. Steinmeier and his successors often referred to Willy Brandt's *Ostpolitik* while speaking about the Ukraine crisis. Steinmeier's (2016a) address to the German–Russian forum in May 2016 provides a prime example.

> I believe that a look at the heritage of Willy Brandt's *Ostpolitik* and his pursuit of détente can help us to find our answers, not least because the starting point of those policies was his very simple observation, which still applies today: 'Russia is our biggest European neighbour'. Or, as Egon Bahr once said, 'America is indispensable. Russia is irremovable'. And this means that lasting security for Europe cannot be achieved without Russia and certainly not against Russia.

In this discourse, Russia was categorised as a 'European neighbour', rather than as a threatening external Other. This use of the discursive strategy of categorisation (see Chapter 2) paved the way for the argument that European security could only be achieved with Russia's participation, which in turn justified the German policy of diplomatic engagement. This policy was pursued also with a view to the broader crisis in European security, which occurred in parallel with and was made more acute by the Ukraine crisis. German leaders appeared particularly concerned about a new arms race in Europe and attempted to preserve the existing arms control treaties between Russia and the United States. Hence, Steinmeier (2016e) contended that:

> precisely in such a situation [Russia's violations of international law in Ukraine] it has to be in our interest to avoid any further escalation and to create transparency where trust has been broken. A re-launch of arms control is not a concession to Russia, but is in the interest of everyone in Europe.

German leaders welcomed Putin's tentative proposal, made in September 2017, to deploy a UN peacekeeping mission in Eastern Ukraine. While expressing some reservations regarding the mandate and practical aspects, Steinmeier's successor Sigmar Gabriel (2017c) portrayed the proposal as a 'true departure' from Putin's earlier position and stated that the EU should welcome it. Significantly, Gabriel (2017d) argued that the West 'should use this [Putin's proposal] to relaunch a policy of détente. Even during the most difficult times of the Cold War, Willy Brandt drew up his policy of détente with Russia and Poland.' According to him, this was necessary not only to solve the Ukraine crisis, but also because the West 'will need Russia in many other issues around the world'.

While the arguments for dialogue with Russia remained prominent in German foreign policy discourse, the failure to make progress in the resolution of the Donbass conflict called into question the German stance. As foreign minister Heiko Maas (2018e) stated in April 2018, 'most of our [Germany's] partners are now very critical of Russia and some doubt whether dialogue is possible. In the past, some were prepared to follow Germany's lead. Now they're asking: what was the point?' The Skripal poisoning led to a further deterioration in relations; Germany expelled four Russian diplomats as part of a coordinated response of several Western countries. In the wake of the crisis, Maas (2018e) stated that 'Russia is, unfortunately, acting in an increasingly hostile manner – the poison gas attack in Salisbury, its role in Syria and eastern Ukraine, and hacker attacks, including against the Federal Foreign Office'. At the same time, he – like his predecessors at the German foreign ministry – insisted that the West 'must remain in dialogue with Russia'. Merkel (2018b) expressed similar views, arguing for the holding of 'permanent talks' with Moscow in the NATO-Russia Council.

Despite repeated ceasefire violations, the German chancellor continued to view the Minsk-2 agreement as the right framework for conflict resolution in the Donbass. For instance, at a gathering of the German diplomatic corps in July 2018, Merkel declared:

> We hope that we will also be able to further implementation of the Minsk Agreement with Ukraine and Russia. France and Germany have taken on responsibility in this field for many years. It grieves us to see that the ceasefire is still broken every single day. But we won't give up hope. We know that relations with Russia could be significantly improved, and this is something that Germany in particular aims to achieve.

As these remarks suggest, Merkel saw the Minsk agreement as an important outcome of joint Franco–German leadership, which Berlin considers a cornerstone of its European policy (hence, it is also an essential constituent of Germany's pro-EU foreign policy identity, see Chapter 3). Most notably, she continued to believe in the possibility of 'significantly' improving relations with Russia and highlighted the importance of this for Germany 'in particular', in a reiteration of Berlin's long-standing policy of seeking cooperation with Moscow.

During the Kerch Strait incident in November 2018, Maas criticised Russia's use of force. According to him 'Russia's actions against Ukrainian ships are unacceptable' and could turn the Sea of Azov into 'a new source of conflict that ultimately threatens our security in Europe'. On the other hand, he claimed that Germany did not want to see 'a militarisation of the conflict and was doing everything in [its] power to put an end to this crisis through diplomacy'. These statements reiterated German leaders' frustration at Russia's use of force and their rejection of military solutions to the crisis. They continued to see diplomacy as the only instrument to solve the conflict. The fact that, as of late 2019, the main concrete steps to solve the Donbass conflict have been based on proposals and agreements negotiated by Germany (Minsk-2, the Steinmeier formula) vindicates the perseverance of its leaders.

The return of the 'Russian threat' in Polish discourse

Poland was one of the most vocal critics of Russian actions in Ukraine within the EU. Polish diplomacy was very active throughout the crisis, but its role changed in the course of 2014. Initially, the Polish foreign minister was directly involved in mediating the crisis. In February 2014, Radoslaw Sikorski flew to Kiev – together with his German and French counterparts – in order to negotiate a compromise between Viktor Yanukovych's government and the Euromaidan demonstrators. However, subsequent negotiations took place in the 'Normandy format', including the leaders of Germany, France, Russia and Ukraine. The end of Poland's role as mediator in the Ukraine crisis roughly coincided with the change of leadership in Warsaw. After seven years in government, in September 2014 Donald Tusk and Radoslaw Sikorski were replaced, respectively, by Ewa Kopacz and Grzegorz Schetyna. Like their predecessors, Kopacz and Schetyna were members of the centre-right Civic Platform. However, their domestic position was constrained by controversies concerning prominent members of their party and the proximity of presidential and parliamentary elections in late spring and fall of 2015 (BBC News 2015a).

In 2014–2015, during the centre-right governments led by the Civic Platform, the dominant Polish official discourse on the crisis criticised Russia harshly for its violations of Ukraine's territorial integrity and advocated robust EU sanctions. It called for a united EU and NATO response, including a military build-up on Polish territory, and for solidarity with and support of Ukraine. However, it backed a diplomatic (rather than military) solution of the crisis and kept communication channels with Moscow open. This stance was formulated during Donald Tusk's government and was later endorsed by Kopacz and Schetyna. However, Kopacz's and Schetyna's rhetoric towards Russia swiftly became more hawkish than that of their predecessors and did not change in the second half of 2015, despite the partial de-escalation of the conflict in the Donbass.

The right-wing Law and Justice government, which took office in November 2015, consolidated and further escalated Russia-critical and anti-Russian discourses. Law and Justice politicians Beata Szydlo and Witold Waszczykowski became prime minister and foreign minister, respectively. Following a government reshuffle in December 2017, they were succeeded by Mateusz Morawiecki (as prime minister) and Jacek Czaputowicz (as foreign minister). During the tenure of Law and Justice, governmental discourses essentialised Russia as the main threat to Poland. Such a radical conceptualisation of Russia affected all areas of the relationship (i.e. security, energy), as shown by numerous examples of interdiscursivity and the linkage of different topics – most notably, through their securitisation. The image of a threatening Russian Other was used also in domestic politics, partly with the goal of discrediting the opposition, which was accused of having conspired with Russia against Polish interests (Davies 2016).

Sanctions and security: Poland's response
to the Ukraine crisis in 2014

The Polish government's condemnation of Russian actions in Ukraine was based primarily on legal arguments. Although Tusk and Sikorski occasionally used historical analogies to interpret current developments, memory politics did not play an important role in their rhetoric. Calls for European and NATO solidarity towards Poland (which was allegedly exposed to potential Russian threats) were justified with pragmatic arguments, notably the increased Russian military activity and the risk of future disruptions in Russian energy supplies. Legality and security were the *topoi* in Tusk's and Sikorski's argumentative strategy, conveying the message that Russia should be sanctioned for its violations of international law, while NATO and the EU should strengthen the military and energy security of their Eastern flank. Support of Ukraine was an essential component of this discourse. This stance resonated with long-standing Polish identity narratives of Russia as a security threat, while the call for EU and NATO solidarity emphasised Poland's identification with the Euro-Atlantic alliance (see Chapter 3).

The dominant Polish official discourse is illustrated in Sikorski's (2014a) interview with the *Washington Post* on 18 April 2014. He argued that 'for the first time since the Second World War, one European country has annexed a province from another European country' and that this was 'a rejection of our entire legal system and international norms and treaties that we have regarded as the foundation of peace'. Sikorski highlighted the significance of Russia's illegal actions in historical perspective and qualified Russia as 'a revisionist power', bent on 'preventing Ukraine from reforming and becoming successful'. In addition, he argued that the US 'should reassure allies in Central and Eastern Europe'. However, he did not support the idea of delivering weapons to Ukraine and specified that Poland was 'not feeling militarily threatened as yet' (2014b). Hence, while security considerations were prominent, they were not accompanied by overly emotional rhetoric or exaggerated claims about the Russian threat.

A similar combination of harsh rhetoric and cold pragmatism emerges from Tusk's statements. Following Russia's occupation of Crimea, he advocated a resolute response from the EU, the imposition of sanctions on Russia and deeper military cooperation with the US (Tusk 2014a and 2014b). Simultaneously, he defended his policy of 'building up good relations' with Russia and argued that the Polish stance towards Moscow should be 'rational' and 'reasonable' (Tusk 2014c). In a context of increasing tensions with Russia, Tusk's statement should be read as a call for a critical, but pragmatic approach. At the same time, Tusk proposed a more strategic EU approach to energy relations with Russia through the formation of an 'energy union' (Tusk 2014d). The proposal originated in response to the EU's dependence on Russian gas and the risk of potential supply disruptions (Siddi 2016b). It combined economic arguments ('Russia's monopolistic position') with political and security considerations (the risks of excessive energy dependence on Russian fossil fuels).

European unity and solidarity were recurrent themes in Tusk's and Sikorski's comments on the Ukraine crisis. In his address to the Polish parliament on 5 March 2014, Tusk stated that 'Poland's aim [was] to maintain a uniform policy of the whole community of the West'. Similarly, Tusk's energy union proposal focused on 'mechanisms guaranteeing solidarity among [EU] member states' (2014d). For the Polish government, calls for European solidarity were functional to obtaining military and strategic support from EU and NATO partners. Furthermore, Polish leaders aimed at steering the unitary EU position towards a more critical stance vis-à-vis Russia. Tusk's and Sikorski's statements reveal that Poland consistently advocated a hard line against Russia within the EU. For instance, this emerges from Tusk's (2014e) comments on the weakness of EU sanctions against Russia (suggesting that he was keen on strengthening them) and in Sikorski's (2014c) claim that 'if the EU had reacted more strongly to Russia's annexation of Crimea and adopted sanction more quickly, as Poland advocated, the current conflict in Donetsk, Ukraine, would not have happened'.

Next to deep-seated fears of Russian imperialism, genuine identification with the Ukrainian cause contributes to explaining the Polish stance in the crisis. Sikorski (2014d) argued that 'the Ukrainians are our [Poland's] neighbours. They are fighting for the same things we did back in 1989 – for a country that is more democratic, less corrupt and is European'. Ukraine was seen as a 'new Poland', replicating the Polish struggle for emancipation from Moscow's sphere of influence in 1989, and – somewhat simplistically – as 'the only place on earth where people have sacrificed their lives for the ideas of European integration' (Tusk 2014a). This discourse resonated with Polish identity narratives of heroism, martyrdom and commitment to the Western cause.

The radicalisation of Civic Platform discourses in 2015

Initially, the change of leadership in Warsaw in September 2014 seemed to have no major effects on Poland's stance towards Russia (Kopacz 2014; cf. Sobczyk and Wasilewski 2014). Like their predecessors, the new ministers came from the ranks of the Civic Platform. However, the analysis of the speeches of the new Polish leaders showed that their criticism of Russia was accompanied by a harsher rhetoric than during Tusk's and Sikorski's tenure. References to history and the use of memory politics to attack Russia became more frequent. Moreover, their support of Ukraine became more vocal and contemplated the provision of military aid.

The foreign policy of the new Polish government was outlined in Schetyna's speech at the Polish parliament on 6 November 2014. He argued that the post-Cold War order in Europe had been questioned by Russia and 'threats that we were confronted with before 1989 re-emerged in Europe: the spectre of military aggression, the unpredictability of a great power, contempt for the rights of sovereign nations and the risk of division of the continent into spheres of influence' (Schetyna 2014a). According to Schetyna (2014a), Russia 'chose the language of aggression, driven by the idea of spheres of influence and giving primacy to force in developing international relations'. In Schetyna's narrative, Russia was personified as an aggressive Other speaking the 'language of aggression'. Moreover, it was categorised as alien to Europe due to 'the rising tide of isolationism and anti-Western feelings and the negation of European values', which 'build a wall that divides Russia from Europe'. Consequently, the continuation of economic sanctions and the strengthening of the military alliance with the United States were presented as the only possible course of action for Poland (see also Schetyna 2015a).

Schetyna occasionally softened his rhetoric by claiming that Poland and Russia 'remain[ed] neighbours and economic partners' (Schetyna 2014a), and Polish leaders would 'try to reverse this [negative] trend and return to normal, good-neighbourly relations' (Schetyna 2015b). These statements highlighted the endurance of the pragmatic stance towards Russia initiated by Tusk and Sikorski in 2007 (Siddi 2017b); they were functional to keeping communication channels open and addressing issues in bilateral relations. However, they were marginal in the broader picture of Polish discourses on Russia. On the whole, the rhetoric of Polish leaders remained hawkish also after the signature of the Minsk-2 agreement. Kopacz (2015a) continued to argue for stricter sanctions on Russia also when German leaders considered them 'unhelpful' (Steinmeier 2015a), while Schetyna (2015b) stated that a renewed escalation of military operations in the Donbass would lead Poland to step up support for Ukraine, 'including its defence'.

In the winter and spring of 2015, the Polish leaders expanded the discursive confrontation with Russia to the field of historical memory. In January 2015, on the seventieth anniversary of the Soviet liberation of the Auschwitz extermination camp, Schetyna argued that the camp had been freed by Ukrainian soldiers. The statement caused a diplomatic row with Russian officials, after which Schetyna corrected his claims and credited a multi-ethnic Soviet army for the liberation of the camp (Easton 2015). History-related disputes continued in the spring, during the commemorations for the seventieth anniversary of the end of the Second World War. The Polish leadership hosted a commemorative event in the Westerplatte peninsula, near Gdansk, where the Second World War had started. The event was organised as an alternative for leaders who intended to boycott victory day celebrations in Moscow, and was attended almost exclusively by representatives of East-Central European countries (BBC News 2015b). Polish president Bronislaw Komorowski (2015) held a speech in which he defined Russia as:

> the forces which bring back memories of the darkest chapters in twentieth century history, the ones which continue to think through the prism of spheres of influence, which strive to maintain their neighbourhood in the condition of vassal's dependency […].

Komorowski's narrative abandoned the spirit of historical reconciliation that had been promoted by Tusk's government in previous years, particularly through the establishment of a Polish–Russian Working Group for Difficult Matters.

During the Kopacz government, Polish official discourses became more radical also in their assessments of the significance of the crisis and the future of Ukraine (Schetyna 2015c). Schetyna argued that 'a sovereign, democratic, pro-European and prosperous Ukraine is an element of the Polish *raison d'état*' (Schetyna 2015b) and asked all Polish political forces to take a united stance on Ukraine. According to Polish leaders, domestic agreement on the issue would allow Poland to further Ukraine's cause internationally. This posture was highlighted by Kopacz's (2015b) statements during a visit to Kiev in January 2015:

> I want to assure our friends in Kiev that we are going to do whatever we can to maintain the uniform position of the European Union on the policy towards Russia [...] We want to be a good ambassador of Ukraine in the EU, and encourage our partners to support Ukraine.

Her claim that Poland would be 'a good ambassador of Ukraine in the EU' illustrated how, by 2015, Warsaw's policy had shifted away from its earlier attempts to play a role as a mediator in the crisis towards the pursuit of pro-Ukraine lobbying in the EU.

'A worse threat than Isis': Law and Justice and the Russian Other

In November 2015, following the defeat of Civic Platform in the national elections, the Kopacz government was replaced by a new one entirely controlled by the Law and Justice party. During the previous Law and Justice government, which held office from 2005 to 2007, Poland's relations with Russia (as well as Germany) deteriorated considerably, partly due to the nationalist rhetoric and politics of memory adopted by Warsaw (Reeves 2010). Following the party's return to power in 2015, Polish discourses on Russia followed a similar negative trajectory, which was aggravated by the tensions related to the Ukraine crisis. Most aspects of Polish–Russian relations were securitised (Sus 2018).

In April 2016, foreign minister Waszczykowski defined Russia as the greatest menace to Poland and Europe. According to him, Russia was more dangerous than Isis because it posed an 'existential threat' and could 'destroy countries' (cited in *Guardian* 2016). This statement highlights how the Law and Justice government essentialised the Russian Other as a threat. It also implied that the West should not seek a rapprochement with Moscow based on a joint anti-terrorism struggle – as suggested by leading politicians in Italy and Germany, for instance (cf. Siddi 2018e: 134) – because Russia was in fact more dangerous than terrorism. Hence, the EU and the West should focus on confronting Russia in Ukraine rather than exploring cooperation in other theatres (see also Chapter 6).

Law and Justice leaders appeared dissatisfied with the approach adopted by the EU, Germany and France in particular, towards the Ukraine crisis, which they considered too 'soft' (cf. Morawiecki 2018b). Referring to the Minsk-2 agreement, Waszczykowski stated that 'Russia and Germany create a distinctive concert of powers over the head of Poland' (cited in Sus 2018: 81–82). This echoed the Polish historical narrative according to which German–Russian dialogue is detrimental to Polish interests. The historical points of reference of this narrative are the Russian–German (and Austrian) partitions of Poland in the eighteenth and nineteenth centuries (indeed, Waszczykowski's use of 'concert of powers' evokes the post-Napoleonic period) and the division of Eastern Europe following the Molotov–Ribbentrop pact in 1939. By taking the Minsk-2 agreement out of its political and historic context, Waszczykowski conveyed the message that Moscow and Berlin were (once again) scheming against Poland.

Russia's aggressive stance against Ukraine was the prism through which Polish leaders assessed other fields of EU–Russia relations. Polish narratives about the Ukraine crisis and energy trade with Russia showed a high degree of interdiscursivity (see also Chapter 5). For instance, Polish minister for European affairs Konrad Szymanski (2016) claimed that 'by supporting Nord Stream 2, the EU in effect gives succour to a regime whose aggression it seeks to punish through sanctions'. Morawiecki (2018b) stated that the pipeline would leave Ukraine 'entirely defenseless' because Russia would 'be able to deliver gas to the West without having to rely on any pipes that go through Ukraine'. Similarly, Waszczykowski (2016a) stated that Nord Stream 2 was a 'blow' against the stability of Ukraine and East-Central Europe; President Duda argued that it was 'a weapon in the hybrid war being conducted against Ukraine' (cited in Radio Poland 2018a). By arguing that energy trade with Russia was a dangerous dependence for the EU, or by portraying it as 'succour' to an aggressive regime, Polish leaders denounced the main form of cooperation between Russia and the EU (energy being the largest component of their bilateral trade).

While the Law and Justice government maintained a pro-Ukrainian stance in the crisis, its widespread use of nationalist memory politics led to the return of Polish–Ukrainian historical disputes to the political agenda. This was partly a response to the politics of history of post-Euromaidan Ukraine, which glorified Ukrainian nationalists that had been responsible *inter alia* for the mass murder of Polish civilians in Volhynia during the Second World War (Portnov 2016). In 2016, the Polish Senate passed a resolution calling the Volhynian massacre a genocide (Siddi 2017a: 474) New legislation introduced in 2018 penalised anyone who denied the crimes committed by Ukrainian nationalists; it was criticised harshly by Ukraine's leadership (Radio Poland 2018b). The combination of Polish empathy and criticism of Ukraine is well reflected in foreign minister Czaputowicz's speech on Polish foreign policy tasks in 2018. On the one hand, Czaputowicz (2018c) argued that 'in Poland, the tragic historic test to which Ukraine is now subject because of Russia's military aggression has inspired a natural feeling of sympathy and solidarity with a nation fighting for "freedom, integrity, and independence"'. On the other hand, in the same speech he noted that 2018 marked the seventy-fifth anniversary of 'the massacres of Poles in Volhynia' and that 'the ban on exhuming the remains of Polish victims of wars and conflicts imposed by Ukraine is, for us, difficult to comprehend, and let me stress, it makes conducting our dialogue more difficult'.

These disputes highlighted the complexity and multiplicity of Polish (and Ukrainian) historical Othering, which involved different nations and communities (see Chapter 3). The adoption of chauvinist rhetoric by several national leaders in the context of the Ukraine crisis catalysed the re-emergence of multiple discursive conflicts. Even so, Russia continued to be the main negative Other in Polish official narratives up until the end of 2018 (cf. Czaputowicz 2018d). Indeed, Polish leaders sometimes evoked joint Polish–Ukrainian struggles against the Russian Other in the past in order to minimise historical disputes with Kiev and foster a shared anti-Russian identity (cf. Baczynska 2018).

Finland: security concerns and dialogue with Russia

The Ukraine crisis had a profound impact on Finnish security and foreign policy debates. Before the crisis, Russia was seen mostly as an economic partner, albeit at times a difficult one and with authoritarian tendencies (Siddi 2017b). In 2013, Russia was Finland's main trade partner and only gas provider. Russian state company Rosatom was involved in the construction of a nuclear power plant on Finnish territory and was thereby acquiring an important stake in the strategic nuclear sector (Reuters 2013, Yle 2015a). Moreover, multilateral cooperation with Russia had grown over the years within several policy frameworks and institutional settings, ranging from the EU's Northern Dimension policy to the Arctic Council. Russia's armed intervention in the Ukraine crisis and its increased military activities in the Baltic region called into question Finland's relationship with Moscow and security posture. The possibility of abandoning military non-alignment and joining NATO was discussed at official level, but support for NATO membership remained relatively low among Finns, not least due to the risk of negative consequences for relations with Russia and hence national security (Yle 2015b). At the same time, Finland's foreign policy leaders focused on the organisation of the commemorations for the fortieth anniversary of the Helsinki Final Act, which took place in the Finnish capital in July 2015. The Helsinki Final Act had marked the high point of détente between the West and Soviet Russia and of Finland's policy of neutrality and international mediation during the Cold War. Moreover, in July 2018 Finland once again provided good offices and played the role of intermediary by hosting a high-level meeting between Vladimir Putin and US President Donald Trump.

Against this background, Finnish official discourses on the Ukraine crisis focused on two main aspects. On the one hand, they highlighted Russia's breaches of international law and collective security. While blaming Russia for the crisis and supporting EU sanctions, Finnish leaders argued that it could be resolved only through diplomacy and dialogue. On the other hand, they attempted to separate the Ukraine crisis from other issues and uphold cooperation with Russia in regional forums concerning the Arctic and the Baltic Sea. Finnish official policy and discourses did not change substantially after the parliamentary elections of 2015, which brought to power a partly new government coalition – including most notably the far-right Finns' Party, whose leader, Timo Soini, became foreign minister.

Countering Russia's illegal actions through diplomacy

Finnish official reactions to Russia's annexation of Crimea focused on its legal and security implications. President Sauli Niinistö argued that it was 'clearly against Ukrainian and international law' (Niinistö 2014a) and 'subjected Europe's security system to intense pressure and damage' (Niinistö 2014b). Similarly, foreign minister Erkki Tuomioja (2014a) stated that the annexation was 'against the fundamental principles of sovereignty, territorial integrity, as well as many binding international agreements', and 'damaging for the long-term stability, security and prosperity of all [Council of Europe] member states and their people'. As a result of Russia's military actions, deep-rooted narratives depicting Russia as a security challenge for Finland became dominant. However, while supporting EU sanctions against Russia, both Niinistö and Tuomioja consistently argued that the crisis could only be solved through diplomacy and dialogue and in accordance with OSCE principles. Legality and cooperative security were the *topoi* of their argumentation strategy.

The relevance of cooperative security and diplomacy in Finnish official discourse on the Ukraine crisis emerges clearly from a speech held by Tuomioja (2014b) in Helsinki on 2 June 2014.

> The Helsinki Final Act provided a framework for dialogue and was considered to be a historic breakthrough at the height of the Cold War. Although the world has tremendously changed since its adoption, the main principles contained in the Helsinki Final Act are still today as universal and relevant as they were at that time. [...] I am fully convinced that more mediation and dialogues, not less, is needed in today's world. This is most recently demonstrated by the crisis in Ukraine. Dialogue, diplomatic efforts and renouncing the use of force are the only way to find a sustainable resolution to that crisis.

Tuomioja's approach to solving the Ukraine conflict and the crisis between Russia and the West was strongly influenced by his understanding of Cold War détente and the Helsinki Final Act, which Finnish policy makers widely regard as one of Finland's greatest diplomatic successes (Tiilikainen 1998: 153–156). Tuomioja considered the OSCE – the institution that represents the main heritage of the Helsinki Final Act – as essential to solving the Ukraine crisis. In a speech held in Vienna in May 2014, he argued that he 'could not think of a better and more relevant mechanism and platform' than the OSCE for discussions on renewing commitments to common security in Europe (Tuomioja 2014c).

By emphasising the role of the OSCE in the resolution of the Ukraine crisis, Finnish policy makers appeared to be playing their traditional role of 'bridge builders' between Russia and the West. However, while emphasising the importance of mediation to solve the crisis, Finnish leaders unequivocally placed themselves in the Western and EU camp and adopted EU sanctions against Russia. In other words, Russia's violations of international law and use of force led Finnish leaders to restate that Finland had placed itself at the Western end of the East–West continuum which had characterised national identity debates in the past (see Browning 2008: 12 and Chapter 3). A speech held by prime minister Alexander Stubb in Berlin in September 2014 illustrates this. After reviewing the history of EU–Russia relations and condemning Russian actions in Ukraine, Stubb (2014) stated that 1995 was 'the most important year' in Finland's recent history:

> Becoming an EU member was long overdue and the most natural thing to happen. We are where we belong. This is also where we firmly place ourselves in the current situation. We are in the EU family, fully committed to our common cause.

Stubb's emphatic remark can only be understood with reference to Finland's Cold War neutrality and Finnish identity debates, including those concerning the decision to join the European Union in 1995. It was a statement of belonging to Europe and the West, which Stubb (2014) associated with liberal democracy and the respect of international law. On the other hand, he argued that Russia had not yet embraced these values, thereby categorising the country as alien to the European and Western communities in which Finland recognised itself.

Finland's support of the EU's official stance towards Russia, combining sanctions with openness to dialogue, remained steady over the years. In January 2016, Soini (2016c) argued that the EU

> should continue to defend the rules-based international order and expect that Russia respects it, as well as its commitments under international law. This relates also to Russia's illegal annexation of Crimea and military activities in Eastern Ukraine. At the same time, the EU should remain open for dialogue with Russia on global challenges and common interests.

Finnish leaders fully supported the Normandy and Minsk negotiations as the best available instruments to solve the Donbass conflict. This was epitomised by president Niinistö's (2017c) statement that there were 'no alternatives to implementing the Minsk Agreement'.

Pragmatism and the isolation of the Ukraine crisis from other policy fields

According to Stubb, Russia's exclusion from the Western community was neither definitive, nor meant that cooperation with Moscow was impossible. He argued that the Soviet period had ended relatively recently, and that democratisation was still possible in the longer run. Until then, Russia and the West could co-exist and consider a strategic partnership as a long-term goal: 'I believe we can co-exist. We need not be alike to be good neighbours, or even strategic partners again. We should aim at that' (Stubb 2014). Moreover, Stubb contended that Russia's current estrangement from Europe did not preclude cooperation, particularly in the economic arena.

> Russia has turned inwards. Many think it is now turning also east and therefore drifting away from Europe. The extent of this turn remains to be seen and, frankly, I do not think such a turn is only a negative thing. In fact, I think it would be wise for Russia to finally make better use of being geographically so Asian. It would profit their economy – and therefore indirectly, also ours. It certainly would not exclude co-operation with Europe.
>
> (Stubb 2014)

Stubb's statement reflected Finland's pragmatic approach to Moscow and the conceptualisation of Russia as an economic partner despite its domestic developments. Pragmatism and economic advantage are the *topoi* in this strategy of argumentation. Stubb also argued that business relations and people-to-people contacts would help solve the crisis between Russia and the European Union – a view that coincided with the key tenets of the German *Ostpolitik* towards Russia, as Stubb (2014) himself noted in his speech in Berlin.

> In fact, Finland and Germany have a very similar approach to the [Ukraine] crisis. But let me make one point very clear. I think we all need to be intellectually mature enough to differentiate between three things in our approach to Russia and things Russian. Firstly, Moscow-level, very hawkish decision-making and its implications. Secondly, mutually beneficial, still functioning business relations and people-to-people contacts; at the end of the day they can be our best guarantee for peace. And thirdly, Russian-speaking minorities living in our own countries. Finland has a longer common border with Russia, 1300 kilometres, than the rest of the EU countries put together. This means that we have a very pragmatic and common-sense approach in all of our Russia policies, knowing we will be in this relationship 'in sickness and in health'.

Stubb's claim that business relations were one of the best guarantees for peace is all the more remarkable because it was made only a few weeks after the EU had imposed sectoral sanctions on Russia. Stubb also reiterated the long-standing argument that Finland needed to have a pragmatic policy towards Russia because of their proximity and long shared border. In the contemporary scenario, this meant distinguishing between Finland's position towards Russia in the Ukraine crisis and in other regional forums. While Finnish policy makers condemned Russian actions in Ukraine, they continued to advocate cooperation with Moscow on Baltic and Arctic issues.

This validity of this approach was reiterated in numerous speeches. At a summit on the EU Strategy for the Baltic Sea Region, Tuomioja (2014d) argued that, despite the Ukraine crisis, 'it should not be in anyone's interest to allow the conflict to negatively affect our pragmatic cooperation in the Council of Baltic Sea states and other regional fora'. Similarly, at a seminar on EU policies towards the Arctic, he argued that it would 'not be in anyone's interest to let the [Ukraine] crisis bring new obstacles for the kind of pragmatic cooperation on environmental, social and economic issues which has benefited all the member states and the people living on the Arctic' (Tuomioja 2014e). Niinistö (2014c) reiterated this argument in a speech held in Reykjavik:

> Russia's actions [in Ukraine] have damaged international security and co-operation especially in Europe. However, I am convinced that we should keep the North and the Arctic Council on a road towards more – not less – co-operation. The Arctic Council is the only circumpolar organization that deals with the specific problems of this region. Should its work get paralysed everybody would lose. We don´t want that.

The new Finnish government that took office in 2015 maintained the same stance to sectoral cooperation with Russia. Soini (2016c) argued that:

> multilateral, regional cooperation fora – such as the Artic Council and Northern Dimension policy – should be used to engage with Russia and to tackle a wide range of security concerns, including environmental protection, maritime safety and public health issues. Regional and cross-border cooperation also provide a framework for enhancing contacts with Russian civil society.

Finnish leaders claimed that the continuation of cooperation in the Baltic and the Arctic was compatible with Finland's stance on the Ukraine crisis because it did not affect the Finnish position on the annexation of Crimea or the EU sanctions. At the same time, it prevented an unnecessary escalation of the crisis between the EU and Russia. As Niinistö (2015c) argued, 'even if there is no return to normal, this does not mean that we should continue moving towards an abnormal situation'. Furthermore, this posture allowed Finnish leaders to play a role as bridge builders between Russia and the EU on regional policies, for instance by asking Russia to accept the EU's application for observer status in the Arctic Council (Tuomioja 2015) and by encouraging EU–Russia cooperation within the Barents Euro-Arctic Council (Soini 2015).

Finland's 'shielding' of Arctic cooperation from the tensions related to the Ukraine crisis became particularly relevant during the country's chairmanship of the Arctic Council from 2017 to 2019. Speaking in Washington in February 2018, Soini (2018) stated that 'there was a moment about four years ago, after the illegal annexation of Crimea and the conflict breaking in Eastern Ukraine, when the normal continuation of Arctic cooperation was also in doubt'.

However, he stressed, 'all Arctic countries concluded that they have so many common interests that they must pursue them together'. Niinistö (2017b) also noted that, despite the Ukraine crisis, Russia remained cooperative on Arctic issues.

Finnish leaders appeared to be particularly concerned about the extension of West–Russia security tensions to the Baltic region. As Soini (2016a) argued in January 2016, 'from Finland's perspective, it is a concern that tensions created by the Ukraine conflict have shifted towards the Baltic region'. While Finland is not a NATO member, Soini declared that it was in 'Finland's interests' that 'NATO clearly shows its commitment to the defence of all of its member states'. Such statements could be read as expressing Finland's identification with the Western cause, despite its military non-alignment. At the same time, Finnish leaders made no commitments to joining the Atlantic alliance, and refused to be pressured into making a decision. Soini (2016a) stated that 'it must be made clear to all parties that Finland will decide on its security policy solutions independently'. Finnish leaders appeared concerned that a substantial increase of NATO troops at Russia's borders may worsen the security situation. For instance, Soini (2016a) stressed that 'NATO's response to Russia's power politics' should be 'proportionate and fundamentally defensive' in order 'not to provoke or escalate the situation'.

Furthermore, Soini argued that tensions over the Ukraine crisis should not prevent cooperation in other contexts. Speaking at the Finnish Institute of International Affairs in January 2016, he contended that 'Russia might be part of the problem in many respects but it is undoubtedly also an essential part of many solutions', citing the Iran nuclear deal as an example of 'Russia as playing a crucial and constructive role' (Soini 2016c). He viewed such a role as 'equally essential in resolving the Syria conflict and other international security issues'. Similarly, Niinistö (2017b) argued that 'although Russia remains inflexible on many issues, it is now looking for a more constructive approach in others', citing 'the improvement of flight safety over the Baltic Sea', 'the problem of black carbon in the Arctic region' and the Northern Dimension as areas of cooperation.

Conclusion

Due to the Kremlin's policies in the Ukraine crisis, dominant discourses in the countries under investigation argued that Russia posed a challenge to the European legal and security order. German, Polish and Finnish official discourses converged towards the unanimous condemnation of Russia's violations of international law. This convergence reflected the broader commonality of views among EU member states on the crisis, which allowed the EU to deliver a coherent response to Russian actions in the form of sanctions. The chapter showed how this response was discursively constructed (and made possible) in three member states that have been particularly active in shaping EU relations with Russia, both before and during the Ukraine crisis. In Germany, Russia's use of force in Ukraine was perceived as a major challenge to European security. The use of force was at odds with the peaceful security culture that has become deeply entrenched in German identity since 1945. Germany's peaceful security culture also influenced the policy enacted in response to the crisis: Berlin imposed economic sanctions on Russia but rejected proposals to send military equipment to Ukraine.

The Polish and Finnish initial response to the crisis largely mirrored the German perspective. The main difference was that, in Poland, the Tusk government adopted a harsher rhetoric vis-à-vis Russia and emphasised the need of strengthening NATO's military presence in Eastern Europe. This reflected the Euro-Atlantic orientation of Polish foreign policy and identity-based conceptualisations of Russia as imperialist and aggressive, which became dominant again in Polish debates during the Ukraine crisis. On the other hand, Finnish discourses portrayed Russia as a security challenge, but maintained that negotiations and cooperative security (most notably through the OSCE) were the most adequate instruments to address the crisis. This stance was driven by Finland's long-standing support for negotiated solutions to crises between Russia and the West. Despite these differences, national leaders agreed on the common EU policy of imposing economic sanctions on Russia and seeking a diplomatic solution to the crisis.

However, Polish narratives began to diverge from German and Finnish discourses on several issues in 2015, especially after the right-wing Law and Justice government took office in Warsaw in November. Following the signing of the Minsk-2 agreement and the de-escalation of the conflict in the Donbass, German leaders pursued a partial relaxation of tensions with Russia. This included the support of the Nord Stream-2 pipeline, the quest of cooperation with Russia in other policy and regional scenarios (negotiations on Iran's nuclear programme, the Syrian crisis) and upholding the policy of historical reconciliation focusing on the memory of the Second World War. While Germany's continued support of EU sanctions meant that it was not back to 'business as usual' with Russia, these developments signalled that the tenets of *Ostpolitik* remained influential in German foreign policy thinking. German leaders continued to consider Russia as a difficult but fundamental interlocutor in the construction of a stable European security system.

Finnish official discourses evolved along similar lines. Finnish leaders remained firm in their condemnation of Russian actions in Ukraine, but argued for upholding cooperation with Moscow in the Arctic, the Baltic Sea and on environmental issues. Shielding this cooperation from tensions related to the Ukraine crisis was an important component of Finland's policy during its chairmanship of the Arctic Council in 2017–2019. German and Finnish official discourses on Russia remained critical until 2018 due to the failure to implement the Minsk-2 agreement and recurrent crises in multiple contexts (see also Chapter 6). Nevertheless, conceptualisations of Russia as a neighbour with whom dialogue and cooperation are indispensable remained dominant.

Polish official discourses developed differently. Beginning in late 2014, Polish governments adopted a harsher rhetoric towards Russia that advocated deeper economic sanctions and contemplated the provision of military aid to Ukraine. Foreign minister Schetyna and president Komorowski resorted to memory politics in order to evoke negative images of the Russian Other that are entrenched in Polish identity. A further radicalisation of discourses took place after Law and Justice won the 2015 parliamentary elections. The new government essentialised Russia as the main security threat to Poland. While German and Finnish policy makers defined the Minsk-2 agreement and the Normandy negotiations as the main instruments to resolve the Ukraine conflict, their Polish colleagues were much more sceptical. Foreign minister Waszczykowski even accused Germany of using the Normandy format to negotiate Ukraine's future 'over the head of Poland'. Poland's dialogue with Russia was restricted to a minimum and Polish leaders securitised numerous aspects of Polish–Russian relations, such as energy relations. Moreover, from the Polish perspective, the Ukraine crisis remained far more important than any other regional scenario where Russia could possibly become a cooperative partner.

These discursive differences highlight the fragility of the EU's posture vis-à-vis the Ukraine crisis. As this chapter has shown, different and deep-rooted constructions of Russia in national identities continue to act as centrifugal forces in the European discursive arena. While EU member states managed to uphold a common policy on the Ukraine crisis at the EU level, their differences led to divergent stances and policies in the strategic field of energy cooperation. This is illustrated in the next chapter, which focuses on the discursive contestation concerning the Nord Stream 2 project.

5   The EU's discursive strife
on Nord Stream 2

Introduction

While European member states appeared to converge on a shared stance towards Russia within the context of the Ukraine crisis, they took radically different positions regarding the energy partnership with Moscow. This became particularly evident when a new project to export Russian gas to the EU, Nord Stream 2, was announced in the summer of 2015. Russian agency in the Ukraine and Syrian crises, as well as its alleged interference in Western elections in 2016–2017, (re)activated long-standing European constructions of the Russian Other as a threat, which also had an impact on discourses and policies in the energy domain (see also Smith 2014, Siddi 2017c). The chapter argues that different, identity-based conceptualisations of Russia as an energy actor at the national level contribute to explaining intra-EU divisions on Nord Stream 2. These conceptualisations also play a role in the construction of material and economic interests in national energy policy.

The following analysis dissects German, Polish and Finnish leaders' discourses on Nord Stream 2 between 2015 and 2018, against the background of the broader European and transatlantic controversy regarding the pipeline. This investigation is integrated with recent scholarly analyses of the contemporary national public debate, which helps contextualise official statements. The main contribution of the chapter consists in revealing the persistence of different, identity-based constructions of the Russian Other in German, Polish and Finnish discourses throughout the period under investigation.

The Nord Stream 2 project

The Nord Stream 2 project was launched in the summer of 2015 by Russia's state energy company Gazprom together with five Western European partner companies – the German BASF and E.ON,[1] the French Engie, the Austrian ÖMV and the Dutch-British Shell. The pipeline will have the capacity to transport 55 billion cubic metres of gas per year (bcm/y) following an offshore route from Russia to Germany via the Baltic Sea. Together with the parallel infrastructure of the already existing Nord Stream pipeline (which became operational in 2011–2012), this energy corridor could carry 110 bcm/y and thus a large part of Russia's gas exports to Europe, which were approximately 180 bcm in 2017 (Henderson and Sharples 2018: 6). The Nord Stream 2 project has caused a vast debate in Europe that has numerous political, economic and legal ramifications. The following paragraphs summarise the main political and economic aspects that are essential to the ensuing discussion, and refer to more comprehensive studies for further details (Goldthau 2016, Henderson and Sharples 2018, Lang and Westphal 2017).

Nord Stream 2 could make EU–Russia gas trade much less dependent on transit pipelines in Ukraine. Ukrainian transit has been essential to gas flows from (Soviet) Russia to Europe since the Cold War, but has become more controversial following the 2006 and 2009 Russian–Ukrainian gas crises, which led to the temporary interruption of gas flows to Europe, and the more fundamental conflict between Moscow and Kiev that began in 2014 (Belyi 2015: 147–151). The future of the ageing Ukrainian transit pipelines remains somewhat unclear, even if Kiev and Moscow have agreed that substantial volumes of Russian gas directed to Europe will continue to be channelled through Ukraine in the first half of the 2020s (Platts 2019). While Nord Stream 2 creates an alternative and arguably more secure gas route than Ukrainian transit, it is seen by many in Europe and the US as highly controversial from a political standpoint. Critics argue that the pipeline would consolidate Europe's energy dependence on Russia at a time when the EU has adopted sanctions against Moscow and supported Ukraine in the conflict with Russia. The potential redirection of gas flows from Ukrainian transit to Nord Stream 2 would indeed imply an economic loss for Ukraine (which currently earns approximately $2 billion per year from transit fees) and weaken its strategic leverage vis-à-vis Russia. Furthermore, economic and environmental arguments have been made against Nord Stream 2. Environmental groups have argued that the EU will not need additional quantities of gas imports if it pursues decarbonisation policies and invests in renewable energy and energy efficiency (Fischer 2016).

Eastern European EU member states such as Poland, Slovakia and the Baltic States are particularly vocal in their criticism of Nord Stream 2 for both political reasons (the damage that it would inflict on Ukraine and the more general objection to deals with Russia) and because it would redirect gas flows and transit revenues away from their territory. The European Commission has criticised the project too, arguing that it contradicts the spirit of its Energy Union initiative, especially the objective of diversifying import partners (Siddi 2016b). Supporters of Nord Stream 2 counter that the pipeline is a commercial project and it should not be undermined by politics. The official position of the German government has focused on this argument. The German posture is substantiated by the fact that EU market rules are based on the concept of competition, and the Commission has the power to act as a watchdog of competition, but cannot influence it for political reasons.

Other arguments that have been made in favour of Nord Stream 2 focus on the stable or increasing European gas demand at a time of diminishing domestic gas production and the need to buy gas where it is cheaper for the sake of commercial competitiveness (ÖMV 2019).[2] It is also argued that additional gas imports would allow reducing coal and oil consumption (which pollute more than gas) and keep gas as a backup for intermittent renewable energy production while Europe pursues the transition to a low carbon economy. In Germany, the decision to switch off nuclear power plants by 2022 put additional pressure on the government to secure other energy sources while making sure that the country meets its decarbonisation targets. These factors are also among the reasons for Germany's support of Nord Stream 2. Berlin does not view further imports of Russian gas as a security issue because Russia has been a reliable energy supplier to Germany for several decades, even at times of high East–West political tensions during the Cold War (Högselius 2013). Russian gas is seen as an affordable energy source for German industrial production. Conversely, German leaders and industry fear that alternative suppliers, such as US producers of liquefied natural gas (LNG), may turn out to be more expensive. This concern has become more acute due to the aggressive trade policy pursued by the US during the Trump presidency. From a Germany business perspective, the US is an industrial competitor (much more so than Russia); hence, buying energy from US producers (at a higher price than competing US companies) may have a negative impact on the competitiveness of the Germany industry. On the other hand, the availability of US LNG supplies creates a potential alternative to Russian gas and limits the risk that Moscow uses its energy exports as an instrument of political influence or coercion vis-à-vis Germany (cf. Fischer 2016, Judge *et al.* 2016).

While this chapter focuses on German, Polish and Finnish discourses, it must be kept in mind that the debate on Nord Stream 2 increasingly acquired an EU (as well as transatlantic) dimension. Hence, the positions of the member states under analysis were defined also in relation to those of other EU members. For this reason, a brief overview of the latter is provided here. Austria's stance on Nord Stream 2 was similar to that of Germany. While Austria does not have an *Ostpolitik* tradition with Russia as influential as that of Germany, it does have a long history of energy trade and cooperative relations with Moscow (Högselius 2013). Together with its economic interests in the project, this long-standing cooperative approach to Russia arguably motivated Austrian support of Nord Stream 2 (cf. ÖMV 2019).

Other EU member states that had a tradition of cooperative commercial relations and energy trade with Russia, such as France and the Netherlands, were less vocal in defending the project but practically took a similar stance to that of Austria and Germany. As French and Dutch companies are part of the Nord Stream consortium and are also indirectly involved in Nord Stream 2, their interests are a factor affecting the stance of France and the Netherlands. Moreover, like Germany, France has a tradition of seeing economic cooperation with Russia positively, and the Macron government has not departed from it (Deutsche Welle 2018; cf. Cadier 2018). Italy initially expressed a critical perspective on Nord Stream 2 due to the fact that it concentrated EU–Russia gas trade along a northern route, as opposed to a southern one reaching Italian territory. However, Rome disapproved of transatlantic efforts to sabotage the project because energy trade with Russia remains a cornerstone of Italy's energy security (Italy is the second largest importer of Russian gas after Germany). Moreover, Italian companies are involved in other energy projects with Russian partners that may be targeted by US sanctions similar to those planned for Nord Stream 2 (Bongiorni 2017, Siddi 2018e).

The United Kingdom has so far kept a neutral and low profile on Nord Stream 2. The new crisis in bilateral relations with Russia following the poisoning of Sergei and Yulia Skripal on British soil has led some UK politicians to support a more critical stance on the project. Nevertheless, Prime Minister Theresa May has refrained from publicly criticising Nord Stream 2 (Sengupta 2018). By refusing to politicise the debate on the pipeline, the British leadership has de facto contributed to keeping it focused on economic considerations. As the potential consequences of the project are likely to be mostly positive for the UK (keeping the North-Western European markets liquid, see Goldthau 2016: 30–31), no strong opposition to it has arisen. Thus, the UK could be seen as a discursive arena where perceptions of the Russian Other are predominantly negative (cf. Nitoiu 2018), but they are not pervasive in national identity and the political debate. This enables economic considerations on themes such as Nord Stream 2 to be more influential than negative identity-driven or political arguments.

Nordic members of the EU (Sweden and Denmark, in addition to Finland) are not directly affected by Nord Stream 2, if one excepts the decision on granting permission to build the pipeline in their Exclusive Economic Zones or, in the case of Denmark, in its territorial waters (Gotkowska and Szymanski 2016). Their national debates on Russia and Nord Stream 2 have become more securitised following the Ukraine crisis. As a result, Denmark delayed the granting of building permits to the Nord Stream 2 consortium and passed a law that allows the country to block the construction of the pipeline in its territorial waters for security reasons (Reuters 2018). However, Sweden and Denmark also face the pressure of maintaining positive relations with Germany and Russia, which are key trade and security actors in their neighbourhood. This issue is even more relevant to Finland, which shares a long border and has important trade links with Russia. Helsinki also maintains a close energy relationship with Moscow, including the recent decision to have Russian company Rosatom build a new nuclear plant on Finnish soil (Aalto *et al.* 2017).

The position of several East-Central European member states tends to be far more critical, if not overtly hostile, to Nord Stream 2 (cf. Lang and Westphal 2017: 29–34). Apart from Poland, five more of them (the Baltic States, Romania and Slovakia) have consistently argued against the project. The position of the Baltic States is very similar to that of Poland, both in terms of official stance and of likely underlying factors. As the Nord Stream project does not divert gas transit away from their territory (and thus transit revenues), their stance is mostly due to the same strategic and political considerations as Poland's, and is similarly influenced by pervasive negative constructions of the Russian Other (for an extensive discussion, see Berg and Ehin 2009).

While Russia, and particularly its Soviet past, has been conceptualised negatively also in the national identities of other East-Central European countries, antagonising constructions of the Russian Other do not appear as pervasive as in Poland or the Baltic States, particularly in current political discourse. Hence, while negative perceptions of Russia are influential also in these countries, their national debates tend to be influenced also by contextual and material factors. In the case of Slovakia, economic considerations appear to be the main reasons for its opposition to Nord Stream 2. Slovakia plays a key role in the transit of gas that reaches the EU via Ukraine (it earned €355 million in transit revenues in 2015), and thus stands to lose if gas flows are redirected to the Nord Stream 2 route. Romania is an important transit country for Russian gas supplies to the Balkans, and will most likely lose this function if Ukrainian transit pipelines are no longer used (Lang and Westphal 2017: 28–30; Loskot-Strachota and Poplawski 2016).

On the other hand, some other East-Central European countries have been more ambivalent towards Nord Stream 2. This is the case of Bulgaria, whose population has closer cultural and linguistic ties with Russia than other regional actors, and thus a less critical conceptualisation of the Russian Other. Material factors play an essential role: Sofia maintains an interest in a new Southern route for Russian gas imports, and is thus wary of undermining its relations with Russia and Gazprom (Lang and Westphal 2017: 34; Smilov 2018). Perspectives on Russia tend to be complex, and by far not as one-sided as in Poland and the Baltics, also in the Czech Republic and Hungary. Economic interests are likely to be significant in both cases. With Nord Stream 2 operational, the Czech Republic could acquire greater importance as a transit country in Central Europe and strengthen its energy security (Groszkowski 2017). After initially voicing a critical stance, Hungary has taken a much more cautious approach to Nord Stream 2. Thanks *inter alia* to the positive relationship between President Viktor Orban and Putin, Budapest is cooperating with Russia in strategic energy projects in the nuclear field and appears interested in further cooperation with Gazprom with regard to gas trade and infrastructural projects (Aalto *et al.* 2017; Hejj 2018, Lang and Westphal 2017: 33).

This constellation of European interests has shaped the debate on Nord Stream 2. While the discussion initially focused on geopolitical and economic considerations, EU-level debates have gradually shifted towards more technical and legal debates regarding the application of EU legislation to the pipeline. This concerns in particular the applicability of the EU's third energy package to Nord Stream-2, which would limit Gazprom's ability to use the pipeline at full capacity. The ensuing legal dispute pitted against each other not only member states supporting and opposing the project, but even European institutions. While the European Commission's Energy Directorate believed that the legislation should apply to Nord Stream 2, both the Commission's and the Council's legal service stated that this was not the case because the EU's regulatory framework covers the EU's internal market, and not offshore pipelines from third countries (Fischer 2017). Nevertheless, in an effort to thwart the project, the

Commission attempted to ensure the applicability of the third energy package by amending existing legislation (the Gas Market Directive). Between the fall of 2017 and early 2019, this reignited the dispute between member states supporting and opposing Nord Stream-2, which had to make a decision on accepting the Commission's amendments within the European Council. Eventually, an apparent compromise was found in February 2019, with an amendment that decreed the applicability of the legislation to the pipeline section in EU territorial waters, but left the member state where the pipeline lands (in this case, Germany) in charge of applying the legislation (Posaner *et al.* 2019).

Moreover, the dispute around Nord Stream 2 acquired a strong transatlantic dimension when the United States attempted to stop the project through sanctions. In the summer of 2017, the US Congress passed a draft bill threatening to sanction European companies involved in the project. This led to the angry reaction of several European countries, led by Germany, France and Austria, which condemned US interference in European energy policy (Reuters 2017b). Following negotiations with European diplomatic envoys, the legislation was softened with the addendum that sanctions would be imposed at the US president's discretion in coordination with US allies. However, new sanctions bills that do now require presidential approval or coordination with European countries were proposed in the US Congress in 2018–2019. While this legislation is unlikely to stop the construction of Nord Stream 2, it has fed tensions between transatlantic partners, particularly between the US and Germany. Advocates of the pipeline see the proposed extraterritorial sanctions as an illegal attempt to interfere in EU energy policy and promote US LNG exports, whereas detractors view them as an instrument to challenge the ambitions of Gazprom and its European partners (Siddi 2018c and 2018f).

Germany: defending a commercial project in line with European rules

In the aftermath of the Ukraine crisis, different national articulations of the Russian Other became relevant and influenced policy debates in EU member states. While the assessment of Russia became more negative throughout the EU, there were different views about the nature of Russian policies and especially about how to engage the Kremlin in the future. Nowhere does this become clearer than in the divergent German and Polish approaches to energy relations with Russia. The German and Polish debate on Nord Stream 2 reflected two radically different perceptions of the Russian Other.

At the time when the Nord Stream 2 project was launched, high-ranking German officials such as then Foreign Minister Frank-Walter Steinmeier (2016d) argued that the West and Russia 'need[ed] each other' to resolve regional conflicts, as negotiations on the Iranian nuclear programme and Syria had shown. Despite tensions and Steinmeier's own critical assessment of Russian behaviour in the Ukraine crisis, he described Russia as 'the EU's largest neighbour', arguing that 'good neighbourly relations [were] in the interests of both sides'. Significantly, he believed that 'after the experiences of the twentieth century, we Germans in particular bear a responsibility to keep finding channels of communication and solutions to conflicts [with Russia]'. This discourse reflected consolidated German narratives about guilt for the Second World War, and particularly for war crimes in Eastern Europe, which had been influential in the framing of *Ostpolitik* in the 1960s and 1970s (Siddi 2018c). In the post-2014 context, this ideational background induced German policy makers to be wary of radicalising the debate on Russia and seek instead a resolution of the crisis through dialogue, diplomacy and neighbourly cooperation.

One of the prominent articulations of this cooperation concerned trade and energy policy, much like during the *Ostpolitik* of the 1970s (Lang and Westphal 2017: 27). The Nord Stream 2 project was seen as an opportunity to constructively engage Russia and simultaneously strengthen German and European energy security. Steinmeier (2016d) argued that:

> Russia was always a reliable energy partner for us – including in difficult times. The Nord Stream 2 project is currently being discussed in depth between the companies involved and the European Commission. And of course we are also taking part in this discussion [...] Our economic ties with Russia remain very close [...] I am pleased that most German companies are continuing to work with Russia despite this difficult environment.

Steinmeier's views were widely shared among top officials in the German coalition government (including the centre-left Social Democratic Party and the centre-right Christian Democratic Union/Christian Social Union). This was especially true of Steinmeier's fellow Social Democrats, who often praised their former party leader Willy Brandt for crafting the *Ostpolitik*. Minister of Economic Affairs and Energy (2013–2017) and then Foreign Minister (2017–2018) Sigmar Gabriel argued that he was 'strongly in favour of a new *Ostpolitik* and a new policy of détente', adding that 'Brandt began his *Ostpolitik* in 1968 after the Soviet Union had invaded Czechoslovakia, in other words, during the most difficult times' (Gabriel 2017a). With regard to Nord Stream 2, in his bilateral meeting with Putin of October 2015, Gabriel argued that '[Nord Stream 2] is in our interests; but it is not just in Germany's interests – it is a very interesting project even beyond Germany's borders' (Gabriel 2015). Gabriel believed that the pipeline and Germany's energy policy towards Russia furthered European interests, rather than just those of Germany. This approach reflected German leaders' belief that the EU's policy towards Russia could benefit from Germany's *Ostpolitik* experience, eventually leading to the framing of a European *Ostpolitik* (cf. Siddi 2018d; the concept of a European *Ostpolitik* was first proposed by Steinmeier in 2007, during the contemporary German presidency of the EU, see Steinmeier 2007).

Gabriel's successor as foreign minister, Social Democrat Heiko Maas, maintained a similar stance concerning both Nord Stream 2 and relations with Russia in general. For instance, he stated that 'the only possible answer [to the crisis with Russia] is a European *Ostpolitik*' (Maas 2018a). With regard to Nord Stream 2, Maas (2018b) argued that 'This is a business project. Nobody would stand to benefit if the German and European companies were to pull out.' At the same time, Maas argued that the transit of Russian gas through Ukraine should continue, and that Germany had 'obtained this assurance from the Russians' (Maas 2018b, see also below). Maas's statements revealed his effort to reconcile the Nord Stream 2 project with Ukraine's economic and strategic interests, thereby also squaring Germany's energy partnership with Russia with its support of post-Euromaidan Ukraine. Moreover, the fact that he cited 'assurances' from his Russian interlocutors highlighted how the German leadership continued to view Russia as a reliable and trustworthy energy partner, despite ongoing political tensions.

While references to Brandt were mostly the domain of Social Democratic ministers, positive or economically-minded opinions on energy cooperation with Russia were widely shared across party lines in the German government (except for a critical minority) and even among most of the opposition. In parliamentary debates, only the Green Party, in opposition, consistently criticised this cooperation (Heinrich 2017: 74–75). The German media debate on the Nord Stream projects was more critical, but this did not seem to alter the stance of political leaders (Heinrich 2017: 75–79). Most notably, Chancellor Angela Merkel emphasised that Nord Stream 2 was a commercial endeavour and should not be undermined by politics (see for instance German Federal Government 2018a). In fact, behind this apparently neutral stance was significant political support for the project, which emerged more clearly over time, as Nord Stream 2 came under attack from Eastern European member states, European institutions and particularly the US.

As early as October 2015, following initial criticism of the project from European officials and other member states, Gabriel asserted that Nord Stream 2 should remain under the competences of German authorities in order to avoid 'external meddling' and 'political interference' in the project (Gabriel 2015). When Polish opposition to Nord Stream 2 became more vocal (see below), Gabriel (2017b) told Polish media that the pipeline was in the broader European interest and conformed to EU market principles: 'Gas pipelines do not only transport Russian gas to Germany, but also to Poland, of course [...] We ask people to understand that we want to stand by the liberalisation of the gas supply undertaken in Europe years ago'. Therefore, Gabriel attempted to defend Nord Stream 2 by arguing that it complied with European rules and made a positive contribution to European energy security. This discourse resembled the narrative employed by German leaders to counter opposition to the Nord Stream project in 2006–2011, which emphasised the European dimension of the pipeline and its economic benefits for the EU as a whole (Siddi 2017d: 73–75).

At the same time, due to the continued opposition of several EU member states to the project, Gabriel and Merkel conceded that Nord Stream 2 would have an impact on gas transit in Ukraine, Poland and other Eastern European countries, and pledged that Germany would support the continuation of this transit (Gabriel 2017b, German Federal Government 2018b). German leaders realised that, in the tense post-Ukraine crisis context, the argument about Nord Stream 2's 'Europeanness' would not be convincing for many of Germany's EU partners. This led to concerns in Berlin that other EU members would question Germany's commitment to important aspects of European integration, such as the construction of an integrated European energy market. Merkel's and Gabriel's reassurance that gas transit in Ukraine would be preserved, as well as their acknowledgement of the concerns of EU members opposing the pipeline, was meant to reaffirm Germany's commitment to EU policies and values, in line with Germany's pro-EU foreign policy identity. On the other hand, German leaders continued to see no contradiction between this commitment and the *Ostpolitik* tenets of German foreign policy, which drove engagement and energy cooperation with Russia.

The German official response was less accommodating towards criticism voiced by the US. The United States were seen as interfering in European energy policy and having a conflict of interests. In June 2017, the US congress prepared a draft bill that included possible sanctions against Western companies participating in the Nord Stream 2 project. At the same time, US President Donald Trump and numerous other US politicians were arguing that the EU should import US liquefied natural gas rather than Russian gas. Soon after the sanctions bill was announced, Gabriel issued a joint statement with Austrian Federal Chancellor Christian Kern arguing:

> We cannot, however, accept the threat of illegal extraterritorial sanctions being imposed on European companies that are participating in efforts to expand Europe's energy supply network! The draft bill of the US is surprisingly candid about what is actually at stake, namely selling American liquefied natural gas [...] This is about the competitiveness of our energy-intensive industries, and about thousands of jobs [...] Europe's energy supply network is Europe's affair, not that of the United States of America!
>
> (Gabriel and Kern 2017)

As the possibility of US sanctions against Nord Stream 2 remained on the table in subsequent months, German diplomacy consistently reiterated its criticism of US meddling in European energy policy. Foreign minister Heiko Maas intervened once again on the dispute in January 2019, arguing that 'Questions of European energy policy must be decided in Europe, not in the U.S. [...] To impose unilateral sanctions against Nord Stream 2 is certainly not the way to go' (cited in Reuters 2019).

Thus, German leaders insisted on the primarily commercial nature of the project, as well as the fact that it respected EU market principles and laws, whereas stopping it for political reasons would counter those very principles. Arguably, the German defence of Nord Stream 2 went beyond commercial and legal issues and backed a policy line which sought a partial rapprochement with Russia on mutually beneficial contact points. The pursuit of Nord Stream 2 amidst contemporary tensions in EU–Russia relations reflected the belief that cooperation with the Russian Other was still possible, and that conflict was neither all-encompassing nor preordained.

Poland: Nord Stream 2 as a hybrid weapon to divide Europe

The Polish debate on Nord Stream 2 and the Russian Other was radically different from the German debate. The Russian Other was essentialised as a security threat and Russia's policies – including energy projects – were seen as having negative security implications. As discussed in Chapter 3, antagonistic Polish narratives of the Russian Other have a long history that predates Moscow's aggressive policies in Ukraine, and are grounded in Polish experiences of Tsarist and Soviet domination (Zarycki 2004; cf. Siddi and Gaweda 2019: 260–261 and 265–266). In the realm of energy policy, these narratives had already been activated earlier in relation to the Nord Stream project (Siddi 2017d: 76–83). In 2006, shortly after the project was announced, then Defence Minister Radoslaw Sikorski called it 'a new Molotov-Ribbentrop pact' (cited in Castle 2006), thus comparing it to the 1939 Nazi–Soviet deal to partition Eastern Europe.

Moscow's post-2014 belligerent foreign policy contributed to reviving the most antagonistic Polish identity narratives about Russia. In this regard, Russian agency was compounded by changes in Polish domestic politics, most notably the rise to power of the nationalist and profoundly anti-Russian Law and Justice party. The electoral victory of Law and Justice in the fall of 2015 ended eight years of centre-right government under the leadership of Donald Tusk's Civic Platform. Law and Justice has a history of antagonising both Russia and Germany in political discourse (Reeves 2010). In 2016, one of its main representatives, then Foreign Minister Witold Waszczykowski, argued that Russia was an existential threat for Europe, one more dangerous than ISIS (cited in *Guardian* 2016). Hence, as a result of both Russian policies and Polish domestic politics, the Polish–Russian bilateral relationship took the form of a confrontational deadlock (for a full account, see Sus 2018). In the Polish domestic debate, Law and Justice politicians used the image of the antagonistic Russian Other against the political opposition Most notably, they argued that the Civic Platform and the Russian leadership had been responsible for the Smolensk plane crash, in which former president and Law and Justice leader Lech Kaczynski died in 2010, together with many other state officials (Davies 2016). Russia's refusal to return the plane wreck to Poland further contributed to mutual distrust and tensions.

Against this domestic and international background, the Polish parliamentary and media debates on Nord Stream 2 have been overwhelmingly negative across party lines. The project is seen as politically motivated and is considered a threat to Poland's energy security and economic and strategic interests (Sus 2018: 85–86). Many of the arguments that had been made against the first Nord Stream project have been reiterated – for instance, the notion that Poland will face political pressure from Russia after the pipeline is built (cf. Heinrich 2017: 65–73). However, as illustrated in the analysis below, the official debate has become more radicalised due to the tenser international context and the fact that Law and Justice is now in power in Warsaw.

When the Nord Stream project was launched in 2005, some Polish politicians still argued that the damage which the pipeline would inflict on Poland was actually limited, and Warsaw could compete with it (also) by promoting alternative routes for Russian gas (such as the Amber pipeline through the Baltic states) (Heinrich 2017: 67–68, 85). In the context of the Nord Stream 2 debate, such moderate considerations were absent: the project was seen as catastrophic for Poland. The only response envisaged was the construction of new infrastructure for the import of non-Russian gas (particularly the Baltic Pipe[3] and LNG terminals) and even the termination of gas imports from Russia after the current long-term contract between Warsaw and Moscow expires in 2022.

The Polish government's position on Nord Stream 2 is well summarised in the op-ed published by Minister for European Affairs Konrad Szymanski in the *Financial Times* in October 2016.

> Poland has opposed Nord Stream 2 since it was first announced by Gazprom in 2015. It undermines European solidarity and the Energy Union, the EU's flagship project. The economic arguments for Nord Stream 2 were always questionable [...] And given Europe's considerable dependence on Russian gas and the damage the project would cause to the Ukrainian economy (which is subsidised by the EU), the political motivations behind it seemed obvious [...] [Nord Stream 2] now looks like a Trojan horse capable of destabilising the economy and poisoning political relations inside the EU [...] By supporting Nord Stream 2, the EU in effect gives succour to a regime whose aggression it seeks to punish through sanctions. This contradiction is unsustainable.
>
> (Szymanski 2016)

Szymanski cited economic factors and European solidarity first, but his key argument was political/strategic and consisted in juxtaposing Nord Stream 2 to Russia's aggressive policy in the Ukraine crisis. The pipeline was not seen in the context of market factors, such as European demand, transit risk and competition among gas suppliers, but exclusively as a Russian instrument in the geopolitical struggle for Eastern Europe. The conceptualisation of Russia as a threatening Other provides the underlying logic for this narrative.

Szymanski's arguments were reiterated in the public statements of Poland's top leadership. President Andrzej Duda argued that Nord Stream 2 'has nothing to do with economics' and 'is an investment of political nature' (Reuters 2016a). Prime Minister Beata Szydlo argued that the project represented a threat to the energy independence of the whole Central and Eastern Europe (PAP 2017). Foreign Minister Witold Waszczykowski claimed that the pipeline undermined trust among EU member states, struck 'a blow against not only CEE [Central and Eastern Europe]'s security of gas supplies, but also Ukraine's stability' (2016a); it may also cause 'geopolitical destabilisation in Central Europe' (2016b).

While the link between identity narratives and energy policy discourse is sometimes a matter of how diplomatic and official statements are interpreted, explicit references to history are often present next to Polish leaders' analyses of current political events. For instance, in an interview focusing on Poland's foreign, security and energy policy, Waszczykowski explained his country's stance by arguing that 'Poland has had bad experiences in its history. We want to be cautious. We have a war behind our doors right now. We have an aggressive neighbour that is openly proclaiming the redrawing of the borders of Europe' (cited in Dempsey 2016). Similarly, in his speech on Polish foreign policy tasks in 2017, he argued that 'Poland will not accept such a vision [the Russian vision] of the political order in Europe, and will not condone the carving up of our continent into spheres of influence. Never again Munich or Yalta!' (whereby he referred to the partitioning of Czechoslovakia in Munich in 1938 and the division of Europe into spheres of influence at Yalta in 1945) (Waszczykowski 2017b).

Waszczykowski also used the Nord Stream 2 controversy to criticise Germany and associate the project with unrelated issues. He argued that Chancellor Angela Merkel was 'working very hard on Nord Stream 2' (cited in Dempsey 2016) and that the pipeline was a way for Berlin and Brussels to punish Poland for a controversial judicial reform – which in the view of the European Commission, undermined the rule of law in the country (Harper 2017). In his address on Polish foreign policy tasks for 2018, Foreign Minister Jacek Czaputowicz (who succeeded to Waszczykowski after a cabinet reshuffle) juxtaposed his criticism of Nord Stream 2 to demands that Germany compensates Poland for the losses the latter suffered during the Second World War (Czaputowicz 2018c).[4] Juxtapositions like this one aimed at mobilising influential Polish identity narratives of the Second World War that constructed Germany as a negative Other and use them in current political debate (cf. Reeves 2010, Siddi and Gaweda 2019).

Polish and German leaders have engaged each other in the attempt to resolve differences concerning the pipeline project, but their visions have remained fundamentally different. In a bilateral meeting between Merkel and Polish Prime Minister Mateusz Morawiecki in February 2018, Merkel continued to defend Nord Stream 2 as an economic project and an import diversification route, whereas Morawiecki reiterated that it entails political and security risks (BiznesAlert 2018, King 2018). In bilateral discussions, German and Polish leaders agreed to disagree and found common ground only on general statements about their shared commitment to 'European solidarity as regards energy security and the need to diversify the energy supply' (Federal Foreign Office 2018).

As the planning of the pipeline went on, Polish leaders further radicalised their rhetoric. President Andrzej Duda called Nord Stream 2 'a weapon in the hybrid war being conducted against Ukraine' (cited in Radio Poland 2018a). Similarly, Morawiecki stated that the pipeline is a weapon of hybrid warfare that Moscow wants to use to undermine European energy security and EU and NATO solidarity, 'a poison pill for European security' (cited in RFE/RL 2018). Thus, from a Polish perspective, the project continued to be a malign activity engineered by the threatening Russian Other for geopolitical purposes. In the discourse of Polish leaders, the only possible response to Nord Stream 2 was efforts to block it at the European level, or counter it with alternative projects without Russian participation, such as the Baltic Pipe (see Waszczykowski 2017b) and LNG deliveries from the United States (Czaputowicz 2018c).

The Finnish debate: economics and the environment trump security concerns

In the Finnish discursive arena, Nord Stream 2 became an important and controversial topic in the news and in think tank debates, which followed the European discussions and disagreements on the project. As during the construction of Nord Stream (in 2005–2012, see Siddi 2017d: 83–89), Finland was only indirectly affected by Nord Stream 2. The pipeline was not designed to supply Finland, it did not divert existing gas trade away from the country and only crossed the Finnish Exclusive Economic Zone in the Baltic Sea, which meant that Helsinki had to issue environmental permits for its construction. Hence, the Finnish government seemed keen to avoid involvement in the European political dispute concerning the pipeline and approached the issue from a purely technical and environmental perspective. As Prime Minister Juha Sipilä put it, 'Finland has no national special interest either for or against the project' (cited in Raivio 2019).

However, due to the heightened international tensions after the Ukraine crisis, security issues were raised in the public discussion more often than during the building of Nord Stream ten years earlier. Ongoing security discussions concerning the pipeline in other Nordic states, particularly Denmark and Sweden, led some Finnish commentators and politicians to argue that similar debates should take place in Finland (Kurki-Suonio 2018). Another relevant, controversial topic was the work of former Finnish Prime Minister Paavo Lipponen (in office from 1995 to 2003) as a consultant for Nord Stream 2 (Raivio 2019). Moreover, in early 2018 Finnish company Fortum, which is majority state-owned, acquired a 47 per cent stake in German company Uniper, one of the supporters of the Nord Stream-2 project (Yle 2018a).

As a result of these developments, two main discourses on the pipeline existed in the Finnish debates, which largely reflected consolidated Finnish narratives about relations with Russia. On the one hand, the political leadership presented Nord Stream-2 as a commercial project that had to be assessed based on economic and environmental considerations. This discourse reflected conceptualisations of Russia as an economic partner (see Chapter 3). On the other hand, some members of the Finnish epistemic community, journalists and politicians emphasised the security implications of the project and eventually induced the political leadership to address them. Their discourse echoed long-standing Finnish constructions of Russia (and its policies) as the main source of insecurity for Finland.

As argued, the first discourse shaped the official position of the Finnish government. In European Council summits, the government took a similar stance to that of Germany. At a Council summit in December 2015, Sipilä declared that 'for Finland, this [Nord Stream 2] is not a political issue. For us, this is a commercial project' (cited in Hartikainen 2015). Finnish President Sauli Niinistö adopted the same rhetoric and stressed that implications for Finland were limited because the pipeline 'does not lie on Finnish territory' (cited in Uhari 2018). Similarly, Foreign Minister Timo Soini toned down the political dimension of the project by focusing on legal and environmental concerns. In a press conference with his Estonian counterpart (who spoke against Nord Stream 2), Soini stated that 'We [Finland] think that this is a legal and environmental process, and we are going through it in accordance with our own legislation' (cited in Hakala 2019).

Nevertheless, as the security debate on Nord Stream 2 intensified, the Finnish government was urged to address security issues within its broader assessment of the project. The government explained its position on Nord Stream-2 extensively in September 2016 in Sipilä's written answer to questions raised by parliamentarians. The document reiterated that Finland viewed the project as a commercial endeavour and based its assessment on environmental and legal standards, in accordance to the UN Convention on the Law of the Sea. Finland had

no specific national interests to oppose or support the project. The project does not affect Finland's energy security and it is not currently expected to have any other direct security implications for Finland. The key thing to evaluate in Finland is its environmental impact.

(Sipilä 2016a)

Sipilä also stressed that most EU member states took the same approach as Finland. At the same time, he conceded that 'the concerns of those who are critical of the project are understandable' because of contemporary Russian policy and the geopolitical implications of large energy projects such as Nord Stream 2. Nevertheless, he argued that blocking the project for political reasons was not an appropriate response; instead, Finland had to guarantee the application of existing international and national legislation. Sipilä also stressed that the construction phase of the pipeline near Finland did not involve security risks because Finnish authorities could monitor the process and oversee related operations in Finnish ports and territorial waters.

Niinistö also dismissed security concerns by arguing that 'from a security policy perspective, it's difficult to understand why a second pipe is a risk when one already exists' (cited in Yle 2019). In his opinion, the first Nord Stream project had not strengthened Russian political influence, and, in any case, alternative energy supplies were available. He also argued that US opposition to Nord

Stream was partly driven by commercial interests (the export of US LNG) and the influence of Eastern European countries that opposed the project (Niinistö cited in Nurminen 2019). Having ruled out security risks, and following an environmental impact assessment, Finland issued construction permits to Nord Stream 2 in 2017 and 2018 (Ministry of Economic Affairs and Employment of Finland 2018, Yle 2018b).

Arguably, the posture of the Finnish government on Nord Stream 2 was also influenced by the recent precedent of the Fennovoima project. The project concerns the building of a nuclear power plant in Hanhikivi, Finland, and includes Russian nuclear energy company Rosatom as a key partner. The Finnish parliament approved the project in 2014 (at the peak of the Ukraine crisis), with the prevailing opinion that political tensions with Russia should not determine the assessment of an energy project (for background and a critical opinion on Fennovoima, see Martikainen and Vihma 2016: 6–7). Also in the case of Fennovoima, the narrative about Russia as an economic partner appeared to prevail over securitised discourses in Finnish decision-making circles. The Finnish stance on Nord Stream 2 appeared to be in continuity with the logic applied to the Fennovoima project. Fortum's involvement in Nord Stream 2 after its acquisition of Uniper in 2017–2018 further consolidated Finland's economic approach to energy relations with Russia. In the wake of the acquisition, Sipilä (cited in Virkki 2017) stated that 'there is no foreign and security policy dimension to this trade [Fortum's acquisition of Uniper]. That leaves just the company's own needs, and the company's Board of Directors has considered it necessary'.

Drivers of the Nord Stream 2 dispute: identity or material factors?

The analysis of national discourses on Nord Stream 2 would be incomplete without addressing the role played by material factors. This is particularly important when it comes to the German and Polish debates, because both Poland and especially Germany have considerable economic interests at stake in the implementation (or cancellation) of Nord Stream 2. While ideas and a greater predisposition to cooperate with Russia on energy policy played a role in Germany's positive stance on Nord Stream 2, so did the material gains expected from the project. Together with the already operational Nord Stream pipelines, Nord Stream 2 would allow Germany to become the main hub for Russian gas in Europe. The pipelines create a direct line between Gazprom and German and Western European consumers, without any transit-related risks and tariffs. From an economic perspective, this is understandable because Germany is the largest importer of Russian gas in Europe, and gas is expected to acquire a more important role in the German energy mix due to the phase-out of nuclear power plants and the need to curb coal consumption.

In addition to satisfying its own gas demand, Germany will probably also be in the position of managing substantial flows of Russian gas towards Western,

Southern and Central Europe (cf. Loskot-Strachota and Poplawski 2016). This can be inferred from the fact that the combined capacity of the Nord Stream pipelines (110 bcm/y) exceeds German gas consumption of Russian gas (which was 53.4 bcm/y in 2017[5]). Potentially, this also means that countries further down the pipelines may have to pay slightly higher prices for gas than Berlin due to the additional transport costs. This has caused some concern in states that are industrial competitors of Germany, such as Italy (Reuters 2016b). It is difficult to assess whether economic factors are more or less important than ideational ones (namely, the historic construction of energy relations with Russia as a good thing, promoting cooperation and détente) in shaping the stance of German leaders towards Nord Stream 2. In fact, it appears that identity-based constructions and material interests reinforce each other and concur in shaping Germany's favourable stance towards Nord Stream 2. Furthermore, according to constructivist scholarship, material interests are socially constructed. Accordingly, the construction of German economic interests in the Nord Stream 2 debate has occurred in a social and discursive context in which, for historical reasons, energy cooperation with Russia is viewed as a positive fact (in both business environments and top policy making circles).

By the same token, material factors also play some role in Poland's opposition to Nord Stream 2 and partly corroborate identity-based discourses. If the project is completed, the transit pipelines channelling Russian gas across Polish territory (Yamal–Europe) could lose economic and strategic relevance – although the main impact will be on Ukrainian transit pipelines, which have a much larger capacity. This would also endanger Polish revenue from transit fees, which however is very modest, around $5.5 million a year (cf. Reuters 2017a). The Polish authorities also fear that, by making large volumes of cheap Russian gas available on the Polish market, Nord Stream 2 would prevent competition and the diversification of Poland's gas imports. In fact, this argument seems to combine economic and political factors. From an economic perspective, regardless of current prices, a more diversified portfolio of suppliers prevents the emergence of a monopolist, and thus reduces the risk of higher prices in the future. At the same time, Poland's diversification away from Russian gas imports is at least partly motivated by political and ideational drivers, particularly at a time when gas from Russia tends to be cheaper than the alternatives envisaged by the Polish government (such as US LNG).

Warsaw's strategic arguments are grounded on a clearer logic. By redirecting volumes of gas away from Ukraine, Nord Stream 2 would weaken Kiev's strategic position vis-à-vis Russia and the EU (which will reduce reliance on Ukrainian transit pipelines) and decrease its income from transit fees (Loskot-Strachota 2015). The overall impact may therefore be the economic and strategic weakening of Ukraine, which Poland sees as an important geopolitical partner curbing Russian influence. However, the Polish conceptualisation of Ukraine as an anti-Russian buffer is also grounded in ideational constructs of both Ukraine and the Russian Other. Similarly, Polish perceptions of Russian–German commercial deals as a threat are not simply due to possible negative economic consequences for Poland; they are also linked to negative ideational constructs of German–Russian cooperation, which are deeply entrenched in Polish identity (cf. Reeves 2010: 527–528). Thus, both the economic and strategic factors guiding Poland's stance appear to be intertwined with ideational constructs.

Hence, it is difficult to argue that material factors are the main determinant of Poland's opposition to Nord Stream 2. Had Warsaw been guided primarily by an economic logic, it may have attempted to compete with Nord Stream 2 by securing its own supplies of cheap Russian gas, for instance through the expansion of the Yamal pipeline. In the current Polish political discourse, however, this course of action appears unthinkable because the pervasively negative constructions of the Russian Other make further energy cooperation with Moscow highly undesirable. Accordingly, Polish leaders formulated only economic arguments (such as the benefits of diversifying imports away from Russia) that could be reconciled with the dominant ideational constructs portraying Russia as a threatening Other, and its energy policy as a source of insecurity for Poland.

Conclusion

Chapter 4 showed that, despite some discursive and rhetorical differences, EU member states converged towards a common diplomatic position vis-à-vis the Ukraine crisis and the imposition of sanctions on Russia. After Russia's annexation of Crimea and support of Donbas separatists, critical narratives and negative representations of the Russian Other prevailed in the national discourses under investigation. This suggested that a coherent foreign policy narrative focused on antagonising an aggressive Russia was emerging within the EU, transcending national discursive arenas. Chapter 5 exposed that this was in fact not the case in the field of energy relations, one of the most strategic and economically significant aspects of the relationship between the EU and Russia. The analysis of national discourses on Nord Stream 2 revealed that, as in the past, EU member states remained divided in their assessment of Russia as an energy provider. Indeed, the dispute between member states such as Germany and Poland became more radical. It was argued that different constructions of the Russian Other and different historical experiences regarding energy trade with Russia contributed to the framing of highly conflictual national views on Nord Stream 2.

In German official discourses, the logic of *Ostpolitik* remained influential, including the long-standing conceptualisation of Russia as a reliable energy supplier. The Nord Stream 2 project was seen as a mutually beneficial way of engaging Russia at a time of severe political tensions. From the perspective of Germany's political leadership, the pipeline strengthened both German and European energy security and respected European legislation. In their responses to political criticism of the project, German leaders stressed that Nord Stream 2 was a commercial venture and, in the spirit of EU market rules, should not be undermined by politics. US criticism and the threat of sanctions were rebuffed as American interference in European sovereign decisions. By framing Nord Stream 2 as a European project (or as a project in Europe's interests), German leaders attempted to reconcile the *Ostpolitik* vector of their foreign policy with Germany's traditional pro-EU orientation. As several East-Central European member states and Ukraine refused to accept this line of argument and the dispute intensified, the German government acknowledged that the project had geopolitical consequences. However, this did not lead to a radical discursive or policy change. German leaders proposed to remedy the issue through guarantees concerning the continuation of gas transit in Ukraine after the construction of Nord Stream 2.

Conversely, Polish discourses essentialised the Russian Other and its policies as a security threat. This was particularly true of the period under investigation (2015–2018), which coincided with the return to power of the profoundly anti-Russian party Law and Justice. The new government defined Russia as Poland's main security threat. It also used the 'Russian threat' in the domestic political debate, where it tried to construct links between the opposition and the Russian leadership in order to blame both for the Smolensk plane crash and Lech Kaczynski's death in 2010. The political discourse of Law and Justice leaders also described Germany as an antagonist to Poland, tapping into a vast repertoire of anti-German Polish historical narratives. This contributes to explaining why Polish opposition to Nord Stream 2, which was perceived as a Russian–German political endeavour, was so vehement. It also helps understand why the Polish discussion on Nord Stream 2 was securitised and deeply imbued with identity politics. The project was described as a geopolitical threat to Poland, Ukraine and Europe, a weapon in Russia's hybrid war against the West and 'a poison pill for European security' (Morawiecki, cited in RFE/RL 2018).

Caught in a dispute between EU partners, Finnish leaders attempted to take an apparently neutral stance, arguing that Finland was only indirectly affected by Nord Stream 2 and would only provide an environmental assessment of the pipeline section in its Exclusive Economic Zone, as required by international law. However, the intensification of the domestic and international debate on the project eventually induced Finnish leaders to address its economic, political and security implications. Echoing the German stance, they argued that Nord Stream 2 was a commercial project that should not be stopped for political reasons. While recognising that the concerns of critical EU member states were understandable, they argued that the pipeline did not involve security risks for Finland. This stance was reaffirmed when Finnish company Fortum acquired an economic interest in Nord Stream 2. In Finnish official narratives, economic considerations prevailed over the security concerns expressed by some politicians and members of the local epistemic community. The two main themes of the debate – economics and security – mirrored the two long-standing and partly contradictory Finnish constructions of the Russian Other as an economic partner and a source of insecurity.

The chapter also assessed the question of whether material interests played a more influential role than ideational and identity factors in shaping national discourses on Nord Stream 2. The question stemmed from German and, to some extent, Finnish economic interests in the project. In fact, ideational and material drivers were not clearly discernible or appeared to concur in the construction of national positions. Moreover, economic interests are also socially constructed. For instance, German economic involvement in, and political support of Nord Stream 2 emerged within a pre-existing social and historical discursive context that framed energy cooperation with Russia in positive terms. Likewise, the existence of an influential narrative constructing Russia as an economic partner in the Finnish public debate allowed Finnish leaders to refute the securitisation of the project and focus on its commercial and environmental aspects. The fact that Polish discourses on Nord Stream 2 and constructions of the Russian Other were so radically different from German and Finnish ones highlighted how a shared EU narrative on central aspects of relations with Russia remained a distant, perhaps unattainable prospect.

Notes

1 E.ON's fossil fuel assets, including its interests in the Nord Stream 2 project, were acquired by Uniper in 2016.
2 See also Nord Stream 2 website, 'Fact-checking myths', www.nord-stream2.com/project/facts-myths/.
3 The Baltic Pipe is a planned pipeline connecting the Polish Baltic coast to Denmark, which would allow Poland to increase imports of Norwegian gas.
4 Czaputowicz stated:

> We consider the Nord Stream 2 project to be a threat to the whole region's energy security, and to the common EU energy market. We will also be discussing the need to compensate Poles for the losses suffered during World War Two.

5 See www.gazpromexport.ru/en/statistics/.

6 The Russian Other in the Syrian crisis and MENA geopolitics

Introduction

This chapter analyses German, Polish and Finnish leaders' discourses on Russia in the context of the Syrian crisis, between 2015 and 2018. The focus is on the period following Russia's military intervention in Syria, which began in September 2015. The chapter shows how discourses on Russia related to other topical and heated contemporary debates, notably those concerning the refugee crisis and terrorism. These debates occurred in the aftermath of the Ukraine crisis, which inevitably influenced perceptions of Russian policies in Syria too. The chapter reveals that national discourses eventually converged on the criticism of Russia's bombing campaign and human rights violations. This criticism was grounded in deep-seated national conceptualisations of the use of force in international politics. However, the national leaders under investigation had different views and put different emphasis on how to address Russia's involvement in the Syrian crisis. After reviewing the main aspects of the crisis, the chapter discusses these differences and how they can be explained through an interpretive approach that links foreign policy discourse to national identity.

Russia and the EU from the Arab Spring to the Syrian crisis

Up until the 2000s, post-Soviet Russia appeared to have limited interest in the MENA region. It had some important customers for its arms exports (particularly Algeria) and an uneasy partnership with Syria, which also hosted the only remaining base of the Russian navy outside the former Soviet Union (Trenin 2018: 34–40, Watanabe 2019). At this time, Moscow's foreign policy focused primarily on the relationship with the West, which remained by far its most important economic and political partner. Russia's approach to the MENA region began to change in the late 2000s, when Vladimir Putin made numerous official visits to the region, reviving contacts with Soviet-time allies and forging new ones (Kozhanov 2018).

The turning point for Russia's MENA policy came in the early 2010s, with the Arab Spring and the Western response to it, particularly in the context of the Libyan crisis. Russia's reaction to the Arab Spring was markedly different from the Western one. While initially welcoming popular requests for political reforms in North Africa, Russian leaders increasingly perceived the ensuing regional destabilisation as a catalyst of Islamist extremism and of a return to traditional values, to the detriment of secular political regimes (Dannreuther 2015). Due to Russia's large internal Muslim minorities, the spread of radicalisation and terrorism in the MENA region was seen as having potentially very serious consequences for Russia's own security. According to some interpretations, the Russian leadership also viewed the Arab Spring through the prism of the 'colour revolutions' that occurred in the post-Soviet space in the 2000s, and hence as a threat to the authoritarian stability promoted by the Kremlin (Trenin 2018: 40–44).

The Western reaction to the Arab Spring aggravated Russian concerns about regional dynamics. In the EU and the United States, the Arab Spring was largely perceived as a pro-democratisation and anti-authoritarian phenomenon, particularly in its early years. Moreover, when Muammar Gaddafi's regime attempted to suppress the protests in Libya in February–March 2011, a group of Western countries headed by France and the United Kingdom intervened militarily, as part of a NATO-led coalition. Their military intervention ostensibly implemented United Nations Security Council Resolution 1973, which authorised the international community to establish a no-fly zone and protect civilians in Libya. In this context, Germany constituted an exception in the Western camp, as it abstained in the Security Council vote on Resolution 1973 and did not take part in the military campaign against Libya (Koenig 2017: 360). Moreover, Poland declared that it supported Resolution 1973 and EU actions to prevent a humanitarian disaster in Libya, but declined to contribute its military forces to any NATO or European operation. This stance marked a departure from Polish foreign policy in the 2000s, which focused on active participation in US- or NATO-led military operations abroad, such as the 2003 war in Iraq (Reeves 2019). In the 2010s, even before the Ukraine crisis, Polish leaders refocused the country's security policy on defending its national territory, rather than contributing to out-of-area operations. Warsaw maintained this posture vis-à-vis the Syrian crisis.

Then Russian president Dmitry Medvedev did not object to the military intervention in Libya, and Russia abstained in the decisive vote at the UN Security Council. However, as NATO coalition forces bombed Gaddafi's troops and military installations, and the country later descended into chaos, Russian opposition to the military intervention became more vocal. Vladimir Putin, who was prime minister in 2011, criticised NATO's intervention and compared it to a crusade (cited in Dannreuther 2019: 732). From the Russian perspective, the intervention was the continuation of the Western policy already implemented during the 1999 bombing of Yugoslavia and the 2003 invasion of Iraq, when the West had promoted regime change and violated international law using the pretext of humanitarian interventions (Averre 2018: 400). According to some commentators, Medvedev's failure to prevent the military campaign weakened his position in the Russian debate and contributed to Putin's return to the presidency in 2012 (Zygar 2016: 197–199, 203–206).

Developments in Libya shaped the subsequent Russian attitude to the Arab Spring and the prospect of further Western intervention. Putin resolved that Russia should avoid the repetition of the Libyan scenario in other contexts, most particularly Syria, where Arab Spring protests and the regime's repression escalated into civil war in 2011 (Dannreuther 2019: 732). Russia, together with China, used its veto power in the UN Security Council in order to deprive the West of a UN authorisation to intervene militarily in Syria. In fact, Western public opinion and political establishments were wary of military initiatives, particularly as the aftermath of the intervention in Libya highlighted the long-term failure of Western military intervention. US president Obama took a cautious approach and attempted to avoid further military entanglements in the Middle East. Among EU members, the French and British governments were the most predisposed to supply arms to the Syrian rebels and launch military strikes against the regime. However, the British government changed its stance after failing to secure parliamentary support for military action in August 2013. Other EU members such as Germany, Austria, Sweden and the Czech Republic were highly sceptical of military action and viewed arms supplies to the Syrian rebels as a dangerous step that could intensify the conflict (Koenig 2017). Furthermore, after 2014 the European Union and its member states were increasingly occupied with the domestic consequences of the destabilisation of the MENA region, most notably the arrival of hundreds of thousands of asylum seekers on EU territory.

Between 2012 and 2015, Moscow sent various forms of aid to the Syrian regime and promoted diplomatic solutions to international crises caused by allegations of the use of chemical weapons by the regime. Most notably, Russia's diplomacy played an essential role in the removal and destruction of Syrian chemical stockpiles in late 2013. In September 2015, as the regime's power continued to erode, Russia decided to launch a direct military intervention in Syria. Russia's military intervention was presented as an anti-terrorism operation authorised by an explicit request of the Syrian government. On the eve of the intervention, Putin invited Western countries to join an anti-terrorism coalition with Russia 'similar to the anti-Hitler coalition' (Putin 2015). The Russian military intervention took the form of a bombing campaign in support of the Syrian regime and its allies on the ground, including Iranian and Hezbollah troops. Thanks to the Russian intervention, the power balance tilted in the regime's favour, and both Isis terrorists and the so-called Free Syrian Army (FSA) were progressively defeated (Siddi 2019).

Initially, the European reaction to Russia's military intervention in Syria was ambivalent. Putin's call for an anti-terrorism coalition was followed by a rise in terror attacks in European cities. Hence, the most affected countries – France in particular – explored options for cooperation with Russia (Cadier 2018: 49–50). Italy also backed anti-terrorism cooperation with Moscow (Siddi 2018e). Eventually, however, the Russian intervention caused new tensions with the West, which generally supported the FSA against Russia's Syrian allies. In the West, Russian air strikes were seen as targeting primarily FSA forces, rather than Isis militants. On the other hand, Russia argued that the FSA included extremists and terrorists. A peak in West–Russia tensions was reached in the fall of 2016, as the Russian air force bombed Aleppo and caused civilian casualties in what was broadly seen as a decisive battle for the defeat of the FSA. In October 2016, the European Council discussed the imposition of new sanctions on Russia related to its military actions in Syria. The United Kingdom and particularly France seemed keen on new restrictive measures against Moscow. However, no new sanctions were imposed due to the opposition of several member states led by Italy (Siddi 2018e: 132). Further tensions between Russia (on one side) and the US, France and the UK (on the other) occurred in April 2017 and April 2018, as the Western powers launched limited missile strikes against Syrian military installations in response to the regime's alleged use of chemical weapons.

More broadly, Russia's intervention in Syria consolidated its return to the MENA region, which is of strategic importance for the Southern flank of the EU (Stepanova 2018a). In December 2016, Moscow launched the Astana peace talks for the resolution of the Syrian conflict, including also Iran and Turkey as leading mediators. According to Russian officials, the talks support the UN-led Geneva peace process on Syria. Within the Astana process, in late 2017, Russia presented a constitutional proposal for the federalisation of Syria and subsequently hosted peace talks in Sochi. While conflict resolution remains a distant prospect, during 2018 Russian efforts increasingly shifted towards the reconstruction process and securing international funding for this purpose. This involved discussions with European actors too, most notably Germany (Ramani 2019).

In the aftermath of its intervention in Syria, Russia boosted its role in MENA regional diplomacy by reaching out to virtually all significant actors, across political fault lines (Zvyagelskaya 2016). It strengthened its position as top provider of arms to the region. In the energy field, it negotiated a crucial deal with OPEC countries to stabilise the oil price, which is key to the Russian economy. It also paved the way for ambitious projects in the civilian nuclear sector with several regional actors, including Egypt, Jordan and Saudi Arabia. As a result, Russia is now perceived as an important interlocutor by most regional players – and often, as a useful partner to diversify foreign policy options and avoid excessive dependence on the West (Katz 2018, Mühlberger and Siddi 2019). Through opportunistic and skilful diplomacy, Russia has also acquired a role in the Libyan crisis and profiled itself as a potential mediator in other regional conflicts (Stepanova 2018b). In European policy debates, all this increasingly pointed to the fact that Russia had become a significant actor in the MENA region, one that Europe needs to address as part of its regional policy.

German discourses: criticism of Russian intervention and the quest for a political solution

In the statements of German leaders, the Syrian civil war was portrayed primarily as a humanitarian crisis that could only be solved through an inclusive political process under the aegis of the United Nations, rather than with military means. The fact that Germany was also the largest recipient of refugees from Syria contributed to a focus on the humanitarian consequences of the conflict. German leaders repeatedly criticised Russia's military intervention, particularly at times of more intense fighting near large cities. Germany's stance was consistent with the identity-based tenets of its foreign policy: the rejection of war as a means to solve international disputes, multilateralism and the primacy of human rights. Berlin rejected any direct involvement of the German military in the fighting, even when it agreed to send a contingent of 1,200 soldiers to the region in order to support its Western allies with reconnaissance and logistics (Peifer 2016). The criticism of Russia's bombing campaign reflected the deep-rooted aversion of German leaders towards this type of warfare, which had already become manifest in the context of the 2003 war in Iraq (Bjola and Kornprobst 2007). On the other hand, following the logic of *Ostpolitik*, they argued that diplomatic engagement with Russia provided the only realistic approach to solving the Syrian conflict.

From the onset of the Syrian civil war, Germany acted as a co-leader with the US, France and the UK in the fields of diplomacy and sanctions, in line with its self-image as a civilian power and the principle of multilateralism (Koenig 2018: 10). The German government objected to Western arms deliveries to the Syrian opposition, arguing that they would worsen the conflict (although it agreed to deliver weapons to the Iraqi Kurdish Peshmerga in August 2014). Most significantly, Germany contributed to the destruction of Syria's chemical weapons arsenal in September 2013, following a US–Russia agreement to have it removed from the country (Koenig 2018: 11). At this stage, despite Russia's support of Syrian leader Bashar al-Assad and uncooperative role in the UN Security Council, Germany and the West viewed Moscow as an important partner in the resolution of the Syrian conflict, as well as in other key international forums such as the E3+3 negotiations concerning the Iranian nuclear programme. Even after the Ukraine crisis started, leading to a general deterioration of EU–Russia relations and reciprocal sanctions, Angela Merkel argued that 'the E3+3 negotiations on reaching a solution to the nuclear conflict with Iran and the elimination of Syrian chemical weapons prove that, despite all crises, we can successfully cooperate with Russia on important topics' (Merkel 2015c).

German perceptions of the Syrian conflict evolved significantly in 2015, as the country was confronted with three major developments: the large inflow of refugees in the summer, Russia's military intervention in September and the Isis-linked terror attacks in Paris in November. In response to the arrival of hundreds of thousands of asylum seekers (mostly from Syria), in August 2015 Merkel decided to suspend the EU's Dublin regulation and allow them to file their asylum applications in Germany. Merkel argued that Germany had the economic and societal resources to cope with the emergency. By late 2015, more than 14,000 volunteer centres were opened to welcome asylum seekers in Germany. These measures were unique in Europe and, while domestically contested (especially by right-wing politicians), they initially received considerable popular endorsement. It has been argued that Merkel's and Germans' 'welcoming culture' were linked to the historical experiences of the Germany nation, particularly at the end of the Second World War, when millions of ethnic Germans fled or were expelled from Eastern Europe and resettled in West and East Germany (Mushaben 2017). In Germany, the memory of these events had been rekindled since the 2000s in books, films and an unprecedented public debate. Having both caused and experienced mass flights from armed conflict in the twentieth century, Germans empathised with Syrian refugees and felt the historical responsibility to help them (Kleikamp 2015, Kossert 2015).

Russia's military intervention in Syria in September 2015 led to a partial reconfiguration of German leaders' discourses. While maintaining a focus on the humanitarian crisis and the need to support a political process for conflict resolution, they highlighted the role and responsibility of international actors, most notably Russia. Merkel joined other European leaders in expressing concern over Russian air attacks on the Syrian opposition and civilians (Merkel 2015j). However, German leaders still hoped that the Syrian crisis could be solved through cooperation with Moscow. Foreign minister Frank-Walter Steinmeier in particular urged Russia and the US to spearhead cooperation. He argued that:

> there is no resolution without Russia. But success is sometimes achieved with Russia. One example is the Iran agreement […] Fully aware that the US and Russia alone could not end the conflict, we nevertheless tried to persuade them to cooperate in Syria.
>
> (Steinmeier 2016a)

Steinmeier stated that cooperation with Russia was necessary also to solve other ongoing crises, such as the Libyan civil war. His call for cooperation with Russia appeared to be endorsed by the German public opinion. According to a poll conducted in early 2016, 81 per cent of Germans supported a closer relationship with Russia, and cooperation on the Syrian crisis topped Germans' list of priorities in EU–Russia cooperation (Bidder 2016).

The Isis terror attacks in Paris in November 2015 further contributed to the evolution of German policy towards the Syrian crisis. German leaders expressed solidarity with France, which has traditionally been perceived as Germany's main European ally since the Second World War. Berlin committed up to 1,200 troops, six reconnaissance tornado jets and a frigate to support France's response against Isis in Syria and Iraq, excluding however an active combat role for the German contingent (Koenig 2018: 12). As Russia's intervention in Syria was officially an anti-terrorist operation, and Putin himself had called for an anti-terror alliance with the West in September 2015, new prospects opened up for cooperation with Moscow. However, they were quickly frustrated by the intensification of Russia's bombing campaign, which – according to Western and German leaders – worsened the humanitarian crisis. For instance, in February 2016 Merkel publicly stated that she was 'appalled at the human suffering of tens of thousands of people caused by bombing raids – bombing raids carried out largely by the Russian side' (Merkel 2016a).

German leaders' criticism of the Russian bombing campaign in Syria reached a peak in the fall of 2016, during the siege of Aleppo. In October 2016, Merkel (2016b) declared that 'the humanitarian situation has become even more disastrous as a direct result of the Syrian and Russian airstrikes against defenceless people, hospitals and doctors'. On the eve of a European Council summit where sanctions against Moscow concerning its Syrian campaign were discussed (cf. Siddi 2018d: 11), Merkel (2016c) blamed the Syrian regime and Russia for 'barbarous actions' against civilians and called for the prosecution of their human rights violations. Steinmeier echoed Merkel's criticism, but adopted a more moderate rhetoric towards Moscow and blamed primarily the Syrian regime and 'radical Islamist groups' for torpedoing ceasefires negotiated by the US and Russia (Steinmeier 2016b).

German criticism of Russia's actions in Syria reflected two essential principles of Germany's foreign policy identity, the respect of international law and the rejection of the use of force (see Chapter 3). German leaders were particularly critical of Russia's bombing campaign. During the bombing of Aleppo, Merkel (2016d) stated that she 'personally do[es]n't believe that it's possible to distinguish terrorists from peaceful persons'. Arguably, Germany's profound aversion towards bombing campaigns such as the one conducted by Russia is 'grounded in German collective memories from World War II, with tales of the horrors of aerial bombardment passed down through the generations and revisited over the last ten years' (Peifer 2016: 271). As the eminent German writer Günter Grass argued, this type of warfare reminded Germans of air raids on German cities, of the 'feeling of impotence and terror'. Similarly, the renowned historian Jörg Friedrich explained that 'since 1945, Germans sympathise and identify with those being bombed and not with those dropping the bombs' (cited in Peifer 2016: 272).

While criticising Russia's military campaign, German leaders incessantly reiterated the need for dialogue and engagement with Moscow as the only way of solving the conflict. This was consistent with Germany's diplomatic approach to solving international crises and the *Ostpolitik* tradition of seeking engagement with Russia. Even at the peak of the crisis over the bombing of Aleppo, Steinmeier (2016c) called for 'cooperation between the major powers, the US and Russia' in Syria. In April 2017, while justifying a US missile strike against an airbase of the Syrian regime (in response to its alleged use of chemical weapons), Merkel advocated working with Russia to launch a political transition process. The same view was reiterated by Sigmar Gabriel, who succeeded to Steinmeier as foreign minister in January 2017. The German government argued that 'there could be no political solution to the conflict without or against Russia' (Federal Chancellor's Office 2017).

The same stance – support for the posture of Germany's Western allies in Syria and calls for dialogue with Russia – was maintained throughout 2018. Moreover, as the Syrian regime and Russia progressively defeated the remnants of the Free Syrian Army, German leaders relaxed their calls for Assad to step down as a precondition for the launch of a political process (Federal Chancellor's

Office 2018). Heiko Maas, Germany's foreign minister since March 2018, stated that Berlin would 'urge Russia to take a constructive stance. Without Russia, the political process will not succeed' (Maas 2018c). In addition, he called for the Russia-led Astana process and the West-led Small Group (including the US, UK, France Saudi Arabia and Jordan) to cooperate on a joint approach to solving the Syrian crisis (Maas 2018d). The US decision to abandon the nuclear deal with Iran, in opposition to Germany's and the EU's stance, made cooperation with Russia in MENA policy even more urgent from the perspective of German leaders. In the second half of 2018, Merkel held several meetings with Putin where Syria and Iran topped the agenda. At the end of October 2018, together with French president Emmanuel Macron, she reached out to both Putin and Turkish president Recep Tayyip Erdogan at a conference in Istanbul, where she advocated an UN-led multilateral process to solve the Syrian conflict (Merkel 2018a). As discussions about the reconstruction of Syria began, Germany maintained a significant presence in the negotiations thanks to its potentially important role in the process.

The Polish stance: keeping the focus on the 'Eastern flank'

In Polish foreign policy discourses, the Syrian crisis and Russia's military activities in the Syrian context appeared as a topic of secondary importance, recurring less frequently than issues such as the war in Ukraine and Poland's security concerns in the EU's Eastern neighbourhood. Poland's geographical proximity to Ukraine and its relative distance from Syria partly explain this imbalance. The reorientation of Polish security policy towards the defence of Poland's national territory in the 2010s, as opposed to its quest for involvement in US- and NATO-led out-of-area operations in the 2000s, is another important explanatory factor (Reeves 2019). Nevertheless, in the light of their traditional posture as leading Russia-critics within the EU (see Chapters 4 and 5 and Siddi 2017b), it may appear surprising that Polish leaders maintained a relatively low profile on Russia's controversial actions in Syria. This is particularly remarkable as Russia's use of military force and bombing of Syrian cities could have plausibly evoked Polish identity constructions about the aggressive and brutal Russian Other (see Chapter 3).

The Polish stance towards the Syrian crisis could be explained by taking into account the agency and motivations of Polish politicians and the peculiarity of the use of the Russian Other in Polish discourse. In 2015, the civil war and the atrocities of Isis terrorists in Syria, as well as the ensuing refugee crisis, became dominant topics in EU politics and public debates. When Putin launched the military operation in Syria and called for an anti-terrorism alliance with the West, Polish leaders feared that Western foreign and security policy might shift its focus from confrontation with Russia in the Ukraine crisis to cooperation with Moscow in Syria. They perceived the danger that, following a potential rapprochement, the West could even lift the sanctions imposed on Russia during the Ukraine crisis and return to a cooperative relationship. While this scenario was in fact implausible, the fear that it could materialise was particularly strong among Polish policy makers in the winter of 2015–2016, when French, German and US leaders appeared to be interested in limited cooperation with Russia in Syria. For instance, foreign minister Witold Waszczykowski (2015a) openly stated that 'We [Poland] are not going to sell Ukraine for Russian assistance to help (in) the Syrian conflict or the IS conflict'. Polish leaders seemed to think that refocusing the relationship between the West and Russia on the Syrian context was not functional to Polish national interests. This helps understand why, even in the tensest periods of the Syrian crisis, Polish foreign policy speeches focused primarily on Ukraine and the Eastern neighbourhood.

An additional explanation relates to the use of the Russian Other in Polish discourses. In both historical and current narratives, Polish constructions of the Russian Other focus on how it was and is a threat to Poland (mostly) and its Eastern neighbours. As seen in Chapter 3, the threat posed by the Russian Other to the Polish Self activates deep-rooted identity narratives about national martyrdom. Therefore, constructions of the Russian Other seem to be an effective discursive strategy only when they are related to the Polish Self. Polish discourses devote much less attention to how the Russian Other may threaten distant and different Others (such as Syrians). Moreover, as the analysis of Polish speeches revealed, Syrians were not conceptualised primarily as victims of an aggressive Russian Other. They were portrayed mostly as being different from (and even threatening for) the Polish Self due to the fact that a majority of them is not of Christian faith. This was highlighted by the decision of the Polish government to only offer asylum to a handful of Christian Syrians (Wasik and Foy 2015).

This decision was made by the centre-right government in the spring of 2015, few months before the Polish presidential and parliamentary elections. At this time, other EU members were calling on Poland to show solidarity and welcome some of the numerous asylum seekers that had reached the EU's Southern members. Due to the domestic unpopularity of the relocations and the impending national elections, then prime minister Ewa Kopacz attempted to justify the decision by appealing to Poland's Christian identity ('Today Christians, who are persecuted in a barbaric way in Syria, deserve that another Christian country, such as Poland, reacts quickly and offers help', Kopacz 2015c). This however did not prevent international criticism of what was seen as a discriminatory approach to refugee policy (Wasik and Foy 2015), nor did it stop the right-wing opposition from winning both the presidential and the parliamentary elections.

Under the new Law and Justice (PiS) government, Poland stopped the relocation of asylum seekers altogether and limited its humanitarian policy to the provision of modest sums of development aid via Polish church organisations that were active in the Middle East. This policy was justified in terms of its alleged better effectiveness. According to the new interior minister, Marius Blaszczak (2017), 'imposing the obligation to admit refugees arriving in Europe does not constitute an effective means of providing aid to people affected by the war'. Prime minister Beata Szydlo (2017) argued that Poland would provide assistance 'where it is most needed, that is in places where the people in need of it live'. Foreign minister Waszczykowski (2015b) even argued that Syrians fleeing from war were not entitled to refugee status in Poland:

> Those people from Syria who fled to Turkey have the status of political refugees right there in Turkey. But once they leave Turkey and go to an EU country, they lose their refugee status and become economic emigrants seeking better pay or social benefits.

Moreover, he attempted to justify Poland's limited financial commitment to the humanitarian crisis in Syria by arguing that Warsaw gave priority to Ukraine and Belarus (Waszczykowski 2017a), an argument that (leaving aside the question of its truthfulness) resonates with Poland's 'Ukraine first' policy.

Indeed, the Syrian crisis was hardly a priority for the PiS government. As shown, shortly after coming to power, Waszczykowski (2015a) stated that the continuation of sanctions against Russia until the full implementation of the Minsk agreement was more important for Poland than cooperation concerning Syria or terrorism. He also ruled out any significant Polish military involvement in the Syrian crisis by arguing that Poland's priorities were in the Eastern neighbourhood: 'With regards to some sort of large involvement, that definitely won't happen. At the moment we need to guard the Eastern flank' (Waszczykowski 2016f). In April 2016, Waszczykowski sharpened his rhetoric by arguing that Russia was an 'existential threat', one more dangerous for Europe than Isis (cited in *Guardian* 2016). Through this statement, he reiterated his view that security issues in Eastern Europe were more urgent than those in the South. Moreover, he entirely dismissed the argument about anti-terrorism cooperation with Russia by contending that Russia was in fact a worse threat than Isis.

This depiction of Russia was functional to the foreign policy agenda of the PiS government, which focused on strengthening military ties with the United States – particularly through the deployment of US troops and weapons on Polish territory – and on opposing the implementation of the Nord Stream 2 pipeline (cf. Sus 2018: 83–88). Both priorities were driven by the perception that Russia's actions in the Eastern neighbourhood were the main threat to Poland. Another recurrent topic was the restitution of the wreck of the Polish governmental plane on which former President Lech Kaczynski died in April 2010 during a failed landing in Smolensk (in Russia). The Polish government repeatedly requested the return of the wreck to Poland; however, the Russian authorities turned down the requests due to an ongoing investigation of the accident in Russia. While being mostly confined to Poland's national interests or Polish–Russian bilateral relations, these topics played a dominant part in the statements of Polish policy makers also in multilateral forums, such as NATO summits, or in discussions with the representatives of third countries. For instance, during his first official trip to the US, Waszczykowski (2016g) stated that the 'the main goal of [his] visit [were] efforts to strengthen Poland's security and that of NATO's entire Eastern flank'. Similarly, in his first meeting with US Secretary of State Rex Tillerson, prime minister Mateusz Morawiecki (who replaced Szydlo in December 2017) focused on Nord Stream 2 and Polish requests to station additional US troops in Poland (Poland's Prime Minister Office 2018).

Polish leaders broached the topic of the war in Syria more rarely, mostly to argue that cooperation with Russia was unlikely to produce positive results. During a visit to Italy in March 2016, Waszczykowski (2016c) argued that Russia's engagement in Syria 'does not contribute to solving the existing situation'. Commenting on the US–Russia talks on Syria a few months later, he stated: 'In my talks with Secretary of State John Kerry, I have been expressing for months my scepticism about the positive outcome of his talks with Russia' (Waszczykowski 2016d). In Waszczykowski's view, the Russian government was not interested in solving the conflict and treated the Syrian campaign as 'a handy tool in Russia's domestic politics'.

Polish leaders' references to the Russian campaign in Syria became more frequent during the peak of the battle of Aleppo, in the fall of 2016. At this point of time, it was evident that Russia's intervention in Syria was leading to additional tensions with the EU and the West, rather than to cooperation. Hence, Polish leaders no longer had grounds to fear a 'reset' in West/EU–Russia relations that might change the Western posture towards the Ukraine crisis. The siege of Aleppo was discussed in the European Council summit of October 2016. On this occasion, Poland aligned with the member states arguing for a harsher response to Russia's military operation, including the option of additional sanctions (Poland's Prime Minister Office 2016). Moreover, Waszczykowski (2016e) stated that 'an appalling tragedy is unfolding in several districts of Aleppo that are besieged by regime forces. The world can put Russia under pressure to stop the hostilities and create safe passages.'

After 2016, Polish diplomacy simply aligned with the US, British and French position whenever tensions with Russia concerning the Syrian crisis escalated. For example, following the US missile strike against Syrian regime forces in April 2018, foreign minister Jacek Czaputowicz (who replaced Waszczykowski in December 2017) expressed his support of the strike and condemned the Syrian regime, which was accused of using chemical weapons in Eastern Ghouta (Czaputowicz 2018a). However, the main focus of Polish leaders' speeches remained on different aspects of relations with Russia. The Syrian crisis was mostly mentioned as one of the areas of tensions between Russia and the West in order to highlight the need to adopt countermeasures against the threatening Russian Other (cf. Czaputowicz 2018b, Morawiecki 2018a). From a Polish perspective, however, military countermeasures were to be taken in Eastern Europe, rather than in the Middle Eastern theatre.

Finnish discourses: from tentative cooperation to humanitarian tragedy

In the first half of 2015, the Syrian crisis was a controversial topic in Finland due to its humanitarian consequences and the rising number of asylum requests that the country was receiving. Finland's position on these issues was complicated by the inclusion of the right-wing Finns Party in the new government that assumed office in Helsinki in May 2015. The Finns Party strongly opposed migration and the EU's policy of relocating asylum seekers. Consequently, despite Finland's traditionally pragmatic and pro-EU stance, the government decided to abstain in the EU's vote concerning the relocation of asylum seekers. Finland was the only EU member that abstained from voting, whereas 20 members voted in favour and four (the Visegrad group) voted against (Wahlbeck 2018).

Russia acquired a more prominent role in the Finnish debate on the Syrian crisis after the launch of its military intervention in September 2015. In Finnish official discourses, Russia's actions in Syria became another important aspect of the complex West–Russia relationship. Finnish leaders attempted to strike a delicate balance between condemning Russia's policies in the Ukraine crisis and maintaining dialogue and cooperation with Moscow concerning trade, the Baltic and the Arctic regions. President Sauli Niinistö defined relations with Russia as one of the pillars on which Finland's security rested, together with national defence, Western integration and a rule-based international system (Niinistö 2015a). Prime Minister Juha Sipilä (2015a) argued that his government would 'continue a constructive dialogue and solid, everyday, neighbourly relations with Russia. Our relationship with Russia is good, even though times are more difficult now, both due to Russia's external actions and the direction of Russia's internal development'. On the one hand, Russia's assertive stance in the international arena increased Finnish threat perceptions. On the other hand, due to the long shared border and its considerable economic interests in Russia, Finland continued to see Moscow as an unavoidable interlocutor. Therefore, while identifying itself with the EU's stance towards Moscow, Finnish diplomacy put particular emphasis on engaging Russia. This posture reflected long-standing self-perceptions of Finland as the West's easternmost outpost and bridge builder in relations with Russia (see Chapter 3).

While the Ukraine crisis and Baltic and Artic security remained Finland's main concerns in relations with Russia, Finnish leaders acknowledged that developments in the Middle East had even greater humanitarian consequences. As Niinistö (2015a) argued, 'Despite the serious nature of the Ukraine conflict, it pales beside the tragedy being enacted in the Middle East'. Finnish leaders identified 'barbaric' and 'horrendous' Isis as the main threat in the region (cf. Niinistö 2015b, Sipilä 2015b). Hence, Finland became involved in the anti-Isis coalition by contributing to the training of the Iraqi armed forces. Moreover, the Finnish government called on the EU to become more active in the resolution of the Syrian crisis 'in collaboration with other key international actors' (Sipilä 2015b), including Russia. Finland initially perceived Russia's involvement in the Syrian crisis as a potential opportunity for engagement with the West, particularly with the US. Niinistö believed that Moscow and Washington could cooperate in the fight against terrorism because 'Isis is an issue on which Russia and the United States largely agree'. Based on the recent success of the negotiations concerning the Iranian nuclear programme, the Finnish president saw the Middle East as a region where US–Russia dialogue could be revived.

> The agreement on the Iranian nuclear programme was this year's best news from the Middle East – not just because of the agreement itself, but also because the United States and Russia pulled together on the issue. The news would be even better if their budding dialogue on the Syrian crisis were to bloom into progress towards a solution.
>
> (Niinistö 2015a)

In November 2015, the resumption of international negotiations on Syria was seen as 'a positive event', where the UN Security Council showed 'responsibility and leadership in advancing the political process' (Niinistö 2015b). Niinistö's optimism concerning US–Russian negotiations to solve the Syrian crisis culminated in his New Year speech on 1 January 2016. In the speech, he argued that 'Presidents Obama and Putin sitting at the same table to discuss a solution to the Syrian crisis' was, together with the Paris climate agreement, the 'good news' from 2015 (Niinistö 2016a). Significantly, Niinistö also stated that 'if such [common] solutions can be found in Syria, this will hopefully enable the relaxation of tensions elsewhere'.

However, the intensification of the Russian bombing campaign in Syria, targeting in particular the FSA, led to additional disagreements with the West and dashed Niinistö's hopes for a relaxation of tensions. Moreover, in early 2016 the bilateral Finnish–Russian relationship underwent a temporary crisis as Russia allowed a growing number of asylum seekers with no Finnish visas to cross the border with Finland. Approximately 1,000 asylum seekers crossed the Finnish–Russian border in January and February 2016, compared to 700 in the whole of 2015. This led to an angry reaction from the Finnish government, particularly from right-wing ministers. Foreign minister and then Finns Party leader Timo Soini stated that problems in border control cooperation with Russia were one of the most serious issues in the bilateral relationship: 'We do not want a new uncontrolled migration route into the Schengen Area through our Eastern border. Our position on this must also be made clear to Russia' (Soini 2016a). Concerns mounted in Helsinki that the crossings might intensify as the weather improved and the Balkan route got harder to access for migrants from the Middle East (as a result of the EU–Turkey refugee deal of March 2016) (Forsell and Rosendahl 2016). The crisis was solved through high-level negotiations in March 2016, after which the number of crossings decreased again. However, the crisis highlighted how migration had become a highly sensitive topic through which Russia could potentially exert pressure on the Finnish government.

The Finnish government continued to pursue dialogue and cooperation with Russia during and after the border control crisis. In the same speech where he criticised Moscow for the crisis, Soini (2016a) described Russia as 'an important neighbour' and 'one of Finland's major economic partners'. He also discussed a long list of fields where he saw potential for cooperation between Russia and the

West, including Iran's nuclear programme, North Korea, energy, climate and environmental issues, technology and Arctic policies. Soini argued that 'Finland's vision is – alongside the fostering of effective bilateral relations – to support Russia's advance towards global and European structures'. This vision was consistent with Finland's long-standing self-conceptualisation as a facilitator of West and EU–Russia relations.

Nevertheless, hopes of significant cooperation with Russia in the Syrian crisis and the fight against terrorism progressively faded. Soini (2016a) aptly summarised the reasons for this shift in perceptions.

> There has been a high degree of unanimity on counter-terrorism measures within the framework of the UN. In practice, cooperation is difficult, however. The situation in Syria illustrates the magnitude of the challenge. There are major differences of opinion between the West and Russia, even about the fundamental issues in Syria and how the current predicament came about. The actions of Russia's armed forces operating in the area of Syria rightly raise a lot of questions and legitimate concerns about the objective of these actions. Russia and the West also have very different views on developments in North Africa as well as the Arab Spring. According to the West, the turmoil in the Arab world had internal causes and was due to the failure of its authoritarian regimes. Russia, on the other hand, has considered the actions of the West to be an intervention into Arab countries' internal affairs and – irrespective of its own activities in Ukraine – a violation of international law.

Different readings of the Arab Spring and of which Syrian armed factions should be branded as terrorists prevented substantial cooperation between West and Russia on the ground. Finnish leaders increasingly saw Russia as playing a geopolitical game that conflicted with Western interests in the Middle East. Following the Russian–Turkish rapprochement in the summer of 2016, Niinistö (2016b) argued:

> The rapid rapprochement between Turkey and Russia represents a major geopolitical change. While it does not necessarily amount to a stable alliance, even a tactical rapprochement poses new challenges to Western actors. It should be borne in mind that both countries have expressed deep frustration with the EU at what they view as an endless process of negotiating a partnership – or a membership.

Subsequently, the focus of Finnish discourses on Syria shifted towards the humanitarian consequences of Russia's and its allies' military operations. As the battle of Aleppo escalated, Sipilä (2016b) condemned the 'indiscriminate bombing of civilians and children'. Soini (2016b) openly blamed Russia: 'The situation in the city of Aleppo is catastrophic. Civilians are at the centre of the fighting. For this, the primary responsibility lies will the al-Assad regime and

Russia, which supports it'. He also accused the Kremlin of using its veto power to block UN resolutions aimed at halting the bombing of the city.

From the perspective of Finnish leaders, the conduct of the Syrian regime and of its allies – including Russia – violated human rights and international humanitarian law, principles that Finnish diplomacy had long cherished. In response to these violations, Soini (2017a) argued that 'the persons responsible for war crimes must be brought to justice. Impunity is never acceptable. We must reassert the primacy of international humanitarian and human rights law and put end to its repeated violations.' Accordingly, Finland became a supporter of the International, Impartial and Independent Mechanism for the crimes committed in Syria, an initiative undertaken after efforts to refer the crimes to the International Criminal Court were vetoed in the UN Security Council (see Soini 2017b). Furthermore, in January 2017 Finland hosted the Conference on Supporting Syrians and the Region, where the UN highlighted the humanitarian priorities for Syria and launched the Regional Refugee and Resilience Plan for 2017–2018 (cf. Sipilä 2017, Soini 2017a).

Therefore, in mid-2016 Finnish leaders came to see the Syrian crisis as part of the problems in West and EU–Russia relations, rather than a theatre where cooperation could be revived. As the fighting in Aleppo subsided and Russia launched the Astana peace talks (co-chairing them with Iran and Turkey), Finnish leaders expressed cautious support for the negotiations (Soini 2017a, Soini 2017c). However, they also criticised the fact that the EU was not included in the negotiations (Niinistö 2017a), and argued that 'the only sustainable solution to the crisis is an inclusive Syrian-led political process under the auspices of the UN' (Soini 2017a). Moreover, they remained deeply critical of the way in which Russia and its allies had tried to solve the Syrian crisis. As Niinistö (2017b) stated in the summer of 2017,

> although violence in the region has now decreased, this state of relative calm has been achieved by means of brutal killing that took place earlier. This extended period of mutual cruelty and hatred is not a good foundation for building the future of Syria.

Conclusion

Russia's military intervention in the Syrian civil war and its growing political and economic engagement in the MENA region have opened up a new important dimension in relations between the EU, its member states and Russia. Russia had been intensifying its presence in the region since the mid-2000s. This vector of Moscow's foreign policy became more prominent in the wake of the Arab Spring and the ensuing turmoil, which Russian leaders perceived as a threat to Russia's geopolitical interests and internal security. The Libyan crisis and Western military intervention against Gaddafi in 2011 were particularly significant in this respect. Vladimir Putin and the Russian foreign ministry deplored the outcome of the Western intervention in Libya and were determined to avoid the repetition of the Libyan scenario in other contexts, most notably Syria.

The MENA region bears considerable political and economic importance for the EU, especially for its Southern members. Despite clear signs of increasing Russian presence in the region, until 2015 the EU's policy towards Moscow remained focused almost entirely on European issues such as the Ukraine crisis and energy security. The humanitarian consequences of the Syrian civil war (particularly the growing numbers of asylum seekers reaching the EU) and Russia's military intervention in September 2015 led to a partial refocus of the EU's policy towards Moscow. While some European leaders initially hoped that the EU and Russia could cooperate in Syria, the crisis eventually became another source of conflict in EU–Russia relations. Moreover, while jointly condemning the humanitarian effects of the Russian bombing campaign, EU member states held different views on how to approach Moscow in the MENA. The attempts of France, the UK and Italy to influence developments in the region appeared to be shaped by national interests and bilateral agendas. This prevented the emergence of a common EU stance on central issues such as Syria-related sanctions on Russia.

This chapter highlighted the different evolution of discourses on Russia in Germany, Poland and Finland, as well as how they relate to identity constructs and conceptualisations of Russia. While other EU member states may have been just as, or even more, active in shaping the relevant European and Western policies, the national case studies under investigation here offered an interesting spectrum of European views on Russia's actions in Syria. Both German and Finnish leaders initially hoped that the resolution of the Syrian crisis would offer an opportunity for cooperation between the West and Russia. This hope was based on recent instances of West–Russia cooperation in the negotiations concerning Iran's nuclear programme and the elimination of Syria's chemical weapons. It also reflected a broader, long-standing approach in Finnish and German foreign policy towards Russia, according to which enduring security can only be achieved in cooperation with Moscow. The terrorist attacks in Paris in November 2015 and Putin's call for an anti-terrorist coalition with the West also contributed to expectations of cooperation.

Nevertheless, during 2016 German and Finnish discourses on the Russian intervention in Syria became increasingly critical. Russia's attempt to resolve the crisis with military means conflicted with Germany's and Finland's normative foreign policy identity and their quest for peaceful, multilateral solutions. In Germany, the Russian bombing of Aleppo revived the deep-rooted aversion of the German public towards aerial bombardments, which is rooted in Germans' own experiences during the Second World War. As during the US-led invasion of Iraq in 2003, Germans sympathised with civilians under bombardment, rather than with the side carrying out the bombing. In Finland, the border control crisis with Russia of early 2016 and the military escalation in Syria convinced the political leadership that Russia was using Middle Eastern politics to pursue geopolitical goals, which made cooperation with the West unlikely.

Subsequently, Finnish policy towards the crisis focused on humanitarian issues and on bringing war criminals to justice. Russia's actions in Syria were seen as an irritant in the broader relationship with Moscow, and no longer as offering a chance for cooperation.

Polish leaders criticised Russia's intervention in Syria from the outset. They rejected the notion that West–Russia cooperation could restart in the Middle East because they feared that this could lead the West to relax its stance towards the Ukraine crisis, Poland's main foreign policy concern. Poland's foreign minister Witold Waszczykowski argued that Russia was a worse threat than Isis, a statement that both highlighted the futility of anti-terrorism cooperation with Moscow (from a Polish perspective) and reflected deep-rooted conceptualisations of the Russian Other as a security threat to Poland. Indeed, the Ukraine crisis remained the main topic of Polish foreign policy speeches throughout the period under investigation, whereas the Syrian crisis was relegated to the margins of the debate. This was possible also because Poland's right-wing government showed little interest or outright contempt towards Syrian asylum-seekers, who were seen as threatening Others rather than as victims of Russia's military escalation.

Overall, the Russian military intervention in the Syrian crisis led to the consolidation of German, Finnish and Polish discourses that were highly critical of Russia's role as a security actor and of its geopolitical goals. These discourses furthered the negative conceptualisations of the Russian Other that had become prevalent after the Ukraine crisis. However, significant differences remained between German and Finnish narratives, on the one hand, and Polish ones, on the other. While Polish leaders rejected engagement with Russia in Syria *a priori* and focused on military deterrence in Poland's Eastern neighbourhood, their German and Finnish colleagues maintained that a solution to the crisis could only be achieved through multilateral dialogue with all the actors involved, including Russia.

Conclusion

(Dis)united we stand? National discourses and the Russian Other, 2014–2018

This book showed that the quick succession of international crises and political developments in which Russia was involved since 2014 reawakened European constructions of the Russian Other that had been forged during the past decades, or even centuries. In turn, these constructions contributed to shaping the foreign policy responses of European states to Russia's policies. The book focused on the relationship between national identity and official discourses about Russia in three member states of the European Union, Germany, Poland and Finland. The analysis showed that national identity and historically constructed images of Russia permeated foreign policy narratives, both in the national and the European discursive arenas. After 2014, negative conceptualisations of the Russian Other became prominent in the three countries under investigation, which allowed them to converge towards a shared discourse on the Ukraine crisis. However, as historical constructions of the Russian Other and ideas on how to approach it differed from country to country, divergent views persisted in foreign policy narratives. This was particularly evident on issues such as energy policy and Russia's role in the European and global security system.

The book has shown that national identities influence the way in which a state engages other international actors and tries to influence the agenda of international organisations such as the EU. Although the EU is sometimes described by scholars as a post-national organisation (cf. Habermas 2003), the analysis in this book has revealed that national identities continue to shape European foreign policy debates. In the EU discursive arena, they reflect the defining cultural, historical and political constituents of a state. Therefore, national identity remains an influential construct that International Relations scholars cannot ignore. Analysing it helps understand the domestic construction of foreign policy and international politics.

Within the study of national identity, the politics of memory deserves special attention. Political elites formulate selective discourses of a country's past in order to forge identities that strengthen social cohesion. These narratives have considerable political significance because they create a reciprocal sense of obligation among the members of a nation over time. They can also be mobilised to justify foreign policy decisions, for instance by interpreting a current political development with reference to past experiences and 'lessons' supposedly learned by a nation during its history. Most significant for this study, the politics of memory plays a central role in the construction of a country's historical Others. Investigating its articulations at the national level is therefore crucial to understand relations between EU member states and Russia, which is one of Europe's main historical Others.

The analysis focused on how national identities and memory politics influenced foreign policy narratives about Russia between 2014 and 2018. This period witnessed unprecedented tensions between post-Soviet Russia and the EU, which led to the expectation that negative representations of the Russian Other would be dominant in all national discursive arenas. The empirical research confirmed this expectation. Russia's violations of international law and military assertiveness during the Ukraine crisis posed a serious challenge to previous narratives focusing on pragmatism and economic partnership. National leaders condemned unanimously Russian breaches of international law, and the EU managed to formulate a united response to the crisis. Moscow's bombing campaign in Syria further fuelled critical discourses, even though the EU ultimately failed to agree on sanctions against Russia related to its actions in Syria.

However, the analysis also highlighted that considerable differences persisted in national discourses. While narratives about economic cooperation were marginalised at the peak of the Ukraine crisis (2014-early 2015), they gradually regained some prominence in Finland and especially Germany, most notably in the context of energy trade and the Nord Stream 2 project. Conversely, in Polish discourses, Russia was essentialised as a threatening Other, which hardly left any room for narratives about economic cooperation. This difference was explained with reference to the multifaceted conceptualisation of the Russian Other in Germany and Finland, where critical discourses have often coexisted with more cooperative ones, whereas in Poland antagonistic constructions have been overwhelmingly dominant. Political leaders' agency also played a role. In Germany and Finland, decision makers believed that engagement with Russia served the purpose of improving relations and defusing crises, even at times of fundamental disagreement. In Poland, the right-wing government that came to power in 2015 did not endorse this logic and, instead, emphasised long-standing negative conceptualisations of Russia in the pursuit of both domestic and foreign policy agendas.

While these differences have not yet impeded a common EU stance towards Russia in the Ukraine crisis, they have contributed to making the formulation of shared policies more contested and controversial. Disagreements between Germany, Poland and some other East-Central European member states on the Nord Stream 2 project epitomise this challenge. The lack of a shared and well-articulated European stance towards Russia's military intervention in Syria also reflected different views of Moscow as a security actor in the EU. More recently, the initiatives of some member states, most notably France, to improve relations with Russia have rekindled long-standing divisions within the Union (Euractiv 2019). Due to the radicalisation of discourses on Russia in some

Eastern EU members and Russia's adoption of a foreign policy stance that stokes its neighbours' fears, reformulating EU narratives around a shared cooperative discourse remains a daunting task.

A social constructivist approach to foreign policy analysis

The book adopted a historicist social constructivist approach to the investigation of the relationship between national identities and foreign policy narratives on Russia. It argued that national identity is an important constituent of international relations and is shaped by the historical interaction with one or more significant Others. EU member states have a long and diverse history of relations with Russia, which had an impact on the construction of their national identities. The book theorised that different discourses on Russia within the EU could be explained by using national identity as an interpretive framework. In order to do this, the research drew primarily on scholarship that conceptualises identity as a cognitive device providing national leaders with an understanding of other countries' motives, interests and actions. National identities were defined as multifaceted and malleable constructs that influence the formulation of national interests and foreign policy decisions. Their relationship with foreign policy is complex and mutually constitutive and can be best analysed as the interaction of discourses, rather than in terms of a unidirectional cause-effect correlation. Concretely, this means that national identity narratives both shape and are influenced by foreign policy discourses.

After reviewing the main theoretical approaches to the study of identity in the discipline of International Relations, the book developed an interpretive model to analyse the interaction between identity and foreign policy discourses. National identity and foreign policy narratives were studied both at the domestic level, in their process of national formation and contestation, and in the context of a country's relations with external actors. The relationship between Self and Other was not framed in exclusively antagonistic terms and Russia was not considered *a priori* as a negative Other. Both positive and negative historical interaction was investigated and framed as part of the process of constructing the Russian Other. Moreover, this study argued that a Self can have multiple Others, and that the boundaries between Self and Other are not always sharply delimited, but can sometimes be blurred.

According to the theoretical model adopted in the book, national identity guides and constrains foreign policy makers' choices. However, political leaders can also make selective and instrumental use of particular identity discourses in order to achieve specific foreign policy goals. In other words, decision makers are not simply at the mercy of dominant identity constructs; their agency also matters in determining which discourses become dominant. Arguably, the focus on policy makers' agency was essential to explaining the evolution of dominant narratives. Furthermore, the model conceptualised material power as a central factor of international relations, which acquires significance within particular political contexts and discursive constructions.

The discourse-historical approach, a variant of critical discourse analysis developed by Ruth Wodak (2002b), was the methodology adopted to investigate foreign policy discourses. This approach had already been applied to examine media and institutional debates about immigration and identity politics (see Krzyzanowski 2010 and 2009, Oberhuber *et al.* 2005, Reisigl and Wodak 2001, Wodak 2009). The book showed that discourse-historical analysis is an apt methodology also for the study of Self/Other relationships in international relations, and can therefore be a useful tool in foreign policy analysis. Thanks to the interdisciplinary nature of the discourse-historical approach, it was possible to integrate the theoretical model with an interpretive framework that was largely derived from the findings of historical scholarship. As argued, national identity construction takes place over a long time span. For most European nations, this process dates back to the nineteenth century or earlier (see Gellner 1983, Guibernau and Hutchinson 2004, Hobsbawm 1990, Smith 1996a). Therefore, the book contended that current discourses are best studied in a *longue durée* perspective. This approach proved appropriate to investigating the historical dimension of foreign policy narratives.

Accordingly, three national discursive arenas were selected for closer inspection based on the depth of countries' historical interaction with Russia, actorness in current EU–Russia relations and the representativeness of the main national positions towards Moscow within the EU. Their being representative of the main stances towards Russia in the broader EU arena also allowed to draw conclusions on prospects for a shared EU posture towards Russia. These prospects were assessed in the context of three topical case studies and key policy areas of EU–Russia relations: the Nord Stream 2 project, the Ukraine crisis and the Syrian crisis.

The historic construction of the Russian Other in German, Finnish and Polish identities

The analysis of national identity construction and historical narratives about Russia revealed significant differences between Finland, Poland and Germany. A common feature of these countries was that the Russian Other played a prominent role in national identity construction. Controversial bilateral relations with Russia in the past left an enduring trace in German, Polish and Finnish identities. However, while in Germany and Finland positive and negative conceptualisations of Russia coexisted and became dominant at different times, mainstream Polish narratives were consistently negative throughout the country's modern history.

In Germany, dominant discourses on Russia criticised its authoritarian and corrupt political system. This criticism concerned both the Tsarist and the Soviet period, even though different views sometimes existed depending on the political orientation of the speaker. Criticism of Soviet and Russian authoritarianism in post-war (West) Germany was a reflection of the country's modern history. Following the disastrous outcome of the Wilhelmine and Nazi regimes, the

Federal Republic of Germany rebuilt German identity around democratic and market principles. As a result, West Germany joined Western institutions that endorsed these principles (notably the European Community) and opposed Soviet state socialism. Hence, from the 1940s to the 1960s, Soviet Russia was West Germany's main antagonistic Other.

During the 1960s, due to increasingly intense public debate about German crimes in the Second World War, dominant West German discourses began to change. Arguably, Germany's authoritarian and genocidal past became the main Other against which West German identity was defined. In this context, the Soviet Union was partly reconceptualised as a victim of German aggressive policies. This reconceptualisation drove West German leaders, starting with Willy Brandt, to pursue reconciliation and a more cooperative approach towards the Soviet Union, which became enshrined in the concept of *Ostpolitik*. The *Ostpolitik* discourse argued that dialogue and cooperation with Moscow would lead to both détente in international relations and positive domestic change in the Soviet Union. *Ostpolitik* was also seen as fostering Germany's economic interests and preference for a multilateral approach to international relations. German narratives depicted Soviet Russia as an influential actor in the international arena; engagement with Moscow was thus seen as unavoidable and in Germany's interests. The *Ostpolitik* discourse became dominant and was endorsed by all the main political parties in the Federal Republic. Hence, following the emergence of *Ostpolitik*, discourses portraying Russia as an important economic and strategic partner coexisted with those denouncing its authoritarianism.

Conversely, dominant Polish historical narratives consistently depicted Russia as Poland's main negative Other. The image of Russia as Poland's main antagonist was functional to the construction of narratives on Polish heroism and martyrdom, which are essential to Polish national identity. According to these narratives, Poland never surrendered to Russian imperialism and authoritarianism, in spite of the overwhelming strength of the Russian Other. The doomed Polish struggle against Tsarist Russia and the Soviet Union was presented as Poland's sacrifice for the sake of Western civilisation. However, this sacrifice was not acknowledged by Poland's Western allies, which (as the narrative goes) abandoned the country to its fate during the Tsarist and Soviet occupations. Religious imagery based on the country's Catholic identity was used to shore up the discourse on martyrdom: Poland was 'the Christ of nations' that sacrificed itself on behalf of the other European peoples.

In Polish discourses, depicting (Soviet) Russia as oriental, undemocratic and corrupt also allowed relativising Poland's cultural distance from the West. Emphasising Polish commitment to 'Western' or 'European' values enabled Polish liberal and nationalist leaders alike to claim that, despite the protracted political subjugation to Russia, Poland belonged to the West. In the foreign policy of post-communist Poland, this discourse translated into a strong Euro-Atlantic orientation and opposition to Russia. Only in the late 2000s did dominant official narratives change partially and temporarily, allowing for the emergence of a discourse that portrayed Russia as a potential partner within a pragmatic foreign policy. However, post-2014 international tensions and the return to power of nationalist politicians in Warsaw led to a new radicalisation of Polish official discourses on Russia.

In Finnish historical narratives, dominant constructions of Russia changed considerably over time, alternating positive and deeply negative representations. In the early nineteenth century, Tsarist Russia was considered mostly a benevolent Other that had granted Finland political autonomy after the period of Swedish domination. This paved the way for the consolidation of a Finnish cultural and national identity. However, positive discourses on Russia lost prominence in the latter part of the century, when the Tsarist Empire attempted to russify ethnic Finns. In the interwar period, following the victory of the Whites in the Finnish civil war, Finnish official discourses conceptualised Soviet Russia as the main threat to Finland. The negative Othering of the Soviet Union reached its peak during the military confrontation that lasted almost uninterruptedly from 1939 until 1944.

Post-war Finland reformulated its identity and foreign policy posture. Nationalist and anti-Russian narratives were held responsible for the escalation that had dragged the country into a disastrous war. Hence, they were marginalised in official discourse, while Soviet Russia was reconceptualised as an important partner. To an extent, the limits imposed by the victorious countries (especially the Soviet Union) on Finnish sovereignty made this reconceptualisation a political necessity in the post-war period. During the Cold War, the cooperative policy towards Moscow allowed Finland to retain independent political and economic structures and simultaneously present itself as a bridge between East and West. Military non-alignment was the practical outcome of Finland's positioning between East and West. It became part of the country's national identity and continued to be endorsed by a majority of Finns after the end of the Cold War. At the same time, Russia's military power continued to be a source of insecurity for the Finnish elite and public opinion. After the disintegration of the Soviet Union, these preoccupations were expressed more openly in official discourse, showing that perceptions of Russia as a potential threat persisted in spite of deeper economic and diplomatic cooperation.

Therefore, the analysis of national identity construction and narratives of the Russian Other highlighted significant differences in the three countries under investigation. Subsequently, the book assessed whether these constructions influenced official foreign policy discourses on Russia in the years 2014–2018. A central question was whether different historical constructions of the Russian Other resulted in different or diverging foreign policy postures vis-à-vis present Russia.

The Ukraine crisis: the return of the Russian threat?

The escalation of the Ukraine crisis and Russia's military assertiveness led to a convergence of national discourses and a united European policy response. Following Russia's annexation of Crimea and the destabilisation of Eastern Ukraine, historical narratives about the threatening Russian Other regained prominence in public German, Finnish and especially Polish political debates. Conversely, narratives portraying Russia as an economic and strategic partner lost dominance. Russia's use of force was at odds with Germany's peaceful security culture, a central tenet of post-1945 German foreign policy identity. The rejection of the use of force also guided Berlin's response to the crisis: German leaders advocated economic sanctions and diplomatic negotiations, but rejected proposals to send military equipment to Ukraine.

In 2014, the Polish and Finnish response to the Ukraine crisis largely mirrored the German one. The main difference was that Polish officials adopted a harsher rhetoric towards Russia, advocated deeper sanctions and a stronger NATO presence in Eastern Europe. This reflected higher threat perceptions concerning Russia and the Euro-Atlantic orientation of Polish foreign policy. Finnish narratives put more emphasis on the need of negotiations and cooperative security. Overall, however, all national discourses under investigation focused on legal and security issues and converged towards the condemnation of Russia's use of force and breach of international law in Ukraine. This paved the way for a joint EU response to the crisis, including sanctions against Russia and the simultaneous quest for a negotiated solution.

On the surface, the consistent support of all EU member states for the sanctions suggests that the Union found a united stance towards Russia, and that national discourses could be reconciled by focusing on the construction of Russia as an antagonistic Other. However, the analysis has highlighted that this unity was precarious. Polish discourses began to diverge from German and Finnish ones on several issues in 2015, especially after the right-wing Law and Justice government took office in Warsaw in November. While upholding the policy of sanctions, German and Finnish leaders highlighted the importance of continuing cooperation with Russia in several strategic policy fields. This was particularly the case after Russia, together with Ukraine, signed the Minsk-2 agreement, allowing a partial de-escalation of the conflict in Donbas. German leaders regarded the agreement as an important, even if fragile, achievement of Franco–German (and thus European) diplomacy.

Thereafter, German officials argued for cooperation with Moscow in energy trade, the Syrian crisis and the fight against international terrorism. They also continued to support the process of historical reconciliation through joint commemorations with their Russian counterparts for the seventieth anniversary of the end of the Second World War. While Germany's continued support for sanctions meant that it was not back to 'business as usual' with Russia, its quest for some economic and political cooperation with Moscow highlighted that the tenets of *Ostpolitik* remained influential in German foreign policy thinking. German leaders continued to view Russia as a difficult but essential interlocutor to achieve a stable European security system. Following a similar approach, Finnish leaders remained firm in their condemnation of Russia's policies in Ukraine, but argued that cooperation with Moscow should continue in regional forums such as those concerning the Baltic and the Arctic. In Finland, maintaining dialogue with Russia was considered fundamental also for national security, due to the long shared border and common environmental challenges. Hence, Finnish leaders shared with their German counterparts the belief that dialogue remained indispensable and was the best available approach to address disagreements with Russia.

Conversely, during 2015 Polish official discourses on Russia took a more confrontational stance. Following Donald Tusk's and Radoslaw Sikorski's departure from power, who had crafted a more balanced and pragmatic foreign policy approach to Moscow between 2007 and 2014 (cf. Siddi 2017b), long-standing narratives of Russia as a threatening Other became omnipresent. Polish leaders portrayed themselves as spokespersons of Ukraine in the EU and contemplated the provision of military aid to Kiev. Polish decision makers were much more sceptical than their German and Finnish colleagues regarding the significance and prospects of the Minsk-2 agreement. Law and Justice ministers even argued that, within the Normandy Four negotiations, Germany purposefully disregarded the interests of Poland, which was not invited to participate in this format. Furthermore, from Warsaw's perspective the Ukraine crisis remained far more important than any other regional scenario. The security threat emanating from Russian actions there could not be alleviated by cooperation in other theatres.

Hence, substantial differences persisted across national narratives concerning the Russian Other. National identities continued to act as centrifugal forces in the European discursive arena. This highlighted the fragility of the EU's united stance vis-à-vis Russia in the Ukraine crisis. The failure to implement the Minsk-2 agreement led EU member states to maintain a common position on the sanctions policy. However, in other fields and regional contexts, national perspectives were too different for a shared position to be agreed. The Nord Stream 2 debate provided an apt example.

Europe (re)divided: the Nord Stream 2 debate

When Russian state energy company Gazprom and a group of Western European business partners launched the Nord Stream 2 project in the summer of 2015, criticism of Russia had already become nearly omnipresent in the European discursive arena due to Russian agency in the Ukraine crisis. Long-standing European constructions of the threatening Russian Other had regained dominance in the public debate and also had an impact on EU–Russia energy cooperation, which had been largely unaffected by earlier (and comparatively less significant) political crises. However, only a few Eastern member states, such as Poland, decided to securitise their energy relationship with Russia, whereas others (Germany *in primis*) continued to see energy trade as a mutually beneficial relationship that kept Russia engaged with Europe. The book contended that different national constructions of energy cooperation with Russia were rooted in conflicting identity narratives and historical experiences.

In German official discourses, both the logic of *Ostpolitik* and the conceptualisation of Russia as a reliable energy supplier remained influential. German officials cited the history of German–Russian energy cooperation since the 1970s to argue that Russia was a trustworthy energy partner. They also stressed that, by creating an additional import route for Russian gas, Nord Stream 2 strengthened both German and European energy security. In their view, the project was a commercial venture that respected European legislation, and should therefore not be undermined by politics. In 2018, German leaders – most notably Merkel – conceded that the pipeline was not simply a commercial endeavour and had geopolitical consequences. However, this did not lead to substantial discursive or policy change. Germany attempted to reconcile its *Ostpolitik* towards Russia with its commitment to Eastern European partners by acknowledging their concerns and increasing diplomatic efforts to ensure that gas transit in Ukraine will continue after Nord Stream 2 becomes operational.

Polish leaders had a radically different view of both Nord Stream 2 and energy cooperation with Russia more broadly. They argued that Nord Stream 2 undermined Polish interests and allowed Russia to use its energy power as an instrument to coerce Poland. The project was described as a geopolitical threat, a 'poison pill' for European security and a weapon in Russia's hybrid war against the West. Mainstream Polish discourses essentialised Russian energy power as a security threat and viewed German–Russian energy cooperation through a distorting historical lens that led to comparisons with Nazi–Soviet cooperation. The political discourse of Law and Justice was rife with anti-Russian and anti-German memory politics narratives. This contributes to explaining why Polish opposition to Nord Stream 2 was so fierce, as well as why the Polish debate on the project was securitised and deeply imbued with identity politics.

Finnish leaders took an apparently neutral stance and argued that Nord Stream 2 did not affect Finland directly, with the exception that Helsinki had to provide an environmental assessment of the pipeline section in the Finnish Exclusive Economic Zone. However, as the European discursive conflict concerning the project intensified and intersected with Finnish domestic debates about energy cooperation with Russia, Finnish officials addressed some economic and security aspects of Nord Stream 2. Finnish discourses reflected the dichotomous construction of Russia in Finnish identity as both an important economic partner and a potential security threat. While recognising that the concerns of Eastern EU member states were understandable, Finnish officials argued that the pipeline did not have negative security consequences for Finland. This argument was reiterated when Finnish company Fortum acquired a stake in the project. Hence, economic considerations ultimately prevailed over security concerns in the Finnish official debate.

Therefore, national discourses on Nord Stream 2 differed depending on how Russia's energy power was constructed in national identity narratives. In Poland, it was framed as an instrument for Russia's geopolitical goals; consequently, dominant narratives were very critical. In Germany and Finland, it was perceived primarily as another articulation of lucrative energy trade with Russia.

The different perceptions of Russia's energy power confirmed the theoretical argument made in Chapter 2 that material power acquires significance only within specific discursive constructions. In the Nord Stream 2 debate, ideational and material drivers of country positions were not clearly discernible and simultaneously concurred in the formulation of national stances.

Furthermore, the analysis of discourses on energy cooperation exposed multiple and ambivalent representations of Russia, which is consistent with Iver Neumann's (1998) claim that Russia is a liminal case of European identity. Depending on the circumstances and the national context, European discourses either externalised Russia as a threat or portrayed it as part of geographic, cultural and economic constructions of Europe. Most significantly, the case study on Nord Stream 2 highlighted that national identities and different constructions of the Russian Other remain highly influential and can lead to conflict in the EU discursive arena. National identities play an important role in interest formation. Hence, if they differ substantially, countries develop divergent foreign policy interests and priorities.

Tentative cooperation and new tensions: the Syrian crisis

The initial European reactions to the Russian military intervention in the Syrian crisis reflected the different perceptions and approaches to Russia described earlier. German and Finnish leaders hoped that Russia, the US and the EU could cooperate in the crisis based on a common anti-terrorism agenda. Their thinking followed long-standing national narratives according to which a stable international security system can only be achieved with Russia's participation and through cooperation with Moscow. Conversely, the Polish leadership refused to even contemplate a rapprochement with Russia based on anti-terrorism cooperation in the Middle East and continued to focus its foreign policy narratives on the Ukraine crisis, where Russia was constructed as Poland's threatening Other.

In Polish official narratives, the Syrian crisis tended to be marginalised for two main reasons. First, Polish leaders feared that Western foreign and security policy might shift its focus from confronting Russia's actions in Ukraine to cooperating with Moscow in Syria. From their perspective, the West should continue to focus on Eastern European geopolitics and on reinforcing its military presence there in order to challenge Russia's aggression. Hence, they attempted to refute the arguments for cooperation in Syria by arguing that it was unlikely to lead to positive outcomes due to Russia's unreliability. Polish foreign minister Waszczykowski tried to undermine the basic logic of any prospective cooperation, the anti-terrorism agenda, by arguing that Russia was in fact a greater threat to Europe than Isis. The other main reason for the marginalisation of the Syrian crisis was that Polish officials seemed to have little interest for the victims of Russian bombing in Syria. The Polish government depicted Syrian asylum-seekers primarily as threatening Others, rather than as victims of the military escalation. Poland's refusal to grant asylum and implement the EU's relocation quotas were the policy outcomes of this depiction.

In fact, Polish fears that the EU might achieve a reset of relations with Russia over Syria were unwarranted. When Russia intensified its bombing campaign, particularly during the autumn of 2016, other European and Western leaders became increasingly critical of Russian actions and ceased to believe that far-reaching cooperation could occur in Syria. In Germany, the bombing campaign revived the deep-rooted aversion of the political leadership and public opinion alike towards the use of military force and aerial bombing, which had already become manifest during earlier international crises (most notably the US-led invasion of Iraq in 2003). Partly as a result of their country's historical experiences during the Second World War, which had become part of dominant national identity narratives, Germans sympathised with civilians under aerial bombardment, rather than with the side that claimed to be bombing terrorists. In Finland, similar narratives focusing on the humanitarian consequences of Russian bombing became dominant. Moreover, the border control crisis with Russia of early 2016 and Moscow's military escalation in Syria led Finnish officials to believe that the Kremlin was using Middle Eastern politics to pursue geopolitical goals, which made cooperation with the West highly unlikely.

Arguably, by the end of 2016 German, Finnish and Polish narratives on Russia's policies in Syria converged towards a shared critical stance. However, some significant differences remained. While Polish leaders marginalised the Syrian crises in their discourses, their German and Finnish counterparts emphasised that it was a major threat to the stability of the EU and its neighbourhood. Despite their criticism of Russian bombing, German and Finnish officials continued to believe that a lasting solution to the crisis could be achieved only through dialogue with Russia, particularly as the Russian intervention influenced decisively the outcome of the civil war. On the contrary, Polish leaders argued that dialogue with Russia over Syria was unlikely to lead to positive results. These differences of opinion between German, Finnish and Polish leaders were part of a broader set of more serious disagreements among EU members on how to respond to Russia's actions in Syria. The disagreements prevented the adoption of a coherent and incisive EU stance towards both the Syrian crisis and Russian policies in that context.

Towards a shared European discourse on the Russian Other?

At first glance, the EU's approach towards Russia in the years 2014–2018 appears coherent and consistent. The EU adopted sanctions in response to Russia's annexation of Crimea and destabilisation of the Donbas region, and has been able to maintain an internal consensus on this stance. The book has argued that this was possible thanks to the convergence of national narratives on a discourse that prioritised the respect of international law and the rejection of the use of force as a means of resolving international disputes. Arguably, these values have been internalised in the national identities and security cultures of most European states due to the disastrous legacy of wars and genocide on the European continent in the twentieth century. Furthermore, the mobilisation of historical narratives about the threatening Russian Other has played an important role in achieving and maintaining unity within the EU.

However, in the longer term, antagonistic constructions of the Russian Other do not seem to offer a solid base for a shared and effective EU policy. The main reason for this is that the Russian Other has been constructed and internalised in different ways in national identities. As the analysis of German, Polish and Finnish narratives has demonstrated, these different constructions induce EU member states to adopt different approaches to Russia. In the three member states under investigation, this was highlighted by their different views on the Minsk-2 agreement, the possibility to cooperate with Russia in the Syrian crisis and, most notably, conflicting ideas concerning the Nord Stream 2 project. Especially in energy relations, which continue to be the most significant area of interaction between the EU and Russia (in economic terms), othering and antagonising Russia has proved to be a divisive factor for EU member states.

However, this research also highlighted that European countries are not at the mercy of identity-driven divisions. The agency of policy makers also determines which particular narrative becomes dominant in a national discursive space. National leaders have the discursive power to marginalise the most polarising constituents of national identity, if they wish to do so. For instance, in 2014 German policy makers steered official debates on the Ukraine crisis in such a way that allowed normative discourses to gain dominance over economic ones. Prior to 2015, Polish discourses on Russia were less radical and hence more similar to German and Finnish ones. While it is unlikely that European narratives on Russia will soon revert to the pre-2014 rhetoric, in which pragmatic and economy arguments prevailed, European leaders could refrain from abusing antagonistic images of the Russian Other to pursue domestic or foreign policy agendas. This would prevent the crystallisation of depictions of Russia as a threatening Other, which fuel distrust and conflict in Europe. Undoubtedly, Russian agency also plays an important role in this respect: a more cooperative, or at least less confrontational Russian stance would facilitate a positive reconceptualisation of the Russian Other in the EU.

As this book has shown, essentialising Russia as a negative Other would mean overlooking the complexities and fluidity of the Self/Other relationship. The boundaries between Self and Other are fluid and positive interaction can occur. Prior to 2014, European policy makers often portrayed Russia as a partner. In some important policy fields – such as energy relations, the Arctic and negotiations on Iran's nuclear programme – cooperation has continued. Concrete steps forward in the resolution of the Ukraine crisis would be essential to return to a more collaborative *modus operandi* in the broader EU–Russia relationship. At the beginning of the 2020s, in the face of major global challenges ranging from the climate crisis to the return of zero-sum geopolitics, neither Russia nor the EU can afford a protracted confrontation driven by backward-looking identity politics.

Bibliography

Aalto, P. and Forsberg, T. (2016) The structuration of Russia's geo-economy under economic sanctions, *Asia Europe Journal* 14(2): 221–237.

Aalto, P., Nyyssönen, H., Kojo, M. and Pal, P. (2017) Russian nuclear energy diplomacy in Finland and Hungary, *Eurasian Geography and Economics* 58(4): 386–417.

Aalto, P. and Tynkkynen, N. (2008) 'The Nordic countries: engaging Russia, trading in energy or taming environmental threats?', in P. Aalto (ed.) *The EU-Russian Energy Dialogue*, Aldershot: Ashgate, pp. 119–143.

Aalto, P. and Westphal, K. (2008) 'Introduction', in P. Aalto (ed.) *The EU-Russian Energy Dialogue*, Aldershot: Ashgate, pp. 1–21.

Adamson, F. and Demetriou, M. (2007) 'Remapping the boundaries of "State" and "National Identity": incorporating diasporas into IR theorizing', *European Journal of International Relations*, 13(4): 489–526.

Adler, E. (1992) 'The emergence of cooperation: national epistemic communities and the international evolution of the idea of nuclear arms control', *International Organization*, 46(1): 101–145.

Adler, E. (1997) 'Seizing the middle ground: constructivism in world politics', *European Journal of International Relations*, 3(3): 319–363.

Ahonen, P. (2011) 'Unity on trial: the Mauerschützenprozesse and the East-West rifts of unified Germany', in A. Fuchs, K. James-Chakraborty and L. Shortt (eds) *Debating German Cultural Identity since 1989*, Rochester (NY): Camden House, pp. 30–45.

Ahrens, A. and Weiss H. (2012) 'The Image of Russia in the editorials of German newspapers (2001–2008)', in R. Krumm, H. Schröder and S. Medvedev (eds) *Constructing Identities in Europe: German and Russian perspectives*, Baden-Baden: Nomos, pp. 147–169.

Albert, R. (1995) 'Das Sowjetunion-Bild in der sozialliberalen Ostpolitik 1969–1975', *Tel Aviver Jahrbuch für Deutsche Geschichte*, 24: 299–326.

Allison, G. and Zelikow P. (1999) *Essence of Decision: Explaining the Cuban missile crisis*, New York: Longman.

Anderson, B. (1991) *Imagined Communities: Reflections on the origin and spread of nationalism*, London: Verso.

Arnold-de Simine, S. (ed.) (2005) *Memory Traces: 1989 and the question of German cultural identity*, Bern: Peter Lang.

Ash, T. G. (1993) *In Europe's Name: Germany and the divided continent*, London: Jonathan Cape.

Ash, T. G. (2002) *The Polish Revolution: Solidarity*, New Haven: Yale University Press.

Assmann, A. (2006) *Der Lange Schatten der Vergangenheit: Erinnerungskultur und Geschichtspolitik*, Munich: C. H. Beck.

Austin, D. F. C. (1996) *Finland as a Gateway to Russia: Issues in European security*, Aldershot: Avebury.

Auswärtiges Amt (2014) 'Partners in Europe'. www.auswaertiges-amt.de/EN/Aussenpolitik/ RegionaleSchwerpunkte/Russland/Russland_node.html (accessed 10 August 2016).

Averre, D. (2009) 'From Pristina to Tskhinvali: The legacy of Operation Allied Force in Russia's relations with the West', *International Affairs*, 85(3): 575–591.

Averre, D. (2018) 'Russia, the Middle East and the Conflict in Syria', in R. Kanet (ed.) *The Routledge Handbook of Russian Security*, Abingdon: Routledge, pp. 399–409.

Aydın-Düzgit, S. (2018) 'Foreign policy and identity change: Analysing perceptions of Europe among the Turkish public', *Politics*, 38(1): 19–34.

Baczynska, G. (2018) 'Poland says war-time killings tarnish ties with Ukraine', Reuters, 11 July. www.reuters.com/article/us-poland-ukraine/poland-says-war-time-killings-tarnish-ties-with-ukraine-idUSKBN1K12J5 (accessed 12 December 2019).

Balmaceda, M. (2012) 'Russia's central and eastern European energy transit corridor', in P. Aalto (ed.) *Russia's Energy Policies: National, interregional and global levels*, Cheltenham: Edward Elgar, pp. 136–155.

Banchoff, T. (1999) 'German identity and European integration', *European Journal of International Relations*, 5(3): 259–289.

Barnett, M. (1996) 'Identity and alliances in the Middle East', in P. Katzenstein (ed.) *The Culture of National Security: Norms and identity in world politics*, New York: Columbia University Press, pp. 400–450.

Bayley, P. and Williams G. (2012) *European Identity: What the media say*, Oxford: Oxford University Press.

BBC News (2012) 'Russian Patriarch Kirill makes historic visit to Poland', 16 August. www.bbc.com/news/world-europe-19281205 (accessed 11 August 2016).

BBC News (2015a) 'Poland leak scandal: Three ministers and Speaker resign', 10 June. www.bbc.com/news/world-europe-33089659 (accessed 23 August 2016).

BBC News (2015b) 'Europe and US mark VE Day anniversary', 8 May. www.bbc.com/ news/world-europe-32619704 (accessed 23 August 2016).

BBC News (2017) Russia warns Poland not to touch Soviet WW2 memorials. BBC, 31 July. www.bbc.com/news/world-europe-40775355 (accessed 5 December 2019).

BBC News (2019) 'Ukraine conflict: Can peace plan in east finally bring peace?', 29 October. www.bbc.com/news/world-europe-49986007 (accessed 5 December 2019).

Bedani, G. and Haddock, B. (eds) (2000) *The Politics of Italian National Identity*, Cardiff: University of Wales Press.

Bell, D. (2006) 'Introduction: memory, trauma and world politics', in D. Bell (ed.) *Memory, Trauma and World Politics*, Basingstoke: Palgrave Macmillan, pp. 1–32.

Belyi, A. (2015) *Transnational Gas Markets and Euro-Russian Energy Relations*, Basingstoke: Palgrave Macmillan.

Benner, E. (2001) 'Is there a core national doctrine?', *Nations and Nationalism*, 7(2): 155–174.

Berg, E. and P. Ehin (eds) (2009) *Identity and Foreign Policy: Baltic-Russian Relations and European Integration*, Farnham: Ashgate.

Berger, S. (1997) *The Search for Normality: National identity and historical consciousness in Germany since 1800*, Oxford: Berghahn.

Berger, T. (1996) 'Norms, identity and national security in Germany and Japan', in P. Katzenstein (ed.) *The Culture of National Security: Norms and identity in world politics*, New York: Columbia University Press, pp. 317–356.

Berger, T. (2002) 'The power of memory and memories of power: the cultural parameters of German foreign policy making since 1945', in J. Müller (ed.) *Memory and Power in Post-War Europe*, Cambridge: Cambridge University Press, pp. 76–99.

Bidder, B. (2016) 'Deutsche wünschen sich engere Partnerschaft mit Russland', S*piegel Online*, 27 April. www.spiegel.de/politik/deutschland/russland-deutsche-wollen-engere-partnerschaft-laut-umfrage-a-1089428.html (accessed 28 May 2019).

Bikont, A. (2012) *My z Jedwabnego*, Wolowiec: Wydawnictwo Czarne.

BiznesAlert (2018) 'Merkel and Morawiecki: We have different views on Nord Stream 2', 19 February. http://biznesalert.com/merkel-morawiecki-nord-stream-2/ (accessed 5 December 2019).

Bjola, C. and Kornprobst M. (2007) 'Security communities and the habitus of restraint: Germany and the United States on Iraq', *Review of International Studies*, 33(2): 285–305.

Blaikie, N. (2010) *Designing Social Research*, Cambridge (MA): Polity Press.

Blaszczak, M. (2017) Statements at the press conference with the Church aid initiative for Syria, 1 March. www.premier.gov.pl/en/news/news/prime-minister-beata-szydlo-the-polish-government-becomes-involved-in-the-church-aid.html (accessed 1 June 2019).

Bongiorni, R. (2017) 'Da Nord Stream a Sakhalin, a rischio 8 progetti europei', *Il Sole 24 Ore*, 26 July. www.ilsole24ore.com/art/mondo/2017-07-25/da-nord-stream-sakhalin-rischio-8-progetti-europei-200606.shtml?uuid=AEYMUD3B (accessed 5 December 2019).

Boyd, C. (1997) *Historia Patria: Politics, history, and national identity in Spain, 1875–1975*, Princeton: Princeton University Press.

Braithwaite, R. (2008) 'Misreading Russia', *Survival*, 50(4): 169–176.

Breuilly, J. (1985) 'Reflections on Nationalism', *Philosophy of the Social Sciences*, 15(1): 65–75.

Brown, J. (2010) 'A Stereotype, Wrapped in a Cliché, Inside a Caricature: Russian Foreign Policy and Orientalism', *Politics*, 30(3), 149–159.

Browning, C. (2002) 'Coming home or moving home? "Westernizing" narratives in Finnish foreign policy and the reinterpretation of past identities', *Cooperation and Conflict*, 37(1): 47–72.

Browning, C. (2003) 'The region-building approach revisited: the continued othering of Russia in discourses of region-building in the European North', *Geopolitics*, 8(1): 45–71.

Browning, C. (2007) 'Branding Nordicity: models, identity and the decline of exceptionalism', *Cooperation and Conflict*, 42(1): 27–51.

Browning, C. (2008) *Constructivism, Narrative and Foreign Policy Analysis*, Bern: Peter Lang.

Browning, C. and Lehti, M. (2007) 'Beyond East–West: marginality and national dignity in Finnish identity construction', *Nationalities Papers*, 35(4): 691–716.

Brubaker, R. (1996) 'Nationalizing states in the old "New Europe" – and the new', *Ethnic and Racial Studies*, 19(2): 411–437.

Brubaker, R. (1996a) *Nationalism Reframed: Nationhood and the national question in the New Europe*, Cambridge: Cambridge University Press.

Brubaker, R. (2009) 'Ethnicity, race and nationalism', *Annual Review of Sociology*, 35: 21–42.

Bryman, A. (2008) *Social Research Methods*, Oxford: Oxford University Press.

Burridge, T. (2016) 'Ukraine conflict: Daily reality of east's "frozen war"', *BBC News*, 15 April. www.bbc.com/news/world-europe-35990401 (accessed 15 August 2016).

Cadier, D. (2014) 'Eastern Partnership vs Eurasian Union? The EU–Russia competition in the shared neighbourhood and the Ukraine crisis', *Global Policy*, 5(Supplement 1): 76–85.

Cadier, D. (2018) 'France's Russia policy from Europeanisation to Macronisation', in Siddi, M. (ed.) *EU Member States and Russia: National and European Debates in an Evolving International Environment*, FIIA Report 53, Helsinki: Finnish Institute of International Affairs, pp. 41–58.

Campbell, D. (1998) *Writing Security: United States foreign policy and the politics of identity*, Minneapolis: University of Minnesota Press.

Casier, T. (2011) 'The rise of energy to the top of the EU-Russia agenda: from interdependence to dependence?', *Geopolitics*, 16(3): 536–552.

Casier, T. (2018) 'The Geopoliticisation of the EU's Eastern Partnership', *Geopolitics*, 24(1), 71–99.

Castle, S. (2006) 'Poles angry at pipeline pact', *The Independent*, 1 May, www. independent.co.uk/news/world/europe/poles-angry-at-pipeline-pact-6102171.html (accessed 18 July 2016).

Chaisty, P. and Whitefield, S. (2012) 'The effects of the global financial crisis on Russian political attitudes', *Post-Soviet Affairs*, 28(2): 187–208.

Checkel, J. (1998) 'The Constructivist turn in IR Theory', *World Politics*, 50(2), 324–348.

Checkel, J. (2004) 'Social Constructivisms in global and European politics: a review essay', *Review of International Studies*, 30(2): 229–244.

Checkel, J. (2006) 'Constructivism and EU politics', in K. E. Jorgensen, M. Pollack and B. Rosamond (eds) *Handbook of European Union Politics*, London: Sage, pp. 57–76.

Checkel, J. (2008) 'Constructivism and foreign policy', in S. Smith, A. Hadfield and T. Dunne (eds) *Foreign Policies: Theories, actors, cases*, Oxford: Oxford University Press, pp. 71–82.

Checkel, J. and Katzenstein, P. (eds) (2009) *European Identity*, Cambridge: Cambridge University Press.

Chouliaraki, L. (2000) 'Political discourse in the news: democratizing responsibility or aestheticizing politics?', *Discourse and Society*, 11(3): 293–314.

Cichocki, B. (2013) 'Poland', in M. David, J. Gower and H. Haukkala, (eds), *National Perspectives on Russia: European foreign policy in the making?*, London: Routledge, 86–100.

Connor, W. (1990) 'When is a nation?', *Ethnic and Racial Studies*, 13(1): 92–103.

Connor, W. (2004) 'The timelessness of nations', *Nations and Nationalism*, 10(1/2): 35–47.

Consolidated Version of the Treaty on European Union (as amended by the Treaty of Lisbon). http://register.consilium.europa.eu/pdf/en/08/st06/st06655.en08.pdf (accessed 24 August 2016).

Copsey, N. and Pomorska, K. (2014) 'The influence of newer member states in the European Union: the case of Poland and the Eastern Partnership', *Europe-Asia Studies*, 66(3): 421–443.

Cornell, S. and Starr, F. (eds) (2009) *The Guns of August: Russia's war in Georgia*, London: M.E. Sharpe.

Curry, J. L. (2008) 'Poland and the politics of God's playground', in S. L. Wolchik and J. L. Curry (eds) *Central and East European Politics*, Plymouth: Rowman and Littlefield, pp. 165–189.

Czaputowicz, J. (2018a) Statements after the Foreign Affairs Council meeting, 17 April. www.msz.gov.pl/en/news/minister_jacek_czaputowicz_attends_foreign_affairs_council_ meeting_ (accessed 1 June 2019).

Czaputowicz, J. (2018b) Statements at the Meeting of NATO ministers of foreign affairs, 27 April. www.msz.gov.pl/en/news/meeting_of_nato_ministers_of_foreign_affairs_in_ brussels (accessed 1 June 2019).

Czaputowicz, J. (2018c) Information of the Minister of Foreign Affairs on Polish foreign policy tasks in 2018, 21 March. www.msz.gov.pl/en/ministry/minister/speeches/information_of_the_minister_of_foreign_affairs_on_polish_foreign_policy_tasks_in_2018 (accessed 5 October 2018).

Czaputowicz, J. (2018d) Address at the OSCE Ministerial Council, 6 December. www.osce.org/whoweare/405539?download=true (accessed 12 December 2019).

Damro, C. (2012) 'Market Power Europe', *Journal of European Public Policy*, 19(5): 682–699.

Dannreuther, R. (2015) 'Russia and the Arab Spring: Supporting the Counter-Revolution', *Journal of European Integration*, 37(1), pp. 77–94.

Dannreuther, R. (2019) 'Understanding Russia's return to the Middle East', *International Politics*, 56(6): 726–742.

David, M., Gower J. and Haukkala, H. (2011) 'Introduction: The European Union and Russia', *Journal of Contemporary European Studies*, 19(2): 183–188.

David, M., Gower J. and Haukkala, H. (eds) (2013) *National Perspectives on Russia: European foreign policy in the making?*, London: Routledge.

David, M. and Romanova, T. (2015) 'Modernisation in EU–Russian Relations: Past, Present, and Future', *European Politics and Society*, 16(1): 1–10.

Davies, C. (2016) 'The conspiracy theorists who have taken over Poland', *Guardian*, 16 February. www.theguardian.com/world/2016/feb/16/conspiracy-theorists-who-have-taken-over-poland (accessed 5 October 2018).

Davies, N. (1996) *Europe: A history*, Oxford: Oxford University Press.

Davies, N. (1996) (2001) *Heart of Europe: The past in Poland's present*, Oxford: Oxford University Press.

Davies, N. (1996) (2005) *God's Playground: A history of Poland*, vol. 2, Oxford: Oxford University Press.

Davis Cross, M. (2013) 'Rethinking epistemic communities twenty years later', *Review of International Studies*, 39: 137–160.

DeBardeleben, J. (2018) 'Introduction: A Transnational Approach to EU-Russia Relations', in T. Casier and J. DeBardeleben (eds) *EU-Russia Relations in Crisis: Understanding Diverging Perceptions*, Abingdon: Routledge, pp. 1–29.

De Cilla, R., Reisigl M. and Wodak, R. (1999) 'The discursive construction of national identities', *Discourse and Society*, 10(2): 149–173.

De Custine, A. (1989) *Empire of the Czar: A journey through eternal Russia*, Auckland: Anchor Books.

Delanty, G. (1995) *Inventing Europe: Idea, identity, reality*, London: Palgrave Macmillan.

De Lazari, A. (2011) 'Polish-Russian difficult matters', *The Polish Quarterly of International Affairs*, 1: 72–82.

Dempsey, J. (2016) Interview with Witold Waszczykowski, *Carnegie Europe*, 17 March. http://carnegieeurope.eu/strategiceurope/63057 (accessed 5 October 2018).

De Quetteville, H. (2008) 'Condoleezza Rice signs missile defence deal with Poland', *Telegraph*, 20 August. www.telegraph.co.uk/news/worldnews/europe/poland/2590043/Condoleezza-Rice-signs-missile-defence-deal-with-Poland.html (accessed 9 August 2016).

Deutsche Welle (2018) French President Emmanuel Macron in Russia proposes joint initiatives with Vladimir Putin, 24 May. www.dw.com/en/french-president-emmanuel-macron-in-russia-proposes-joint-initiatives-with-vladimir-putin/a-43920043 (accessed 5 October 2018).

Dunlop, J. (2011) 'The August 2008 Russo-Georgian war: which side went first?', in M. R. Freire and R. Kanet (eds) *Russia and its Near Neighbours. Identity, interests and foreign policy*, Basingstoke: Palgrave Macmillan, pp. 89–108.

Easton, A. (2015) 'Poland-Russia row sours Auschwitz commemoration', *BBC News*, 26 January. www.bbc.com/news/blogs-eu-30957027 (accessed 23 August 2016).

ECFR (European Council on Foreign Relations) (2014) *European Foreign Policy Scorecard 2014*, London: European Council on Foreign Relations.

Eder, K. (2005) 'Remembering national memories together: the formation of a transnational identity in Europe', in W. Spohn and K. Eder (eds) *Collective Memory and European Identity*, Aldershot: Ashgate, pp. 197–220.

Ehala, M. (2009) 'The Bronze Soldier: identity threat and maintenance in Estonia', *Journal of Baltic Studies*, 40(1): 139–158.

Elder, M. (2011) 'Vladimir Putin set to lose majority amid complaints of electoral violations', *Guardian*, 4 December. www.theguardian.com/world/2011/dec/04/vladimir-putin-majority-complaints-violations (accessed 10 August 2016).

Elder, M. (2012) 'Vladimir Putin's return to presidency preceded by violent protests in Moscow', *Guardian*, 6 May. www.theguardian.com/world/2012/may/06/vladimir-putin-presidency-violent-protests-moscow (accessed 10 August 2016).

Emmott, R. (2016), 'EU to extend Russia sanctions, divided over next steps', 20 June, *Reuters*. www.reuters.com/article/us-ukraine-crisis-eu-sanctions-idUSKCN0Z61QE (accessed 17 July 2016).

Etzold, T. and Haukkala H. (2011) 'Is there a Nordic Russia Policy? Swedish, Finnish and Danish relations with Russia in the context of the European Union', *Journal of Contemporary European Studies*, 19(2): 249–260.

Euractiv (2019) 'EU divisions over Russia mount as France, Germany seek peace in Ukraine', 7 October. www.euractiv.com/section/europe-s-east/news/eu-divisions-over-russia-mount-as-france-germany-seek-peace-in-ukraine/ (accessed 15 January 2020).

European Council (2014) 'Statement of the Heads of State or Government on Ukraine', 6 March. www.consilium.europa.eu/workarea/downloadAsset.aspx?id=15199 (accessed 15 August 2016).

European Council (2016) 'EU restrictive measures in response to the crisis in Ukraine'. www.consilium.europa.eu/en/policies/sanctions/ukraine-crisis/ (accessed 15 August 2016).

Evans, A. B. (2012) 'Protests and civil society in Russia: The struggle for the Khimki forest', *Communist and Post-Communist Studies*, 45(3–4): 233–242.

Evans, R. (2003) 'Introduction. Redesigning the past: history in political transitions', *Journal of Contemporary History*, 38(1): 5–12.

Ewans, M. (ed.) (2004) *The Great Game: Britain and Russia in Central Asia*, London: Routledge.

Federal Chancellor's Office (2017) Merkel stresses need to push ahead with political process, 11 April. www.bundeskanzlerin.de/bkin-en/news/merkel-stresses-need-to-push-ahead-with-political-process-448876 (accessed 29 May 2019).

Federal Chancellor's Office (2018) 'Only a political solution will bring peace', 16 April. www.bundeskanzlerin.de/bkin-en/news/only-a-political-solution-will-bring-peace-1007084 (accessed 29 May 2019).

Federal Foreign Office of Germany (2018) Working with Poland for a strong and united Europe, 2 November. www.auswaertiges-amt.de/en/aussenpolitik/laenderinformationen/polen-node/german-polish-intergovernmental-consultations/2157410 (accessed 5 August 2018).

Fedorowicz, K. (2007) 'National identity and national interest in Polish Eastern Policy, 1989–2004', *Nationalities Papers*, 35(3): 537–553.

Feklyunina, V. (2012) 'Russia's foreign policy towards Poland: seeking reconciliation? A social constructivist analysis', *International Politics*, 49(4): 434–448.

Fischer, S. (2016) 'Nord Stream 2: Trust in Europe', *Policy Perspectives*, Zurich: ETH. https://css.ethz.ch/content/dam/ethz/special-interest/gess/cis/center-for-securities-studies/pdfs/PP4-4.pdf (accessed 6 December 2019).

Fischer, S. (2017) 'Lost in regulation: The EU and Nord Stream 2', *Policy Perspectives*, Zurich: ETH. https://css.ethz.ch/content/dam/ethz/special-interest/gess/cis/center-for-securities-studies/pdfs/PP5-5.pdf (accessed 6 December 2019).

Fogu, C. and Kansteiner W. (2006) 'The politics of memory and the poetics of history', in R. N. Lebow, W. Kansteiner and C. Fogu (eds) *The Politics of Memory in Post-war Europe*, Durham (NC): Duke University Press, pp. 284–310.

Forsberg, T. (ed.) (1995) *Contested Territory: Border disputes at the edge of the former Soviet empire*, Aldershot: Edward Elgar.

Forsberg, T. (2006) 'Finnish-Russian security relations: is Russia still seen as a threat?', in H. Smith (ed.) *The Two-Level Game: Russia's relations with Great Britain, Finland and the European Union*, Helsinki: Aleksanteri Institute, pp. 141–154.

Forsberg, T. (2016) 'From Ostpolitik to "Frostpolitik"? Merkel, Putin and German Foreign Policy towards Russia', *International Affairs*, 92(1): 21–42.

Forsberg, T. and Haukkala, H. (2016) *The European Union and Russia*, Basingstoke: Palgrave Macmillan.

Forsberg, T. and Pesu, M. (2016) 'The "Finlandisation" of Finland: The Ideal Type, the Historical Model, and the Lessons Learnt', *Diplomacy & Statecraft*, 27(3): 473–495.

Forsberg, T. and Seppo A. (2011) 'The Russo-Georgian war and EU mediation', in R. Kanet (ed.) *Russian Foreign Policy in the 21st Century*, Basingstoke: Palgrave Macmillan, pp. 121–137.

Forsell, T. and Rosendahl, J. (2016) 'Flow of migrants into Finland from Russia dries up: Helsinki', *Reuters*, 17 March. www.reuters.com/article/us-europe-migrants-finland-russia/flow-of-migrants-into-finland-from-russia-dries-up-helsinki-idUSKCN0WJ1NP (accessed 5 June 2019).

Friedrich, J. (2002) *Der Brand: Deutschland im Bombenkrieg 1940–1945*, Munich: Propyläen.

Fulbrook, M. (1995) *Anatomy of a Dictatorship: Inside the GDR 1949–1989*, Oxford: Oxford University Press.

Fulbrook, M. (1999) *German National Identity after the Holocaust*, Malden: Blackwell.

Fulbrook, M. (2011) *Dissonant Lives: Generations and violence through the German dictatorships*, Oxford: Oxford University Press.

Gabriel, S. (2015) Transcript of meeting with Putin, 28 October. http://en.kremlin.ru/events/president/news/50582 (accessed 6 December 2019).

Gabriel, S. (2017a) Interview with Focus, 14 July. www.auswaertiges-amt.de/en/newsroom/news/170714-bm-focus/291394 (accessed 6 December 2019).

Gabriel, S. (2017b) Interview with Gazeta Wyborcza, 8 March. www.auswaertiges-amt.de/en/newsroom/news/170308-bm-gazetawyborcza/288368 (accessed 6 December 2019).

Gabriel, S. (2017c) Speech at the opening of the conference Making Conventional Arms Control Fit for the 21st Century, 6 September. www.auswaertiges-amt.de/en/newsroom/news/170906-bm-conventional-arms-control/292366 (accessed 9 December 2019).

Gabriel, S. (2017d) Interview with Nordkurier, 7 September. www.auswaertiges-amt.de/en/newsroom/news/170907-bm-nordkurier/292328 (accessed 9 December 2019).

Gabriel, S. and C. Kern (2017) Statement on the imposition of Russia sanctions by the US Senate, 15 June. www.auswaertiges-amt.de/en/newsroom/news/170615-kern-russland/290666 (accessed 6 December 2019).

Gartzke, E. and Gleditsch, K. S. (2006) 'Identity and conflict: ties that bind and differences that divide', *European Journal of International Relations*, 12(1): 53–87.

Gaweda, B. (2017) No country for losers? Gender, (in)equality, and the discursive construction of subjects and values in Polish politics. PhD Dissertation, University of Edinburgh, https://era.ed.ac.uk/handle/1842/25940 (accessed 6 December 2019).

Gaweda, B. (2019) 'The Polish Grand Canyon? Gendered Cleavages in Politics and Society', in U. Gućrot and M. Hunklinger (eds) *Old and New Cleavages in Polish Society*, Krems: Edition Donau-Universität Krems, pp. 73–92.

Gebhard, C. (2011) 'Coherence', in C. Hill and M. Smith (eds) *International Relations and the European Union*, Oxford: Oxford University Press, pp. 102–127.

Gellner, E. (1983) *Nations and Nationalism*, Ithaca (NY): Cornell University Press.

Gellner, E. (1996) 'Ernest Gellner's reply: "Do nations have navels?"', Nations and Nationalism, 2(3): 366–370.

Gellner, W. and Douglas, J. (eds) (2003) *The Berlin Republic: German unification and a decade of changes*, London: Frank Cass.

Gel'man, V. (2013) 'Cracks in the wall. Challenges to electoral authoritarianism in Russia', *Problems of Post-Communism*, 60(2): 3–10.

Gel'man, V. (2016) 'The politics of hear: how Russia's rulers counter their rivals', *Russian Politics*, 1(1): 27–45.

German, T. (2010) 'Pipeline politics: Georgia and energy security', in P. Rich (ed.) *Crisis in the Caucasus: Russia, Georgia and the West*, London: Routledge, pp. 94–112.

German Federal Government (2018a) Press release on Polish prime minister's visit, 16 February. www.bundesregierung.de/Content/EN/Artikel/2018/02_en/2018-02-16-morawiecki-in-berlin_en.html?nn=709674 (accessed 6 December 2019).

German Federal Government (2018b) Press release on Angela Merkel's visit to Vladimir Putin in Sochi, 18 May. www.bundesregierung.de/Content/EN/Reiseberichte/2018_en/2018-05-18-merkel-sotschi_en.html (accessed 6 December 2019).

Gildea, R. (2002a) 'Myth, memory and policy in France since 1945', in J. Müller (ed.) *Memory and Power in Post-War Europe*, Cambridge: Cambridge University Press, pp. 59–75.

Gildea, R. (2002b) *France since 1945*, Oxford: Oxford University Press.

Giles, K. and Eskola, S. (2009) *Waking the neighbour: Finland, NATO and Russia*, Shrivenham: Defence Academy of the United Kingdom.

Gill, G. (2012) 'The decline of a dominant party and the destabilization of electoral authoritarianism', *Post-Soviet Affairs*, 28(4): 449–471.

Gillis, J. (1994) 'Memory and identity: the history of a relationship', in J. Gillis (ed.) *Commemorations: The politics of national identity*, Princeton: Princeton University Press, pp. 3–26.

Goldman, M. F. (2006) 'Polish-Russian relations and the 2004 Ukrainian presidential elections', *East European Quarterly*, 40(4): 409–429.

Goldthau, A. (2016) Assessing Nord Stream 2: regulation, geopolitics & energy security in the EU, Central Eastern Europe & the UK, EUCERS Strategy Paper 10, London: King's College.www.kcl.ac.uk/sspp/departments/warstudies/research/groups/eucers/pubs/strategy-paper-10.pdf (accessed 6 December 2019).

Gordon, M. R., Smale, A. and Erlanger, S. (2015) 'Western Nations Split on Arming Kiev Forces', *New York Times*, 7 February. www.nytimes.com/2015/02/08/world/europe/divisions-on-display-over-western-response-to-ukraine-at-security-conference.html?_r=0 (accessed 15 August 2016).

Gorska, J. A. (2010) *Dealing with a Juggernaut: Analyzing Poland's policy toward Russia 1989–2009*, Plymouth: Lexington.

Gotev, G. (2015) 'Seven EU countries oppose Nord Stream', *Euractiv*, 30 November. www.euractiv.com/section/energy/news/seven-eu-countries-oppose-nord-stream/ (accessed 15 August 2016)

Gotkowska, J. (2010) 'The German-Russian modernisation partnership – failing to meet great expectations', *Eastweek*, 25, Warsaw: Centre for Eastern Studies, pp. 2–4.

Gotkowska, J. and Szymanski, P. (2016) 'The Nordic countries on Nord Stream 2: between scepticism and neutrality', *Energy Post*, 3 November. http://energypost.eu/nordic-countries-nord-stream-2-scepticism-neutrality/ (accessed 6 December 2019).

Grass, G. (2002) *Im Krebsgang*, Göttingen: Steidl.

Greene, S. (2013) 'Beyond Bolotnaya. Bridging old and new in Russia's election protest movement', *Problems of Post-Communism*, 60(2): 40–52.

Greenfeld, L. (1990) 'The formation of the Russian national identity: the role of status insecurity and ressentiment', *Comparative Studies in Society and History*, 32(3): 549–591.

Greenhill, B. (2008) 'Recognition and collective identity formation in international politics', *European Journal of International Relations*, 14(2): 343–368.

Grigas, A. (2013) *The Politics of Energy and Memory between the Baltic States and Russia*, Farnham: Ashgate.

Gromyko, A. (2015) 'Russia–EU relations at a crossroads: preventing a new Cold War in a polycentric world', *Southeast European and Black Sea Studies*, 15(2): 141–149.

Groszkowski, J. (2017) 'Czech support for Nord Stream 2', OSW Analysis, 29 November. www.osw.waw.pl/en/publikacje/analyses/2017-11-29/czech-support-nord-stream-2 (accessed 6 December 2019).

Guardian (2012) 'Hundreds detained after Moscow anti-Putin protest', 5 March. www.theguardian.com/world/blog/2012/mar/05/russian-election-reaction-putin-live (accessed 11 August 2016).

Guardian (2016) Russia is more dangerous than Isis, says Polish foreign minister, 15 April. www.theguardian.com/world/2016/apr/15/russia-more-dangerous-isis-polish-foreign-minister-witold-waszczykowski (accessed 6 December 2019).

Guibernau, M. (2004) 'Anthony D. Smith on nations and national identity: a critical assessment', *Nations and Nationalism*, 10(1/2): 125–141.

Guibernau, M. and Hutchinson, J. (2004) 'History and national destiny', *Nations and Nationalism*, 10(1/2): 1–8.

Guzzini, S. (2000) 'A reconstruction of constructivism in international relations', *European Journal of International Relations*, 6(2): 147–182.

Haas, P. (1992) 'Introduction: epistemic communities and international policy coordination', *International Organization*, 46(1): 1–35.

Haas, P. (2004) 'When does power listen to truth? A constructivist approach to the policy process', *Journal of European Public Policy*, 11(4): 569–592.

Habermas, J. (1988) 'Concerning the public use of history', *New German Critique*, 44: 40–50.

Habermas, J. (1998) *The inclusion of the Other. Studies in political theory*, Cambridge (MA): MIT Press.

Habermas, J. (2003) 'Toward a cosmopolitan Europe', *Journal of Democracy*, 14(4): 86–100.

Hahn, G. M. (2012) 'Perestroyka 2.0: toward non-revolutionary regime transformation in Russia?', *Post-Soviet Affairs*, 28(4): 472–515.

Halbwachs, M. (1992) *On collective memory*, Chicago: University of Chicago Press.

Hakala, H. (2019) 'Suomi ja Viro yhä eri linjoilla Nord Stream 2 –hankkeesta', Verkkouutiset, 23 February, www.verkkouutiset.fi/suomi-ja-viro-yha-eri-linjoilla-nord-stream-2-hankkeesta/ (accessed 6 December 2019).

Haller, J. (1917) *Die russische Gefahr im deutschen Haus*, Stuttgart: Engelhorn.

Hamilton, R. (2010) 'The bear came through the tunnel: an analysis of Georgian planning and operations in the Russo-Georgian war and implications for U.S. policy', in P. Rich (ed.) *Crisis in the Caucasus: Russia, Georgia and the West*, London: Routledge, pp. 202–234.

Hansen, L. (2006) *Security as Practice: Discourse analysis and the Bosnian war*, London: Routledge.

Harnisch, S. and Maull H. (eds) (2001) *Germany as a Civilian Power? The foreign policy of the Berlin Republic*, Manchester: Manchester University Press.

Harper, J. (2017) 'Nordstream II gas pipeline in deep water', *Deutsche Welle*, 14 November. www.dw.com/en/nordstream-ii-gas-pipeline-in-deep-water/a-41372833 (accessed 6 December 2019).

Hartikainen, J. (2015) 'Nord Stream 2 gave birth to a deep divide', *Kauppalehti*, 21 December. www.kauppalehti.fi/uutiset/nord-stream-2-synnytti-syvan-eripuran/381cb695-43b1-3720-bf0b-460c988ad216 (accessed 6 December 2019).

Haukkala, H. (2005) 'Clash of boundaries? The European Union and Russia in the Northern Dimension', in M. Lehti and D. J. Smith (eds) *Post-Cold War Identity Politics: Northern and Baltic experiences*, London: Frank Cass, pp. 273–296.

Haukkala, H. (2010a) *The EU-Russia Strategic Partnership: The limits of post-sovereignty in international relations*, London: Routledge.

Haukkala, H. (2010b) 'A close encounter of the worst kind? The logic of situated actors and the statue crisis between Estonia and Russia', *Journal of Baltic Studies*, 40(2): 201–213.

Haukkala, H. (2015) 'From Cooperative to Contested Europe? The Conflict in Ukraine as a Culmination of a Long-Term Crisis in EU–Russia Relations', *Journal of Contemporary European Studies*, 23(1): 25–40.

Haukkala, H. and Ojanen, H. (2011) 'The Europeanization of Finnish foreign policy: pendulum swings in slow motion', in R. Wong and C. Hill (eds) *National and European Foreign Policies: towards Europeanization*, London and New York: Routledge, pp. 149–166.

Hegel, G. W. F. (1999) 'The German Constitution', in L. Dickey and H. B. Nisbet (eds) *Hegel: political writings*, Cambridge: Cambridge University Press, pp. 6–101.

Heikka, H. (2005) 'Republican Realism: Finnish strategic culture in historical perspective', *Cooperation and Conflict*, 40(1): 91–119.

Heinrich, A. (2017) 'Securitisation in the gas sector: Energy security debates concerning the example of the Nord Stream pipeline', in K. Szulecki, ed. *Energy Security in Europe*. Basingstoke: Palgrave Macmillan, pp. 61–91.

Heinrich, H. and Tanaev K. (2009) 'Georgia and Russia: contradictory media coverage of the August war', *Caucasian Review of International Affairs*, 3(3): 244–260.

Henderson, J. and J. Sharples (2018) 'Gazprom in Europe – two "Anni Mirabiles", but can it continue?' Oxford: Oxford Institute for Energy Studies, March. www.oxfordenergy.org/wpcms/wp-content/uploads/2018/03/Gazprom-in-Europe-%E2%80%93-two-Anni-Mirabiles-but-can-it-continue-Insight-29.pdf (accessed 6 December 2019).

Herman, R. (1996) 'Identity, norms and national security: the Soviet foreign policy revolution and the end of the Cold War', in P. Katzenstein (ed.) *The Culture of National Security: Norms and identity in world politics*, New York: Columbia University Press, pp. 271–316.

Hermann, R., Risse, T. and Brewer, M. (eds) (2004) *Transnational Identities: Becoming European in the EU*, Oxford: Rowman and Littlefield.

Herf, J. (1997) *Divided Memory: The Nazi past in the two Germanys*, Harvard: Harvard University Press.

Hejj, D. (2018) 'Hungary does not support Poland in the area of gas', *Biznes Alert*, 3 April. http://biznesalert.com/hejj-poland-hungary-gas-nord-stream-2/ (accessed 6 December 2019).

Hildermeier, M. (2003) 'Germany and the Soviet Union', in E. Mühle (ed.) *Germany and the European East in the Twentieth Century*, Oxford and New York: Berg, pp. 29–44.

Hill, C. and Smith, M. (2005) *International Relations and the European Union*, Oxford: Oxford University Press.

Hillgruber, A. (1986) *Zweierlei Untergang: Die Zerschlagung des Deutschen Reichs und das Ende des europäischen Judentums*, Berlin: Siedler.

Hobsbawm, E. (1990) *Nations and Nationalism since 1780: Programme, myth, reality*, Cambridge: Cambridge University Press.

Hobsbawm, E. and Kertzer D. J. (1992) 'Ethnicity and nationalism in Europe today', *Anthropology Today*, 8(1): 3–8.

Hodgin, N. and Pearce, C. (2011) *The GDR Remembered: Representations of the East German state since 1989*, Rochester (NY): Camden House.

Högselius, P. (2013) *Red Gas: Russia and the origins of European energy dependence*, Basingstoke: Palgrave Macmillan.

Hopf, T. (1998) 'The promise of constructivism in international relations theory', *International Security*, 23(1): 171–200.

Hopf, T. (2002) *Social Construction of International Politics: Identities and foreign policies, Moscow, 1955 and 1999*, Ithaca (NY): Cornell University Press.

Hunt, N. (2010) *Memory, War and Trauma*, Cambridge: Cambridge University Press.

Huntington, S. (1997) *The Clash of Civilizations and the Remaking of World Order*, New York: Simon and Schuster.

Hutchinson, J. (2000) 'Ethnicity and modern nations', *Ethnic and Racial Studies*, 23(4): 651–669.

Huyssen, A. (1995) 'After the Wall: the failure of German intellectuals', in A. Huyssen (ed.) *Twilight Memories: Marking time in a culture of amnesia*, New York: Routledge, pp. 37–65.

Huyssen, A. (2003) *Present Pasts. Urban palimpsests and the politics of memory*, Stanford: Stanford University Press.

Hyde-Price, A. (2000) *Germany and European order: Enlarging NATO and the EU*, Manchester: Manchester University Press.

IIFFMCG (Independent International Fact-Finding Mission on the Conflict in Georgia) Report (2009), vol. 1. http://news.bbc.co.uk/2/shared/bsp/hi/pdfs/30_09_09_iiffmgc_report.pdf (accessed 24 August 2016).

Isnenghi, M. (ed.) (2010) *I Luoghi della Memoria: Simboli e miti dell'Italia unita*, Roma: Laterza.

James, H. (1989) *German Identity 1770–1990*, London: Weidenfeld and Nicolson.

Jarausch, K. (1994) *The Rush to German Unity*, Oxford: Oxford University Press.

Jarausch, K. (ed.) (1999) *Dictatorship as Experience: Towards a socio-cultural history of the GDR*, Oxford: Berghahn.

Jarausch, K. (2010) 'Nightmares or daydreams? A postscript on the Europeanisation of memories', in M. Pakier and B. Stråth (eds) *A European Memory? Contested histories and politics of remembrance*, Oxford: Berghahn, pp. 309–320.

Jarausch, K. and Geyer, M. (2003) *Shattered past: Reconstructing German histories*, Princeton: Princeton University Press.

Jarausch, K. and Lindenberger, T. (eds) (2007) *Conflicted Memories: Europeanising contemporary histories*, Oxford: Berghahn.

Jepperson, R., Wendt, A. and Katzenstein, P. (1996) 'Norms, identity and culture in national security', in P. Katzenstein (ed.) *The Culture of National Security: Norms and identity in world politics*, New York: Columbia University Press, pp. 33–78.

Jervis, R. (1978) 'Cooperation under the security dilemma', *World Politics*, 30(2): 167–214.

Joenniemi, P. (2002) 'Finland in the New Europe: a Herderian or Hegelian project?', in L. Hansen and O. Wæver (eds) *European Integration and National Identity: The challenge of the Nordic states*, London and New York: Routledge, pp. 182–213.

Joenniemi, P. (2010) 'Finland: Always a borderland?', in M. Hurd (ed.) *Bordering the Baltic: Scandinavian boundary-drawing processes, 1900–2000*, Berlin: Lit Verlag, pp. 41–68.

Johnston, A. I. (1999) 'Realism(s) and Chinese security policy in the post-Cold War period', in E. Kapstein and M. Mastanduno (eds) *Unipolar Politics. Realism and state strategies after the Cold War*, New York: Columbia University Press, pp. 261–318.

Jokela, J. (2010) *Europeanisation and Foreign Policy: State identity in Finland and Britain*, London and New York: Routledge.

Jones, S. (2013) *War and Revolution in the Caucasus: Georgia ablaze*, New York: Routledge.

Judge, A., Maltby, T. and Sharples, J. (2016) 'Challenging Reductionism in Analyses of EU-Russia Energy Relations', *Geopolitics* 21(4): 751–762.

Judt, T. (1992) 'The past is another country: myth and memory in post-war Europe', *Daedalus*, 121(4): 83–118.

Kagan, R. (2008) *The Return of History and the End of Dreams*, New York: Knopf.

Kamen, H. (2008) *Imagining Spain: Historical myth and national identity*, New Haven: Yale University Press.

Katz, M. (2018) 'What do they see in him? How the Middle East views Putin and Russia', Russian Analytical Digest 219, Zurich: Centre for Security Studies.

Katzenstein, P. (ed.) (1996) *The Culture of National Security: Norms and identity in world politics*, New York: Columbia University Press.

Keith, N. (2006) *Britain, Soviet Russia and the Collapse of the Versailles order, 1919–1939*, Cambridge: Cambridge University Press.

King, F. (2018) 'German and Polish leaders clash over Nord Stream 2 pipeline', *Politico*, 16 February. www.politico.eu/article/nord-stream-2-german-and-polish-leaders-clash/ (accessed 6 December 2019).

Kleikamp, A. (2015) 'Als Millionen Deutsche selber Flüchtlinge waren', *Die Zeit*, 19 May. www.welt.de/geschichte/zweiter-weltkrieg/article141112932/Als-Millionen-Deutsche-selber-Fluechtlinge-waren.html (accessed 29 May 2019).

Klessmann, C. (1999) 'Rethinking the second German dictatorship', in K. Jarausch (ed.) *Dictatorship as Experience: Towards a socio-cultural history of the GDR*, Oxford: Berghahn.

Kloth, H. M. (2006) 'Indirect Hitler comparison: Polish minister attacks Schröder and Merkel', *Spiegel Online*, 1 May. www.spiegel.de/international/indirect-hitler-comparison-polish-minister-attacks-schroeder-and-merkel-a-413969.html (accessed 7 August 2016).

Klymenko, L. (2019) 'Forging Ukrainian national identity through remembrance of World War II', *National Identities*, online first.

Knafo, S. (2008) 'Critical approaches and the problem of social construction: reassessing the legacy of the agent/structure debate in IR', Working Paper No. 3, Brighton: University of Sussex.

Knowlton, J. and Cates, T. (eds) (1993) *Forever in the Shadow of Hitler? Original documents of the Historikerstreit, the controversy concerning the singularity of the Holocaust*, London: Humanities Press International.

Kocka, J. (1996) 'Crisis of unification: how Germany changes', in M. Mertes, S. Muller and H. A. Winkler (eds) *In Search of Germany*, New Brunswick and London: Transaction Publishers, pp. 191–210.

Koczanowicz, L. (1997) 'Memory of politics and politics of memory. Reflections on the construction of the past in post-totalitarian Poland', *Studies in East European Thought*, 49(4), pp. 259–270.

Koczanowicz, L. (2008) *Politics of time. Dynamics of identity in post-Communist Poland*, New York and Oxford: Berghahn Books.

Koenig, N. (2017) 'Libya and Syria: At the crossroads of European Neighbourhood Policy and EU crisis management', in T. Schumacher, A. Marchetti and T. Demmelhuber (eds) *The Routledge Handbook on the European Neighbourhood Policy*, Abingdon: Routledge, pp. 358–368.

Koenig, N. (2018) 'Leading Beyond Civilian Power: Germany's Role Re-conception in European Crisis Management', German Politics, doi: 10.1080/09644008.2018.149 6240.

Komorowski, B. (2015) Address at the Westerplatte Commemoration Ceremony, 8 May. www.president.pl/en/president-komorowski/news/art,830,address-at-the-westerplatte-commemoration-ceremony.html (accessed 21 July 2016).

König, H. (2008) 'Erinnern und vergessen. Vom Nutzen und Nachteil für die Politik', *Osteuropa*, 6: 27–40.

Koesel, K. and Bunce, V. (2012) 'Putin, popular protests and political trajectories in Russia: a comparative perspective', *Post-Soviet Affairs*, 28(4): 403–423.

Kopacz, E. (2014) Speech at the Sejm, 1 October. www.premier.gov.pl/en/policy-statement-by-prime-minister-ewa-kopacz-stenographic-record.html (accessed 23 August 2016).

Kopacz, E. (2015a) Press conference, 25 June. www.premier.gov.pl/en/news/news/prime-minister-kopacz-on-deployment-of-us-weapons-in-poland-it-strengthens-natos-eastern.html (accessed 23 August 2016).

Kopacz, E. (2015b) Press conference with Arseniy Yatsenyuk, 19 January. www.premier. gov.pl/en/news/news/support-for-reforms-in-ukraine.html (accessed 23 August 2016).

Kopacz, E. (2015c) Poland will accept 60 families from the conflict-torn Syria, 26 May. www.premier.gov.pl/en/news/news/prime-minister-ewa-kopacz-poland-will-accept-60-families-from-the-conflict-torn-syria.html (accessed 31 May 2019).

Korosteleva, E. A. (2016) 'Eastern partnership and the Eurasian Union: bringing "the political" back in the eastern region', *European Politics and Society*, 17(Supplement 1): 67–81.

Kossert, A. (2015) 'Böhmen, Pommern, Syrien', Zeit Online, 12 February. www.zeit. de/2015/05/fluechtlinge-boehmen-pommern-nachkriegszeit (accessed 29 May 2019).

Kozhanov, N. (2018) Russian Policy Across the Middle East: Motivations and Methods, London: Chatham House.

Kratochwil, F. (2000) 'Constructing a new orthodoxy? Wendt's "Social Theory of International Politics" and the constructivist challenge', *Millennium – Journal of International Studies*, 29(1): 73–101.

Krumm, R. (2012) 'The rise of Realism: Germany's perception of Russia from Gorbachev to Medvedev', in R. Krumm, H. Schröder and S. Medvedev (eds) *Constructing Identities in Europe: German and Russian perspectives*, Baden-Baden: Nomos, pp. 114–123.

Krumm, R., Schröder, H. and Medvedev, S. (eds) (2012) *Constructing Identities in Europe: German and Russian perspectives*, Baden-Baden: Nomos.

Krzyzanowski, M. (2009) 'Europe in crisis: discourses on crisis-events in the European press 1956–2006', *Journalism Studies*, 10(1): 18–35.

Krzyzanowski, M. (2010) *The Discursive Construction of European Identities*, Frankfurt am Main: Peter Lang.

Kuhn, T. (2015) *Experiencing European Integration: Transnational Lives and European Identity*, Oxford: Oxford University Press.

Kulish, N. (2008) 'Georgian crisis brings attitude change to a flush in Poland', *New York Times*, 21 August. www.nytimes.com/2008/08/21/world/europe/21poland.html?pagewanted= alland_r=0 (accessed 9 August 2016).

Kundera, M. (1984) 'The tragedy of Central Europe', *New York Review of Books*, 31(7): 33–38.

Kurki-Suonio (2018) 'Kokoomuksen mepeiltä vahva kanta: "Nord Stream 2:sta ei pitäisi rakentaa"', *Uusi Suomi*, 12 January. www.uusisuomi.fi/kotimaa/239232-kokoomuksen-mepeilta-vahva-kanta-nord-stream-2sta-ei-pitaisi-rakentaa (accessed 6 December 2019).

Laffey, M. and Weldes, J. (1997) 'Beyond belief: ideas and symbolic technologies in the study of international relations', *European Journal of International Relations*, 3(2): 193–237.

Lang, K. O. and Westphal, K. (2017) *Nord Stream 2 – A Political and Economic Contextualisation*. Berlin: Stiftung Wissenschaft und Politik.

Langenbacher, E. (2008) 'Twenty-first century memory regimes in Germany and Poland. An analysis of elite discourses and public opinion', *German Politics and Society*, 26(4): 50–81.

Langenbacher, E. (2010) 'The mastered past? Collective memory trends in Germany since unification', *German Politics and Society*, 28(1): 42–68.

Lasas, A. (2012) 'When history matters: Baltic and Polish reactions to the Russo-Georgian War', *Europe-Asia Studies*, 64(6): 1061–1075.

Lebow, R. N. (2006) 'The memory of politics in post-war Europe', in R. N. Lebow, W. Kansteiner and C. Fogu (eds) *The Politics of Memory in Post-War Europe*, Durham (NC): Duke University Press, pp. 1–39.

Lebow, R. N. (2008a) *A Cultural Theory of International Relations*, Cambridge: Cambridge University Press.

Lebow, R. N. (2008b) Identity and International Relations. *International relations*, 22(4): 473–492.

Lebow, R. N., Kansteiner W. and Fogu, C. (eds) (2006) *The Politics of Memory in Post-War Europe*, Durham (NC): Duke University Press.

Legro, J. and Moravcsik, A. (1999) 'Is anybody still a realist?', *International Security*, 24(2): 5–55.

Leonard, M. and Popescu, N. (2007) *A Power Audit of EU-Russia Relations*, London: European Council on Foreign Relations.

Levintova, E. (2010) 'Good neighbours? Dominant narratives about the "Other" in contemporary Polish and Russian newspapers', *Europe-Asia Studies*, 62(8): 1339–1361.

Lippert, W. (2011) *The Economic Diplomacy of Ostpolitik: Origins of NATO's energy dilemma*, New York: Berghahn Books.

Liu, J. and Hilton, D. (2005) 'How the past weighs on the present: social representations of history and their role in identity politics', *British Journal of Social Psychology*, 44: 537–556.

Lo, B. (2009) 'Medvedev and the European security architecture', Policy Brief, London: Centre for European Reform.

Loew, P. O. (2008) 'Helden oder Opfer. Erinnerungskulturen in Polen nach 1989', *Osteuropa*, 6: 85–102.

Loskot-Strachota, A. (2015) 'The case against Nord Stream 2', *Energy Post*, 23 November. http://energypost.eu/case-nord-stream-2/ (accessed 6 December 2019).

Loskot-Strachota, A. and K. Poplawski (2016) 'EUGAL: the unknown German branch of Nord Stream 2 will make Germany the key gas hub in Europe', *Energy Post*, 6 July. http://energypost.eu/eugal-project-unknown-german-branch-nord-stream-2-will-make-germany-key-gas-hub-europe/ (accessed 6 December 2019).

Luhn, A. (2014) 'The Ukrainian nationalism at the heart of Euromaidan', *The Nation*, 21 January, www.thenation.com/article/178013/ukrainian-nationalism-heart-euromaidan (accessed 26 August 2016).

Maas, H. (2018a) Speech at the Tiergarten Conference of the Friedrich-Ebert-Stiftung, 27 June. www.auswaertiges-amt.de/en/newsroom/news/maas-fes-tiergarten-konferenz/2113728 (accessed 6 December 2019).

Maas, H. (2018b) Interview with Neue Osnabrücker Zeitung, 1 December. www.auswaertiges-amt.de/en/newsroom/news/maas-noz-ukraine-climate-inf/2166620 (accessed 6 December 2019).

Maas, H. (2018c) Speech at the Bundestag, 18 April. www.auswaertiges-amt.de/en/newsroom/news/maas-bundestag-syrien/2001802 (accessed 29 May 2019).

Maas, H. (2018d) Speech at the Bundestag, 16 May. www.auswaertiges-amt.de/en/newsroom/news/maas-bundestag-budgetdebate/2083732 (accessed 29 May 2019).

Maas, H. (2018e) Interview with Der Spiegel, 14 April. www.auswaertiges-amt.de/en/newsroom/news/heiko-maas-spiegel-interview/1992522.

Makarychev, A. and Meister, S. (2015) 'The modernisation debate and Russian-German normative cleavages', *European Politics and Society*, 16(1): 80–94.

Malesevic, S. (2011) 'The chimera of national identity', *Nations and Nationalism*, 17(2): 272–290.

Mälksoo, M. (2009) 'The memory politics of becoming European. The East European subalterns and the collective memory of Europe', *European Journal of International Relations*, 15(4): 653–680.

Mankoff, J. (2012) 'The politics of US missile defence cooperation with Europe and Russia', *International Affairs*, 88(2): 329–347.

Manners, I. (2002) 'Normative Power Europe: a contradiction in terms?', *Journal of Common Market Studies*, 40(2): 235–258.

March, L. (2011) 'Is nationalism rising in Russian foreign policy? The case of Georgia', *Demokratizatsiya*, 19(3): 187–208.

March, L. (2012) 'The Russian Duma "opposition": no drama out of crisis?', *East European Politics*, 28(3): 241–255.

Markovits, A. and Reich S. (1997) *The German Predicament: Memory and power in the new Europe*, Ithaca (NY): Cornell University Press.

Marson, J. (2012) 'Gazprom cuts gas price for Poland', *Wall Street Journal*, 6 November. http://online.wsj.com/news/articles/SB1000142405297020434940457810223013532952 0 (accessed 11 August 2016).

Martikainen, T. and Vihma, A. (2016) 'Dividing the EU with energy? Unpacking Russia's energy geoeconomics', FIIA Briefing Paper 191, Helsinki: Finnish Institute of International Affairs.

Matveeva, A. (2016) 'No Moscow stooges: identity polarization and guerrilla movements in Donbass', *Europe-Asia Studies*, 16(1): 25–50.

McManus-Czubinska, C. and Miller, W. (2008) 'European civilization or European civilizations: the EU as a "Christian club"? Public opinion in Poland in 2005', in M. Myant and T. Cox (eds) *Reinventing Poland: Economic and political transformation and evolving national identity*, London and New York: Routledge, pp. 128–149.

Medvedev, S. (1999) 'Russia as the subconsciousness of Finland', *Security Dialogue*, 30(1): 95–107.

Megill, A. (2011) 'History, memory, identity', in J. Olick, V. Vinitzky-Seroussi and D. Levy (eds) *The Collective Memory Reader*, Oxford: Oxford University Press, pp. 193–197.

Meier, O. (2007) 'Europeans split over U.S. missile defence plans', *Arms Control Today*, 2 April, www.armscontrol.org/print/2333 (accessed 18 July 2016).

Meister, S. (2012) 'An alienated partnership. German-Russian relations after Putin's return', FIIA Briefing Paper 105, Helsinki: Finnish Institute of International Affairs.

Meister, S. (2014) 'Reframing Germany's Russia policy. An opportunity for the EU', ECFR Policy Brief, London: European Council on Foreign Relations Policy.

Merkel, A. (2014a) Speech at the Bundestag, 13 March. www.auswaertiges-amt.de/EN/Infoservice/Presse/Meldungen/2014/140314-Merkel-Ukraine.html (accessed 18 August 2016).

Merkel, A. (2014b) Statement announcing EU economic sanctions against Russia, 29 July. www.bundesregierung.de/Content/EN/Artikel/2014/07_en/2014-07-29-eu-sanktionen_en.html (accessed 18 August 2016).

Merkel, A. (2014c) Statement at the European Council meeting, 18 December. www.bundesregierung.de/Content/EN/Artikel/2014/12_en/2014-12-18-ukraine-merkel-regierungserklaerung.html (accessed 18 August 2016).

Merkel, A. (2014d) New Year address, 31 December. www.bundesregierung.de/Content/EN/Artikel/2015/01_en/2014-12-31-merkel-ansprache-ukraine_en.html (accessed 18 August 2016).

Merkel, A. (2015a) Statement at meeting with NATO Secretary-General in Berlin, 14 January. www.bundeskanzlerin.de/Content/EN/Artikel/2015/01_en/2015-01-14-besuch-nato-gs-stoltenberg_en.html (accessed 18 August 2016).

Merkel, A. (2015b) Statement following talks in Kiev and Moscow, 5 February. www.bundeskanzlerin.de/Content/EN/Reiseberichte/2015/2015-02-05-merkel-hollande-kiew-moskau_en.html (accessed 18 August 2016).

Merkel, A. (2015c) Speech at the Munich Security Conference, 7 February. www.bundesregierung.de/Content/EN/Reden/2015/2015-02-07-merkel-sicherheitskonferenz_en.html (accessed 18 August 2016).

Merkel, A. (2015d) Statements concerning the Minsk-2 agreement, 11 February. www.bundeskanzlerin.de/Content/EN/Reiseberichte/2015/2015-02-11-merkel-minsk_en.html (accessed 19 August 2016).

Merkel, A. (2015e) Statement on the occasion of Petro Poroshenko's visit to Berlin, 16 March. www.bundeskanzlerin.de/Content/EN/Artikel/2015/03_en/2015-03-16-poroschenko-bei-merkel_en.html (accessed 19 August 2016).

Merkel, A. (2015f) Speech at the Bundestag, 19 March. www.bundeskanzlerin.de/Content/EN/Artikel/2015/03_en/2015-03-19-ukraine-regierungserklaerung_en.html (accessed 19 August 2016).

Merkel, A. (2015g) Statements following consultations with Jean-Claude Juncker, 5 March. www.bundeskanzlerin.de/Content/EN/Artikel/2015/03_en/2015-03-05-ukraine_en.html (accessed 19 August 2016).

Merkel, A. (2015h) Statements at joint press conference with Vladimir Putin in Moscow, 10 May. www.bundeskanzlerin.de/Content/EN/Reiseberichte/2015/2015-10-05-bkin-zu-gedenken-min-moskau.html (accessed 19 August 2016).

Merkel, A. (2015i) Statements at the G7 summit, 7 June. www.bundeskanzlerin.de/Content/EN/Artikel/2015/06_en/2015-06-07-auftakt-g7-gipfel-1_en.html (accessed 19 August 2016).

Merkel, A. (2015j) Government statement, 15 October. www.bundeskanzlerin.de/Content/EN/Regierungserklaerung/2015-10-15-regierungserklaerung-bundestag.html (accessed 19 August 2016).

Merkel, A. (2015k) Statements at the European Council in Brussels, 16 October. www.bundeskanzlerin.de/bkin-en/news/european-union-cooperates-with-tukey-on-refugees-600874 (accessed 28 May 2019).

Merkel, A. (2016a) Statements at the joint press conference with Turkish Prime Minister Ahmet Davutoğlu, 8 February. www.bundeskanzlerin.de/bkin-en/news/angela-merkel-offers-turkey-assistance-for-border-region-404262 (accessed 29 May 2019).

Merkel, A. (2016b) Statements on the eve of a meeting with Vladimir Putin, 17 October. www.bundeskanzlerin.de/bkin-en/news/humanitarian-assistance-is-the-top-priority-414672 (accessed 29 May 2019).

Merkel, A. (2016c) Statements following the European Council, 20 October. www.bundeskanzlerin.de/bkin-en/news/responding-to-international-crises-604256 (accessed 29 May 2019).

Merkel, A. (2016d) Statements after the Normandy format talks, 20 October. www.bundeskanzlerin.de/bkin-en/news/merkel-believes-russia-must-acknowledge-responsibility-387466 (accessed 29 May 2019).

Merkel, A. (2018a) Statements at the Istanbul Conference, 27 October. www.bundeskanzlerin.de/bkin-en/news/syria-only-a-political-solution-will-be-successful-1543152 (accessed 29 May 2019).

Merkel, A. (2018b) Speech at the reception for the Diplomatic Corps in Meseberg, 6 July. www.bundeskanzlerin.de/bkin-en/news/speech-by-federal-chancellor-angela-merkel-at-the-reception-for-the-diplomatic-corps-in-meseberg-on-6-july-2018-1513686

Mertes, M., Muller, S. and Winkler, H. A. (eds) (1996) *In Search of Germany*, New Brunswick and London: Transaction Publishers.

Mickiewicz, A. (1833) *Books of the Polish Nation and Polish Pilgrimage*, London: James Ridgway.

Miller, C. (2019) 'Explainer: What Is The Steinmeier Formula – And Did Zelenskiy Just Capitulate To Moscow?', *Radio Free Europe*, 2 October. www.rferl.org/a/what-is-the-steinmeier-formula-and-did-zelenskiy-just-capitulate-to-moscow-/30195593.html (accessed 6 December 2019).

Miller, D. (1997) *On Nationality*, Oxford: Oxford University Press.

Ministry of Economic Affairs and Employment of Finland (2018) Government gives consent to Nord Stream 2 gas pipeline project, 5 April. https://tem.fi/en/article/-/asset_publisher/valtioneuvostolta-suostumus-nord-stream-2-kaasuputkihankkeelle (accessed 6 December 2019).

Mitzen, J. (2006) 'Ontological security in world politics: state identity and the security dilemma', *European Journal of International Relations*, 12(3): 341–370.

Moeller, R. (2003a) *War Stories: The search for a usable past in the Federal Republic of Germany*, Berkeley and Los Angeles: University of California Press.

Moeller, R. (2003b) 'Sinking ships, the lost Heimat and broken taboos: Günter Grass and the politics of memory in contemporary Germany', *Contemporary European History*, 12(2): 147–181.

Möller, U. and Bjereld, U. (2010) 'From Nordic neutrals to post-neutral Europeans: differences in Finnish and Swedish policy transformation', *Cooperation and Conflict*, 45(4): 363–386.

Moore, M. (1996) 'Miller's ode to national homogeneity', *Nations and Nationalism*, 2(3): 422–429.

Morawiecki, M. (2018a) Statements at the Munich Security Conference, 17 February. www.premier.gov.pl/mobile/en/news/news/prime-minister-mateusz-morawiecki-on-the-future-of-europe-during-the-munich-security.html (accessed 1 June 2019).

Morawiecki, M. (2018b) Interview with Der Spiegel, 20 February. www.spiegel.de/international/europe/interview-with-polish-prime-minister-mateusz-morawiecki-a-1194264.html (accessed 12 December 2019).

Morozov, V. (2018) 'Identity and Hegemony in EU-Russia Relations: Making Sense of the Asymmetrical Entanglement' in T. Casier and J. DeBardeleben (eds) *EU-Russia Relations in Crisis: Understanding Diverging Perceptions*, Abingdon: Routledge, pp. 30–49.

Mühlberger, W. and Siddi, M. (2019) In from the Cold: Russia's Agenda in the Middle East and Implications for the EU, Euromesco Policy Brief 91. www.euromesco.net/wp-content/uploads/2019/02/Brief91-In-from-the-cold_Russia_Agenda_In_The_Middle_East-1.pdf (accessed 28 May 2019).

Müller, H. (2004) 'Arguing, bargaining and all that: communicative action, rationalist theory and the logic of appropriateness in international relations', *European Journal of International Relations*, 10(3): 395–435.

Müller, J. (2002) 'The power of memory, the memory of power and the power over memory', in J. Müller (ed.) *Memory and Power in Post-War Europe*, Cambridge: Cambridge University Press, pp. 1–36.

Müller, R. and Ueberschär, G. R. (2009) *Hitler's War in the East: A critical assessment*, Oxford: Berghahn.

Mushaben, J. M. (2017) 'Wir schaffen das! Angela Merkel and the European Refugee Crisis', *German Politics*, 26(4): 516–533.

Naarden, B. (1992) *Socialist Europe and Revolutionary Russia: Perception and prejudice, 1848–1923*, Cambridge: Cambridge University Press.

Naimark, N. (1995) *The Russians in Germany: A history of the Soviet zone of occupation 1945–1949*, Cambridge (MA): Harvard University Press.

Nau, H. (2002) *At Home Abroad: Identity and power in American foreign policy*, Ithaca (NY): Cornell University Press.

Neumann, I. (1996) 'Self and Other in International Relations', *European Journal of International Relations*, 2(2): 139–174.

Neumann, I. (1998) *Uses of the Other: The East in European identity formation*, Minneapolis: University of Minnesota Press.

Neumann, I. (2006) 'European identity and its changing others', Paper 710, Oslo: Norwegian Institute of International Affairs.

Neumann, I. and Medvedev, S. (2012) 'Identity issues in EU-Russian relations', in R. Krumm, H. Schröder and S. Medvedev (eds) *Constructing Identities in Europe: German and Russian perspectives*, Baden-Baden: Nomos, pp. 9–29.

Neumann, I. (2014a) Speech at the dinner for the state visit by President of the Swiss Confederation Didier Burkhalter, 7 April. www.eilen.fi/en/3192/?language=en (accessed 25 August 2016).

Neumann, I. (2014b) Speech at a dinner for the diplomatic corps at Helsinki City Hall, 29 April. www.eilen.fi/en/3193/?language=en (accessed 25 August 2016).

Neumann, I. (2014c) Speech at the opening session of the Arctic Circle Assembly 2014, 31 October. www.eilen.fi/en/3241/?language=en (accessed 25 August 2016).

Neumann, I. (2015a) Speech at the Ambassador Seminar, 25 August 2015. www.eilen.fi/en/3357/?language=en (accessed 4 June 2019).

Neumann, I. (2015b) Statement at the 60th anniversary of Finland's membership to the United Nations, 9 December 2015. www.eilen.fi/en/3415/?language=en (accessed 4 June 2019).

Neumann, I. (2015c) Speech at the diplomatic corps dinner at the Presidential Palace, 23 April. www.eilen.fi/en/3324/?language=en (accessed 26 August 2016).

Neumann, I. (2016a) New Year Speech, 1 January. www.eilen.fi/en/3418/?language=en (accessed 5 June 2019).

Neumann, I. (2016b) Speech at the Ambassador Seminar, 23 August. www.eilen.fi/en/3454/?language=en (accessed 5 June 2019).

Neumann, I. (2017a) New Year Speech, 1 January 2017. www.eilen.fi/en/3567/?language=en (accessed 5 June 2019).

Neumann, I. (2017b) Speech at the Ambassador Seminar on 22 August. www.eilen.fi/en/3594/?language=en (accessed 5 June 2019).

Neumann, I. (2017c) Speech at a dinner in honour of the President of Ukraine at the Presidential Palace, 24 January. www.eilen.fi/en/3568/?language=en (accessed 5 June 2019).

Niinistö, S. (2012) Speech at the plenary session of Saint Petersburg International Economic Forum, 21 June. www.eilen.fi/en/1785/?language=en (accessed 11 August 2016).

Niinistö, S. (2014a) Speech at the dinner for the state visit by President of the Swiss Confederation Didier Burkhalter, 7 April. http://www.eilen.fi/en/3192/?language=en (accessed 22 March 2020).

Niinistö, S. (2014b) Speech at a dinner for the diplomatic corps at Helsinki City Hall, 29 April. http://www.eilen.fi/en/3193/?language=en (accessed 22 March 2020).

Niinistö, S. (2014c) Speech at the opening session of the Arctic Circle Assembly 2014, 31 October. http://www.eilen.fi/en/3241/?language=en (accessed 22 March 2020).

Niinistö, S. (2015a) Speech at the Ambassador Seminar, 25 August 2015. https://www.eilen.fi/en/3357/?language=en (accessed 4 June 2019).

Niinistö, S. (2015b) Statement at the 60th anniversary of Finland's membership to the United Nations, 9 December 2015. https://www.eilen.fi/en/3415/?language=en (accessed 4 June 2019).

Niinistö, S. (2015c) Speech at the diplomatic corps dinner at the Presidential Palace, 23 April. http://www.eilen.fi/en/3324/?language=en (accessed 22 March 2020).

Niinistö, S. (2016a) New Year Speech, 1 January. https://www.eilen.fi/en/3418/?language=en (accessed 5 June 2019).

Niinistö, S. (2016b) Speech at the Ambassador Seminar, 23 August. https://www.eilen.fi/en/3454/?language=en (accessed 5 June 2019).

Niinistö, S. (2017a) New Year Speech, 1 January 2017. https://www.eilen.fi/en/3567/?language=en (accessed 5 June 2019).

Niinistö, S. (2017b) Speech at the Ambassador Seminar on 22 August. https://www.eilen.fi/en/3594/?language=en (accessed 22 March 2020).

Niinistö, S. (2017c) Speech at a dinner in honour of the President of Ukraine at the Presidential Palace, 24 January. https://www.eilen.fi/en/3568/?language=en (accessed 22 March 2020).

Nitoiu, C. (2016) 'The Ukraine crisis and the conflict/cooperation dichotomy in EU-Russia relations', *Southeast European and Black Sea Studies*, 16(3): 375–390.

Nitoiu, C. (2018) 'The United Kingdom: from pragmatism to conflict?', in Siddi, M. (ed.) *EU Member States and Russia: National and European Debates in an Evolving International Environment*, FIIA Report 53, Helsinki: Finnish Institute of International Affairs, pp. 93–105.

Nolte, E. (1986) 'Die Vergangenheit, die nicht vergehen will', *Frankfurter Allgemeine Zeitung*, 6 June. www.staff.uni-giessen.de/~g31130/PDF/Nationalismus/ErnstNolte. pdf (accessed 29 August 2016).

Nora, P. (1989) 'Between memory and history. Les lieux de mémoire', *Representations*, 26: 7–24.

Nora, P. (1992) *Realms of memory: The construction of the French past*, New York: Columbia University Press.

Nurminen, T. (2019) 'USA yrittää pysäyttää Nord Stream 2 -hankkeen, uhkaa myös pakotteilla – Presidentti Niinistö: "Yhdysvaltain kritiikki on ollut aika voimakasta"', *Kauppalehti*, 16 February. https://bit.ly/2LvPa3s (accessed 6 December 2019).

Oberhuber, F., Bärenreuter, C., Krzyzanowski, M., Schönbauer, H. and Wodak, R. (2005) 'Debating the European Constitution. On representations of Europe/EU in the press', *Journal of Language and Politics*, 4(2): 227–271.

ÖMV (2019) Demystifying Nord Stream 2: OMV's rationale for participating in the project, 13 May. www.omv.com/en/blog/190513-demystifying-nord-stream-2-omvs-rationale-for-participating-in-the-project (accessed 6 December 2019).

Olick, J. (2007) *The Politics of Regret: On collective memory and historical responsibility*, New York: Routledge.

Olick, J., Vinitzky-Seroussi, V. and Levy, D. (eds) (2011) *The Collective Memory Reader*, Oxford: Oxford University Press.

Onken, E. (2007) 'The Baltic States and Moscow's 9 May commemoration: analysing memory politics in Europe', *Europe-Asia Studies*, 59(1): 23–46.

Onuf, N. (2001) 'The politics of constructivism', in K. Fierke and K. E. Joergensen (eds) *Constructing International Relations: The next generation*, Armonk (NY): Sharpe, pp. 236–254.

Orla-Bukowska, A. (2006) 'New threads on an old loom. National memory and social identity in postwar and post-Communist Poland', in R. N. Lebow, W. Kansteiner and C. Fogu (eds) *The Politics of Memory in Post-war Europe*, Durham (NC) and London: Duke University Press, pp. 177–210.

Ozbay, F. and Aras, B. (2008) 'Polish-Russian relations: history, geography and geopolitics', *East European Quarterly*, 42(1): 27–42.

Pakier, M. and Stråth, B. (2010) 'Introduction: a European memory?', in M. Pakier and B. Stråth (eds) *A European Memory? Contested histories and politics of remembrance*, Oxford: Berghahn, pp. 1–20.

PAP (Polish Press Agency) (2017) 'PM Szydlo urges EU to "hasten steps" on Nord Stream 2', 20 October. www.pap.pl/en/news-/news,1132702,i-asked-eu-for-faster-action-on-nord-stream-2--pm-szydlo-in-brussels.html (accessed 6 December 2019).

Paul, A. (2010) *Katyn: Stalin's massacre and the triumph of truth*, DeKalb: Northern Illinois University Press.

Pech, L. (2011) 'The institutional development of the EU post-Lisbon: a case of plus ça change …?', *UCD Dublin European Institute Working Paper*, 11(5), Dublin: University College Dublin.

Peifer, D. (2016) 'Why Germany Won't Be Dropping Bombs on Syria, Iraq or Mali', *Orbis*, 60(2): 266–278.

Peterson, J. (2012) 'The EU as a global actor', in E. Bomberg, J. Peterson and R. Corbett (eds) *The European Union: How does it work?*, Oxford: Oxford University Press, pp. 203–223.

Pieper, C. (2012) 'Statements at the opening of the exhibition "Russen und Deutsche – 1000 Jahre Kunst, Geschichte und Kultur"'. www.auswaertiges-amt.de/DE/Infoservice/Presse/Reden/2012/120620-StM_P_Ausstellung_St_H_M.html (accessed 10 August 2016).

Pirani, S. (2012) 'Russo-Ukrainian gas wars and the call on transit governance', in C. Kuzmenko, A. Belyi, A. Goldthau and M. F. Keating (eds) *Dynamics of Energy Governance in Europe and Russia*, Basingstoke: Palgrave Macmillan, pp. 169–186.

Platts (2019) 'Russia to transit 65 Bcm of gas through Ukraine in 2020 under new deal: Gazprom', Platts, 21 December. www.spglobal.com/platts/en/market-insights/latest-news/natural-gas/122119-russia-to-transit-65-bcm-of-gas-through-ukraine-in-2020-under-new-deal-gazprom (accessed 17 January 2020).

Poe, M. (2003) 'A distant world: Russian relations with Europe before Peter the Great', in C. Whittaker (ed.), *Russia Engages the World, 1453–1825*, Cambridge (MA): Harvard University Press, pp. 2–23.

Poland's Ministry of Foreign Affairs (2012) 10th meeting of Polish-Russian Group for Difficult Matters, 17 December. www.mfa.gov.pl/en/news/10th_meeting_of_polish_russian_group_for_difficult_matters (accessed 11 August 2016).

Poland's Prime Minister Office (2016) Press release, 21 October. www.premier.gov.pl/en/news/news/prime-minister-beata-szydlo-discussion-opens-on-reform-and-modification-of-the-european.html (accessed 1 June 2019).

Poland's Prime Minister Office (2018) Meeting of Prime Minister Mateusz Morawiecki with the United States Secretary of State Rex Tillerson, 27 January. www.premier.gov.pl/en/news/news/meeting-of-prime-minister-mateusz-morawiecki-with-the-united-states-secretary-of-state-rex.html (accessed 1 June 2019).

Portela, C. (2019) The State of EU Sanctions on Russia, Euren Brief 1/2019. https://eeas.europa.eu/sites/eeas/files/euren_brief_no._1.pdf (accessed 5 December 2019).

Porter, B. (2000) *When Nationalism Began to Hate: Imagining modern politics in nineteenth century Poland*, Oxford: Oxford University Press.

Portnov, A. (2016) 'Bandera mythologies and their traps for Ukraine', *openDemocracy*, 22 June. www.opendemocracy.net/en/odr/bandera-mythologies-and-their-traps-for-ukraine/ (accessed 5 December 2019).

Posaner, J., Gurzu, A. and Tamma, P. (2019) 'Franco-German alliance survives Nord Stream 2 scare', *Politico*, 8 February. www.politico.eu/article/france-germany-alliance-survives-nord-stream-2-scare/ (accessed 6 December 2019).

Pouliot, V. (2008) 'The logic of practicality: a theory of practice of security communities', *International Organization*, 62(2): 257–288.

Powers, C. (1990) 'Czech-Polish-Hungarian Accord Urged: Europe: Havel proposes "spirit of solidarity" in aftermath of Soviet domination', *Los Angeles Times*, 26 January. http://articles.latimes.com/1990-01-26/news/mn-726_1_central-europe (accessed 17 July 2016).

Prizel, I. (1998) *National Identity and Foreign Policy: Nationalism and leadership in Poland, Russia and Ukraine*, Cambridge: Cambridge University Press.

Putin, V. (2007) 'Vladimir Putin's prepared remarks at 43rd Munich Conference on Security Policy', *Washington Post*, 12 February. www.washingtonpost.com/wp-dyn/content/article/2007/02/12/AR2007021200555.html (accessed 8 August 2016).

Putin, V. (2015) Remarks at the 70th session of the UN General Assembly, 28 September. http://en.kremlin.ru/events/president/news/50385 (accessed 13 June 2019).

Radio Poland (2018a) 'Planned Russia-Germany pipeline a "political project": senior EU official', 13 March. www.thenews.pl/1/10/Artykul/353727,Planned-RussiaGermany-pipeline-a-%E2%80%98political-project%E2%80%99-senior-EU-official (accessed 6 December 2019).

Radio Poland (2018b) 'Ukrainian nationalists plan protests against Polish anti-defamation law', 5 February. http://archiwum.thenews.pl/1/10/Artykul/347692 (accessed 12 December 2019).

Raivio, P. (2019) 'Nord Stream 2: The Russian gas pipeline splitting the European Union in two', *Baltic Rim Economies*, 29 May. https://sites.utu.fi/bre/nord-stream-2-the-russian-gas-pipeline-splitting-the-european-union-in-two/ (accessed 6 December 2019).

Ramani, S. (2019) 'Russia's Eye on Syrian Reconstruction' Carnegie Endowment, 31 January. https://carnegieendowment.org/sada/78261 (accessed 28 May 2019).

Ray, L. (2006) 'Mourning, melancholia and violence', in D. Bell (ed.) *Memory, Trauma and World Politics*, Basingstoke: Palgrave Macmillan, pp. 135–154.

Reeves, C. (2010) 'Reopening the wounds of history? The foreign policy of the "Fourth" Polish Republic', *Journal of Communist Studies and Transition Politics*, 26(4): 518–541.

Reeves, C. (2019) 'From Intervention to Retrenchment: Poland's Strategic Culture and the 2011 Libyan Campaign', *Europe-Asia Studies*, DOI:10.1080/09668136.2019.1627290.

Reichel, P. (2005) *Schwarz-Rot-Gold: Kleine Geschichte deutscher Nationalsymbole nach 1945*, Munich: C. H. Beck.

Reisigl, M. and Wodak, R. (2001) *Discourse and Discrimination*, London: Routledge.

Reuters (2013) 'Finland's Fennovoima signs reactor deal with Rosatom', 21 December. www.reuters.com/article/us-fennovoima-rosatom-idUSBRE9BK05G20131221 (accessed 25 August 2016).

Reuters (2016a) 'Duda says Nord Stream 2 pipeline undermines EU solidarity', 18 January. www.reuters.com/article/poland-energy-eu-nordstream/duda-says-nord-stream-2-pipeline-undermines-eu-solidarity-idUSL8N1521RZ (accessed 6 December 2019).

Reuters (2016b) 'ENI CEO says Nord Stream 2 would raise gas prices in Italy', 26 May. https://de.reuters.com/article/energy-nordstream-eu-idUKL5N18K4KG (accessed 6 December 2019).

Reuters (2017a) 'Poland not concerned about Yamal transit fees –Naimski', 20 June. https://af.reuters.com/article/commoditiesNews/idAFL8N1JH27B (accessed 6 December 2019).

Reuters (2017b) 'La France juge illicites les sanctions US contre la Russie', 26 July. https://fr.reuters.com/article/companyNews/idFRL5N1KH4LV (accessed 6 December 2019).

Reuters (2018) 'Russia-led Nord Stream 2 seeks new route to avoid Danish waters', 10 August. https://uk.reuters.com/article/uk-eu-gazprom-nordstream/nord-stream-2-seeks-alternative-route-to-avoid-danish-waters-idUKKBN1KV118 (accessed 6 December 2019).

Reuters (2019) 'U.S. sanctions against Nord Stream 2 wrong solution: Germany's Maas', 10 January. www.reuters.com/article/us-germany-russia-pipeline/us-sanctions-against-nord-stream-2-wrong-solution-germanys-maas-idUSKCN1P42IH (accessed 6 December 2019).

Reynolds, P. (2008) 'New Russian world order: the five principles', *BBC News*, 1 September. http://news.bbc.co.uk/1/hi/world/europe/7591610.stm (accessed 9 August 2016).

RFE/RL (Radio Free Europe/Radio Liberty) (2018) 'Polish PM Calls Nord Stream 2 "Weapon" Of Hybrid Warfare', 28 May. www.rferl.org/a/polish-pm-calls-nord-stream-2-weapon-of-hybrid-warfare/29255392.html (accessed 6 December 2019).

Rich, P. (ed.) (2010) *Crisis in the Caucasus: Russia, Georgia and the West*, London: Routledge.

Ringmar, E. (1996) *Identity, Interests and Action: A cultural explanation of Sweden's intervention in the Thirty Years War*, Cambridge: Cambridge University Press.

Ringmar, E. (1996a) 'Russia: territory and identity crises', *Nations and Nationalism*, 2(3): 453–460.

Risse, T. (2007) 'Deutsche Identität und Aussenpolitik', in S. Schmidt, G. Hellmann and R. Wolf (eds) *Handbuch zur deutschen Aussenpolitik*, Wiesbaden: Verlag für Sozial-wissenschaften, pp. 49–61.

Risse, T. (2010) *A Community of Europeans? Transnational identities and public spheres*, Ithaca (NY): Cornell University Press.

Risse-Kappen, T. (1996) 'Collective identity in a democratic community. The case of NATO', in P. Katzenstein (ed.) *The Culture of National Security: Norms and identity in world politics*, New York: Columbia University Press, pp. 357–399.

Roberts, S. and Moshes, A. (2016) 'The Eurasian Economic Union: a case of reproductive integration?', *Post-Soviet Affairs* 32(6): 542–565.

Robertson, G. (2013) 'Protesting Putinism. The election protests of 2011–2012 in broader perspective', *Problems of Post-Communism*, 60(2): 11–23.

Robinson, N. (2013) 'Russia's response to crisis: the paradox of success', *Europe-Asia Studies*, 65(3): 450–472.

Romanova, T. (2016) 'Sanctions and the Future of EU–Russian Economic Relations', *Europe-Asia Studies*, 68(4): 774–796.

Rousseau, D. (2007) 'Identity, power and threat perception. A cross-experimental study', *Journal of Conflict Resolution*, 51(5): 744–771.

Ruchniewicz, K. (2007) *'Noch ist Polen nicht Verloren': Das historische Denken der Polen*, Münster: LIT Verlag.

Ruggie, J. G. (1998) 'What makes the world hang together? Neo-utilitarianism and the social constructivist challenge', *International Organization*, 52(4): 855–885.

Rumelili, B. and Morozov, V. (2012) 'The external constitution of European identity: Russia and Turkey as Europe-makers', *Cooperation and Conflict*, 47(1): 28–48.

Rumelili, B. and Todd, J. (2018) 'Paradoxes of identity change: Integrating macro, meso, and micro research on identity in conflict processes', *Politics*, 38(1): 3–18.

Rupnik, J. (1994) 'Europe's new frontiers: Remapping Europe', *Daedalus*, 123(3): 91–114.

Sabrow, M. (2009) *Erinnerungsorte der DDR*, Munich: C.H. Beck.

Sadecki, A. and Kardas, S. (2014) 'Russian-Hungarian nuclear agreement', OSW Analysis, Warsaw: Centre for Eastern Studies.

Said, E. W. (1978) *Orientalism*, New York: Vintage Books.

Sakwa, R. (2008) 'New Cold War or twenty years' crisis? Russia and international politics', *International Affairs*, 84(2): 241–267.

Sakwa, R. (2012) 'Conspiracy narratives as a mode of engagement in international politics: the case of the 2008 Russo-Georgian war', *The Russian Review*, 71(4): 581–609.

Sakwa, R. (2015) *Frontline Ukraine: Crisis in the borderlands*, London: I.B. Tauris.

Sakwa, R. (2017) *Russia against the Rest: The Post-Cold War Crisis of World Order*, Cambridge: Cambridge University Press.

Samokhvalov, V. (2017) *Russian-European Relations in the Balkans and Black Sea Region: Great Power Identity and the Idea of Europe*, Cham: Palgrave.

Satjukow, S. (2008) *Besatzer: »Die Russen« in Deutschland 1945–1994*, Göttingen: Vandenhoeck and Ruprecht.

Schetyna, G. (2014a) Speech at the Sejm, 6 November. www.msz.gov.pl/en/news/minister_grzegorz_schetyna_on_polish_foreign_policy_priorities (accessed 23 August 2016).

Schetyna, G. (2015a) Speech at lunch with ambassadors of EU member states, 6 February. www.msz.gov.pl/resource/dde8b343-005e-4e9a-af17-80a5a69eae4f:JCR (accessed 23 August 2016).

Schetyna, G. (2015b) Speech at the Sejm, 23 April. http://msz.gov.pl/en/news/minister_grzegorz_schetyna_addresses_priorities_of_polish_diplomacy (accessed 23 August 2016).

Schetyna, G. (2015c) Speech at the presentation of the ECFR European Foreign Policy Scorecard, 9 February. www.msz.gov.pl/resource/14f87508-729d-45f0-b86b-a1dd910 00901:JCR (accessed 23 August 2016).

Schmitt, C. (1976) *The Concept of the Political*, New Brunswick (NJ): Rutgers University Press.

Schildt, A. (2003) 'Mending Fences: The Federal Republic of Germany and Eastern Europe', in E. Mühle (ed.) *Germany and the European East in the Twentieth Century*, Oxford and New York: Berg, pp. 153–179.

Schröder, H. (2012) 'Portraying the "strangest country": evolution of the German image of Russia', in R. Krumm, H. Schröder and S. Medvedev (eds) *Constructing Identities in Europe: German and Russian perspectives*, Baden-Baden: Nomos, pp. 97–113.

Schwirtz, M. (2010) 'Putin Marks Soviet Massacre of Polish Officers', *New York Times*, 7 April, www.nytimes.com/2010/04/08/world/europe/08putin.html?ref=europe (accessed 23 January 2017).

Sebenius, J. K. (1992) 'Challenging conventional explanations of international cooperation: negotiation analysis and the case of epistemic communities', *International Organization*, 46(1): 323–365.

Sengupta, K. (2018) 'Message of defiance against Russia from UK allies may yet dissolve into inaction', *The Independent*, 15 March. www.independent.co.uk/news/world/europe/russia-spy-poisoning-sergei-skripal-joint-statement-uk-us-trump-putin-germany-france-a8258191.html (accessed 6 December 2019).

Service, R. (2007) *Comrades! A history of world Communism*, Cambridge (MA): Harvard University Press.

Shekhovtsov, A. (2018) *Russia and the Western Far Right: Tango Noir*, Abingdon: Routledge.

Shevtsova, L. (2012) 'Russia under Putin: Titanic looking for its iceberg?', *Communist and Post-Communist Studies*, 45 (3–4): 209–216.

Shilliam, R. (2006) 'The "other" in classical political theory: re-contextualizing the cosmopolitan/communitarian debate', in B. Jahn (ed.) *Classical Theory in International Relations*, Cambridge: Cambridge University Press, pp. 207–232.

Shiraev, E. (2013) *Russian government and politics*, Basingstoke: Palgrave Macmillan.

Shuster, S. (2011) 'Russia–Poland tensions rise with crash report', *The Time*, 19 January, www.time.com/time/world/article/0,8599,2043130,00.html (accessed 19 July 2016).

Siddi, M. (2012) Russia and the forging of memory and identity in Europe. *Studia Diplomatica*, 65(4): 77–103.

Siddi, M. (2014) 'The abuse of history in the Ukrainian crisis', *Open Democracy*, 5 May, http://opendemocracy.net/can-europe-make-it/marco-siddi/abuse-of-history-in-ukrainian-crisis (accessed 10 May 2014).

Siddi, M. (2016a) 'German foreign policy towards Russia in the aftermath of the Ukraine crisis: a new Ostpolitik?', *Europe-Asia Studies*, 68(4): 665–677.

Siddi, M. (2016b) 'The EU's Energy Union: a sustainable path to energy security?', *The International Spectator*, 51(1): 131–144.

Siddi, M. (2017a) 'The Ukraine crisis and European memory politics of the Second World War', *European Politics and Society*, 18 (4): 465–479.

Siddi, M. (2017b) *National Identities and Foreign Policy in the European Union: The Russia Policy of Germany, Poland and Finland*, Colchester: ECPR Press.

Siddi, M. (2017c) 'Identities and Vulnerabilities: The Ukraine Crisis and the Securitisation of the EU-Russia Gas Trade', in K. Szulecki (ed.) *Energy Security in Europe*, Basingstoke: Palgrave Macmillan, pp. 251–273.

Siddi, M. (2017d) *National Identities and Foreign Policy in the European Union. The Russia Policy of Germany, Poland and Finland*, Colchester: ECPR Press.

Siddi, M. (2018a) *EU member states and Russia: National and European debates in an evolving international environment*. FIIA Report 53. Helsinki: Finnish Institute of International Affairs.

Siddi, M. (2018b) 'The Role of Power in EU–Russia Energy Relations: The Interplay between Markets and Geopolitics', *Europe-Asia Studies*, 70(10): 1552–1571.

Siddi, M. (2018c) 'An evolving Other: German national identity and constructions of Russia', *Politics*, 38(1): 35–50.

Siddi, M. (2018d) 'A Contested Hegemon? Germany's Leadership in EU Relations with Russia', *German Politics*, online first.

Siddi, M. (2018e) 'Italy's "Middle Power" Approach to Russia', *The International Spectator* 54(2): 123–138.

Siddi, M. (2018f) *Russia's evolving gas relationship with the European Union: Trade surges despite political crises*, FIIA Briefing Paper 246, Helsinki: Finnish Institute of International Affairs.

Siddi, M. (2019) 'The Mediterranean Dimension of West-Russia Security Relations', in A. Futter (ed.), *Threats to Euro-Atlantic Security: Views from the Young Generation Leaders Network*, Basingstoke: Palgrave Macmillan, pp. 165–177.

Siddi, M. and Gaweda, B. (2019) 'The national agents of transnational memory and their limits: the case of the Museum of the Second World War in Gdańsk', *Journal of Contemporary European Studies*, 27(2): 258–271.

Sidorenko, E. (2008) 'Which way to Poland? Re-emerging from Romantic unity', in M. Myant and T. Cox (eds) *Reinventing Poland: Economic and political transformation and evolving national identity*, London and New York: Routledge, pp. 109–127.

Sikorski, R. (2014a) Interview with Washington Post, 18 April. www.washingtonpost.com/opinions/talking-with-polands-foreign-minister-about-the-ukraine-crisis-and-russias-next-moves/2014/04/17/f1811e84-c5ad-11e3-bf7a-be01a9b69cf1_story.html?utm_term=.325294e861d1 (accessed 22 August 2016).

Sikorski, R. (2014b) Interview with CNN, 16 March. http://cnnpressroom.blogs.cnn.com/2014/03/16/radek-sikorski-russia-is-leaving-the-european-council-no-choice-on-monday/ (accessed 22 August 2016).

Sikorski, R. (2014c) Interview with Euractiv, 12 September. www.msz.gov.pl/en/news/they_wrote_about_us/minister_radoslaw_sikorski_discusses_european_union_and_ukraine_conflict_with_euractiv__12_september_2014;jsessionid=17517406CD51F0C34681CC15BD27E432.cmsap1p (accessed 22 August 2016).

Sikorski, R. (2014d) Interview with Spiegel, 10 March. www.spiegel.de/international/europe/polish-foreign-minister-discusses-weak-eu-position-in-ukraine-crisis-a-957812.html (accessed 22 August 2016).

Sikorski, R., Olex-Szczytowski, M. and Rostowski, J. (2007) 'Russian gas pipeline would be geopolitical disaster for EU', *Financial Times*, 28 May. www.ft.com/intl/cms/s/0/db259cf2-0cb7-11dc-a4dc-000b5df10621.html (accessed 7 August 2016).

Sipilä, J. (2015a) Speech during a parliamentary discussion on foreign policy, 20 October. www.eilen.fi/en/3372/?language=en (accessed 5 June 2019).

Sipilä, J. (2015b) Lecture at the Paasikivi Society, 3 September. www.eilen.fi/en/3367/?language=en (accessed 5 June 2019).

Sipilä, J. (2016a) 'Vastaus kirjalliseen kysymykseen Nord Stream 2 -hankkeen turvallisuuspoliittisen ulottuvuuden huomioimisesta', 28 September. www.eduskunta.fi/FI/vaski/Kysymys/Documents/KKV_426+2016.pdf (accessed 6 December 2019).

Sipilä, J. (2016b) Speech at the Helsinki Finnish Club EU, 18 October. www.eilen.fi/en/3642/?language=en (accessed 5 June 2019).

Sipilä, J. (2017) Welcoming remarks at the Conference on Supporting Syria and the Region, 24 January. www.eilen.fi/en/3653/?language=en (accessed 5 June 2019).

Sivan, E. and Winter, J. (1999) 'Setting the framework', in E. Sivan and J. Winter (eds) *War and Remembrance in the Twentieth Century*, Cambridge: Cambridge University Press, pp. 6–39.

Smilov (2018) 'Bulgaria torn between Russia and the West', *Deutsche Welle*, 31 May. www.dw.com/en/bulgaria-torn-between-russia-and-the-west/a-44027331 (accessed 6 December 2019).

Smith, A. (2014) 'Politicising energy security: Russia and the European Union', in S. Oxenstierna and V. P. Tynkkynen, *Russian Energy and Security up to 2030*. Abingdon: Routledge, pp. 77–94.

Smith, A. D. (1988) 'The myth of the "modern nation" and the myths of nations', *Ethnic and Racial Studies*, 11(1): 1–26.

Smith, A. D. (1991) *National identity*, Reno (NV): University of Nevada Press.

Smith, A. D. (1992) 'National identity and the idea of European unity', *International Affairs*, 68(1): 55–76.

Smith, A. D. (1994) 'The problem of national identity: ancient, medieval and modern?', *Ethnic and Racial Studies*, 17(3): 375–399.

Smith, A. D. (1996a) 'Opening statement: Nations and their pasts', *Nations and Nationalism*, 2(3): 358–365.

Smith, A. D. (1996b) 'Memory and modernity: reflections on Ernest Gellner's theory of nationalism', *Nations and Nationalism*, 2(3): 371–388.

Smith, A. D. (2004) 'History and national destiny: responses and clarifications', *Nations and Nationalism*, 10(1/2): 195–209.

Smith, A. D. (2011) 'National identity and vernacular mobilisation in Europe', *Nations and Nationalism*, 17(2): 223–256.

Smith, H. (2012) 'Russian foreign policy and energy: the case of the Nord Stream as pipeline', in P. Aalto (ed.) *Russia's Energy Policies: National, interregional and global levels*, Cheltenham: Edward Elgar, pp. 117–135.

Smyth, R., Sobolev, A. and Soboleva, I. (2013) 'A well-organised play. Symbolic politics and the effect of the pro-Putin rallies', *Problems of Post-Communism*, 60(2): 24–39.

Snyder, T. (2003) *The Reconstruction of Nations: Poland, Ukraine, Lithuania, Belarus, 1569–1999*, New Haven and London: Yale University Press.

Sobczyk, M. and Wasilewski, P. (2014) 'Poland's new premier signals shift in Ukraine policy', *The Wall Street Journal*, 1 October. www.wsj.com/articles/poland-to-update-foreign-policy-1412155939 (accessed 23 August 2016).

Socor, V. (2013) 'Russia plans massive expansion of Nord Stream pipelines', *Eurasia Daily Monitor*, 10(68).

Soini, T. (2015) Statement at the meeting of the Barents Euro-Arctic Council, 15 October. www.eilen.fi/en/3394/?language=en (accessed 26 August 2016).

Soini, T. (2016a) Speech at the Helsinki Finnish Club foreign policy, 20 January. www.eilen.fi/en/3432/?language=en (accessed 5 June 2019).

Soini, T. (2016b) Speech at Tampere Paasikivi Society, 19 October. www.eilen.fi/en/3523/?language=en (accessed 5 June 2019).

Soini, T. (2016c) Speech at the Finnish Institute of International Affairs, 28 January. www.eilen.fi/en/3436/?language=en (accessed 5 December 2019).

Soini, T. (2017a) Remarks at the Conference on Supporting Syrians and the Region, 24 January. www.eilen.fi/en/3667/?language=en (accessed 5 June 2019).

Soini, T. (2017b) Remarks at the High-level meeting on the Syria Crisis in New York, 21 September. www.eilen.fi/en/3704/?language=en (accessed 5 June 2019).

Soini, T. (2017c) Speech at Turkeys' Annual Ambassadors' Conference, 11 January. www.eilen.fi/en/3666/?language=en (accessed 5 June 2019).

Soini, T. (2018) Speech at at the Center for Strategic and International Studies, 7 February. www.eilen.fi/en/3797/?language=en (accessed 12 December 2019).

Soldatkin, V. (2018) 'Gazprom says gas transit via Ukraine to Europe may fall to 10–15 bcm per year', *Reuters*, 10 April. www.reuters.com/article/us-russia-ukraine-gas/gazprom-says-gas-transit-via-ukraine-to-europe-may-fall-to-10-15-bcm-per-year-idUSKBN1HH2HL (accessed 6 December 2019).

Spanger, H. (2011) 'Die deutsche Russlandpolitik', in T. Jäger, A. Höse and K. Oppermann (eds) *Deutsche Außenpolitik*, Wiesbaden: Verlag für Sozialwissenschaften, pp. 648–672.

Spiegel Online (2008) 'Merkel redet Medwedew ins Gewissen', 15 August 2008. www.spiegel.de/politik/ausland/georgien-krise-merkel-redet-medwedew-ins-gewissen-a-572360.html (accessed 8 August 2016).

Spohn, W. (2005) 'National identities and collective memory in an enlarged Europe', in W. Spohn and K. Eder (eds) *Collective Memory and European identity*, Aldershot: Ashgate, pp. 1–14.

Standard Eurobarometer 83 (2015), Tables of Results, QD1.1 and QD4, pp. T112 and T123. http://ec.europa.eu/public_opinion/archives/eb/eb83/eb83_anx_en.pdf (accessed 17 July 2016).

Stauter-Halsted, K. (2001) *The Nation in the Village: The genesis of peasant national identity in Austrian Poland 1848–1914*, Ithaca (NY): Cornell University Press.

Steinmeier, F. W. (2007) 'Verflechtung und Integration: Die neue Phase der Ostpolitik der EU', *Internationale Politik*, 1 March. https://zeitschrift-ip.dgap.org/de/ip-die-zeitschrift/archiv/jahrgang-2007/maerz/verflechtung-und-integration (accessed 6 December 2019).

Steinmeier, F. W. (2014a) Speech at the German-Russian Forum, 19 March. www.auswaertiges-amt.de/EN/Infoservice/Presse/Reden/2014/140319-BM_dtrus-Forum.html (accessed 18 August 2016).

Steinmeier, F. W. (2014b) Frankfurter Allgemeine Zeitung, 6 May. www.auswaertiges-amt.de/EN/Infoservice/Presse/Interview/2014/140506-BM_UKR_FAZ.html (accessed 18 August 2016).

Steinmeier, F. W. (2014c) Speech at the Bundestag, 7 May. www.auswaertiges-amt.de/EN/Infoservice/Presse/Reden/2014/140507-BM_BT_Ukraine.html (accessed 18 August 2016).

Steinmeier, F. W. (2014d) Interview with Frankfurter Allgemeine Zeitung, 30 May. www.auswaertiges-amt.de/EN/Infoservice/Presse/Interview/2014/140530-BM_FAZ.html (accessed 18 August 2016).

Steinmeier, F. W. (2014e) Interview with Rzeczpospolita, 22 July. www.auswaertiges-amt.de/EN/Infoservice/Presse/Interview/2014/140722-BM_Rzesczpospolita.html (accessed 18 August 2016).

Steinmeier, F. W. (2014f) Interview with Deutschlandfunk, 27 July. www.auswaertiges-amt.de/EN/Infoservice/Presse/Interview/2014/140727_BM_DLF.html (accessed 18 August 2016).

Steinmeier, F. W. (2014g) Interview with Bild, 26 March. www.auswaertiges-amt.de/EN/Infoservice/Presse/Interview/2014/140326-BM_Bild.html (accessed 18 August 2016).

Steinmeier, F. W. (2014h) Interview with Spiegel, 28 July. www.auswaertiges-amt.de/EN/Infoservice/Presse/Interview/2014/140728-BM_Spiegel.html (accessed 18 August 2016).

Steinmeier, F. W. (2015a) Interview with Neue Osnabrücker Zeitung, 4 June. www.auswaertiges-amt.de/EN/Infoservice/Presse/Interview/2015/150604_NOZ.html (accessed 19 August 2016).

Steinmeier, F. W. (2015b) Interview with Handelsblatt, 5 March. www.auswaertiges-amt.de/EN/Infoservice/Presse/Interview/2015/150305-BM_Hbl.html (accessed 19 August 2016).

Steinmeier, F. W. (2015c) Speech at Volgograd to commemorate the end of the Second World War, 7 May. www.auswaertiges-amt.de/EN/Infoservice/Presse/Reden/2015/150507_Wolgograd.html (accessed 19 August 2016).

Steinmeier, F. W. (2015d) Interview with Neue Westfälische, 4 November. www.auswaertiges-amt.de/EN/Infoservice/Presse/Interview/2015/151104_NeueWestfaelische.html (accessed 19 August 2016).

Steinmeier, F. W. (2015e) Interview with Bild am Sonntag, 22 November. www.auswaertiges-amt.de/EN/Infoservice/Presse/Interview/2015/151122_BamS.html (accessed 19 August 2016).

Steinmeier, F. W. (2016a) Address at the German-Russian Forum/Potsdam Encounters, 30 May. www.auswaertiges-amt.de/en/newsroom/news/160530-bm-deu-rus-forum/280962 (accessed 28 May 2019).

Steinmeier, F. W. (2016b) Speech at the 12th Petersberg Talks, 8 October. www.auswaertiges-amt.de/en/newsroom/news/161008-petersberg/284204 (accessed 29 May 2019).

Steinmeier, F. W. (2016c) Speech on 'Crisis diplomacy in full swing – prospects for the future of Syria and the Middle East', 22 November. www.auswaertiges-amt.de/en/newsroom/news/161122-bm-krisendiplomatie/285560 (accessed 29 May 2019).

Steinmeier, F. W. (2016d) Interview with the Russian news agency Interfax, 23 March. www.auswaertiges-amt.de/en/newsroom/news/-/279458 (accessed 6 December 2019).

Steinmeier, F. W. (2016e) Interview, 31 August. www.auswaertiges-amt.de/en/newsroom/news/160831-bm-rnd/283030 (accessed 6 December 2019).

Stepanova, E. (2018a) 'Russia and Conflicts in the Middle East: Regionalisation and Implications for the West', *The International Spectator*, 53(4): 35–57.

Stepanova, E. (2018b) 'Russia's Approach to the Conflict in Libya, the East-West Dimension and the Role of the OSCE', in A. Dessi and E. Greco (eds), *Search for Stability in Libya: OSCE's Role between Internal Obstacles and External Challenges*, Roma: Edizioni Nuova Cultura, pp. 89–111.

Stern, J. (2006) 'Natural gas security problems in Europe: the Russian–Ukrainian crisis of 2006', *Asia-Pacific Review*, 13(1): pp. 32–59.

Stewart, S. (2012) 'Coherence in EU policy towards Russia: identities and interests', in R. Krumm, H. Schröder and S. Medvedev (eds) *Constructing Identities in Europe: German and Russian perspectives*, Baden-Baden: Nomos, pp. 185–204.

Stubb, A. (2014) Speech at the Körber-Stiftung in Berlin, 29 September. www.eilen.fi/en/3247/?language=en (accessed 25 August 2016).

Suny, R. G. (1994) *The Making of the Georgian Nation*, Bloomington: Indiana University Press.

Sus, M. (2018) 'Poland: leading critic or marginalized hawk?', in Siddi, M. (ed.) *EU Member States and Russia: National and European Debates in an Evolving International Environment*, FIIA Report 53, Helsinki: Finnish Institute of International Affairs, pp. 77–92.

Szabo, E. M. (2011) 'Background vocals: what role for the rotating presidency in the EU's external relations post-Lisbon?', *EU Diplomacy Papers*, 5/2011, Bruges: College of Europe.

Szydlo, B. (2017) Press conference with the Church aid initiative for Syria, 1 March. www.premier.gov.pl/en/news/news/prime-minister-beata-szydlo-the-polish-government-becomes-involved-in-the-church-aid.html (accessed 1 June 2019).

Szymanski, K. (2016) 'Russia's gas pipeline threatens European unity', *Financial Times*, 21 October. www.ft.com/content/25a17928-96c3-11e6-a1dc-bdf38d484582 (accessed 6 December 2019).

Telegraph (2015) 'Minsk agreement on Ukraine crisis: text in full', 12 February. www. telegraph.co.uk/news/worldnews/europe/ukraine/11408266/Minsk-agreement-on-Ukraine-crisis-text-in-full.html (accessed 15 August 2016).

Thumann, M. (1997) 'Vom Einmarsch in der Tschechoslowakei bis zum Moskauer Vertrag. Das Russlandbild westdeutscher Zeitschriften 1968–1970', in K. Meyer (ed.) *Deutsch, Deutschbalten und Russen: Studien zu ihren gegenseitigen Bildern und Beziehungen*, Lüneburg: Nordostdeutsches Kulturwerk, pp. 201–227.

Tiilikainen, T. (1998) *Europe and Finland: Defining the political identity of Finland in Western Europe*, Aldershot: Ashgate.

Tiilikainen, T. (2006) 'Finland – An EU Member with a small state identity', *Journal of European Integration*, 28(1): 73–87.

Timmins, G. (2011) 'German–Russian bilateral relations and EU policy on Russia: between normalisation and the "multilateral reflex"', *Journal of Contemporary European Studies*, 19(2): 189–199.

Torbakov, I. (2011) 'History, memory and national identity: understanding the politics of history and memory wars in post-Soviet lands', *Demokratizatsiya*, 19(3): 209–232.

Torfing, J. (2005) 'Discourse theory: achievements, arguments and challenges', in D. Howarth and J. Torfing (eds) *Discourse Theory in European politics*, Basingstoke: Palgrave Macmillan, pp. 1–32.

Trenin, D. (2018) *What is Russia up to in the Middle East?* Cambridge: Polity Press.

Troebst, S. (2008) '1945 – Ein gesamt-europäischer Erinnerungsort?', *Osteuropa*, 6: 67–76.

Troebst, S. (2010) 'Halecki revisited: Europe's conflicting cultures of remembrance', in M. Pakier and B. Stråth (eds) *A European Memory? Contested histories and politics of remembrance*, Oxford: Berghahn, pp. 56–63.

Tsygankov, A. (2008) 'Self and Other in International Relations theory: learning from Russian civilizational debates', *International Studies Review*, 10(4): 762–775.

Tsygankov, A. (2009) *Russophobia: Anti-Russian lobby and American foreign policy*, Basingstoke: Palgrave Macmillan.

Tuomioja, E. (2014a) Speech at the meeting of the Council of Europe Foreign Ministers, 6 May. www.eilen.fi/en/3211/?language=en (accessed 25 August 2016).

Tuomioja, E. (2014b) Opening words at Helsinki Policy Forum, 2 June. http://formin.finland.fi/public/default.aspx?contentid=307277&contentlan=2&culture=e (accessed 25 August 2016).

Tuomioja, E. (2014c) Speech at the Diplomatic Academy of Vienna, 27 May. http://formin.finland.fi/public/default.aspx?contentid=307075&contentlan=2&culture=en-US (accessed 25 August 2016).

Tuomioja, E. (2014d) Speech at the Fifth Annual Forum of the EU Strategy for the Baltic Sea Region, 4 June. www.eilen.fi/en/3206/?language=en (accessed 26 August 2016).

Tuomioja, E. (2014e) Speech at the final seminar of the EU Arctic Information Centre, 11 September. www.eilen.fi/en/3280/?language=en (accessed 26 August 2016).

Tuomioja, E. (2015) Speech at a seminar on the Arctic in Helsinki, 18 March. www.eilen. fi/en/3329/?language=en (accessed 26 August 2016).

Tusk, D. (2014a) Speech at Sejm, 5 March. www.premier.gov.pl/en/news/news/prime-minister-tusk-at-the-sejm-on-ukraine.html (accessed 22 August 2016).

Tusk, D. (2014b) Statements after the European Council, 6 March. www.premier.gov.pl/en/news/news/european-council-in-brussels-discussion-results-in-line-with-polands-postulates.html (accessed 22 August 2016).

Tusk, D. (2014c) Press conference, 4 March. www.premier.gov.pl/en/news/news/donald-tusk-on-ukraine-our-strategy-does-bring-results.html (accessed 22 August 2016).

Tusk, D. (2014d) 'A united Europe can end Russia's energy stranglehold', *Financial Times*, 21 April. www.ft.com/cms/s/0/91508464-c661-11e3-ba0e-00144feabdc0.html (accessed 22 August 2016).

Tusk, D. (2014e) Press conference, 25 July. www.premier.gov.pl/en/news/news/the-prime-minister-on-european-union-sanctions-against-russia-weaker-sanctions-of-the. html (accessed 22 August 2016).

Uhari, M. (2018) 'Presidentti kaasuputkesta Ylellä: "Putki ei kulje Suomen alueella" – Tutkija: Suomi ei halua laittaa näppejään väliin', 28 April. www.aamulehti.fi/uutiset/presidentti-kaasuputkesta-ylella-putki-ei-kulje-suomen-alueella-tutkija-suomi-ei-halua-laittaa-nappejaan-valiin-200909751 (accessed 6 December 2019).

Vajda, M. (1989) 'Who excluded Russia from Europe?', in G. Schoepflin and N. Wood (eds) *In Search of Central Europe*, Totowa (NJ): Barnes and Noble, pp. 168–182.

Van Dijk, T. (2002) 'Multidisciplinary CDA: a plea for diversity', in R. Wodak and M. Meyer (eds) *Methods of Critical Discourse Analysis*, London: Sage, pp. 95–120.

Vandecasteele, B., Bossuyt, F. and Orbie, J. (2013) 'Unpacking the influence of the Council Presidency on European Union external policies: the Polish Council Presidency and the Eastern Partnership', *European Integration online Papers*, 17(1): 1–28.

Vehviläinen, O. (2002) *Finland in the Second World War: Between Germany and Russia*, Basingstoke: Palgrave Macmillan.

Vihavainen, T. (2006) 'Does history play a role in Finnish-Russian relations?', in H. Smith (ed.) *The two-level Game: Russia's relations with Great Britain, Finland and the European Union*, Helsinki: Aleksanteri Institute, pp. 27–48.

Virkki, P. (2017) 'Juha Sipilä MTV:llä: Kaasuputki ei ole ulkopoliittinen asia – "menee ihan muualle kuin Suomeen"', *Verkkouutiset*, 14 October. www.verkkouutiset.fi/juha-sipila-mtvlla-kaasuputki-ei-ole-ulkopoliittinen-asia-menee-ihan-muualle-kuin-suomeen/ (accessed 6 December 2019).

Volkhonskiy, M. (2009) 'Medvedev-Sarkozy's six points: the diplomatic aspect of the South Ossetian settlement', *Central Asia and the Caucasus*, 4–5(58–59): 200–212.

Volkov, D. (2012) 'The protesters and the public', *Journal of Democracy*, 23(3): 55–62.

Von Haxthausen, A. (1972) *Studies on the Interior of Russia*, Chicago: University of Chicago Press.

Waltz, K. (1979) *Theory of International Politics*, Reading: McGraw-Hill.

Waever, O. (1992) 'Nordic nostalgia: Northern Europe after the Cold War', *International Affairs*, 68(1): 77–102.

Waever, O. (2002) 'Identity, communities and foreign policy: discourse analysis as foreign policy theory', in O. Waever and L. Hansen (eds) *European Integration and National Identity: The challenge of the Nordic states*, London: Routledge, pp. 20–49.

Waever, O. (2005) 'European integration and security: analysing French and German discourses on state, nation and Europe', in D. Howarth and J. Torfing (eds) *Discourse Theory in European Politics*, Basingstoke: Palgrave Macmillan, pp. 33–67.

Wahlbeck, Ö. (2018) 'To Share or Not to Share Responsibility? Finnish Refugee Policy and the Hesitant Support for a Common European Asylum System', *Journal of Immigrant and Refugee Studies*, 1–18, doi:10.1080/15562948.2018.1468048.

Wasik, Z. and Foy, H. (2015) 'Poland favours Christian refugees from Syria', *Financial Times*, 21 August. www.ft.com/content/6edfdd30-472a-11e5-b3b2-1672f710807b (accessed 31 May 2019).

Waszczykowski, W. (2015a) Interview with the Associated Press, 12 December. www.msz.gov.pl/en/news/ap_interview__polish_minister__russia_sanctions_must_remain__1 (accessed 31 May 2019).

Waszczykowski, W. (2015b) Interview with the Berliner Zeitung and Frankfurter Rundschau, 15 December 2015. www.msz.gov.pl/en/news/minister_witold_waszczykowski_in_an_interview_with_the_berliner_zeitung_and_frankfurter_rundschau (accessed 31 May 2019).

Waszczykowski, W. (2016a) Op-ed for the Frankfurt Allgemeine Zeitung 'The today and tomorrow of European integration: Warsaw's perspective', 4 April 2016. https://mfa.gov.pl/en/news/minister_witold_waszczykowski_for_faz___the_today_and_tomorrow_of_european_integration__warsaw_s_perspective_(accessed 6 December 2019).

Waszczykowski, W. (2016b) Interview with Die Welt, 28 May. www.msz.gov.pl/en/news/the_eu_should_not_aspire_to_become_a_superstate__minister_witold_waszczykowski_speaks_to_die_welt (accessed 6 December 2019).

Waszczykowski, W. (2016c) Interview with RaiNews24, 8 March. www.msz.gov.pl/en/news/they_wrote_about_us/minister_witold_waszczykowski_interviewed_by_rai_news_24?channel=www (accessed 1 June 2019).

Waszczykowski, W. (2016d) Statements at TVN24's 'Jeden na jeden' programme, 4 October. www.msz.gov.pl/en/news/minister_witold_waszczykowski_on_tvn24_s__jeden_na_jeden__programme (accessed 1 June 2019).

Waszczykowski, W. (2016e) Statements at Radio Wnet, 15 December. www.msz.gov.pl/en/news/mfa_hosts_special_edition_of_radio_wnet_s_morning_programme (accessed 1 June 2019).

Waszczykowski, W. (2016f) Remarks before the Munich Security Conference, 13 February. www.msz.gov.pl/en/news/minister_witold_waszczykowski_on_the_munich_security_conference__nato_will_be_the_main_focus_of_my_talks (accessed 31 May 2019).

Waszczykowski, W. (2016g) Press conference in Washington, 17 February. www.msz.gov.pl/en/foreign_policy/other_continents/north_america/minister_witold_waszczykowski_in_washington__the_main_goal_of_my_visit_are_efforts_to_strengthen_poland_s_security_and_that_of_nato_s_entire_eastern_flank_ (accessed 1 June 2019).

Waszczykowski, W. (2017a) Interview with Polish Radio Three, 6 April. www.msz.gov.pl/en/news/minister_witold_waszczykowski_on_polish_radio_three_s_salon_polityczny_programme (accessed 31 May 2019).

Waszczykowski, W. (2017b) Information of the Minister of Foreign Affairs on Polish foreign policy tasks in 2017. www.msz.gov.pl/en/ministry/minister/archive_speeches/information_of_the_minister_of_foreign_affairs_on_polish_foreign_policy_tasks_in_2017 (accessed 6 December 2019).

Watanabe, L. (2019) 'Russia's Renaissance in the Arab World', in J. Thompson and O. Thränert (eds), *Strategic Trends 2019: Key Developments in Global Affairs*, Zurich: Centre for Security Studies, pp. 65–82.

Webber, M. (2009) 'Russia and the European security governance debate', in J. Gower and G. Timmins (eds) *Russia and Europe in the Twenty-first Century: An uneasy partnership*, London: Anthem Press, pp. 267–288.

Weidenfeld, W. (2001) 'Geschichte und Identität', in K. Korte and W. Weidenfeld (eds) *Deutschland-Trendbuch: Fakten und Orientierungen*, Opladen: Leske and Budrich, pp. 29–58.

Weitz, R. (2009) 'Russia and NATO maneuver over Georgia', *Central Asia-Caucasus Institute Analyst*, 11(9): 6–8.

Wendt, A. (1992) 'Anarchy is what states make of it: the social construction of power politics', *International Organization*, 46(2): 391–425.

Wendt, A. (1994) 'Collective identity formation and the international state', *American Political Science Review*, 88(2): 384–396.

Wendt, A. (1995) 'Constructing international politics', *International Security*, 20(1): 71–81.

Wendt, A. (1999) *Social Theory of International Politics*, Cambridge: Cambridge University Press.

Westphal, K. (2008) 'Germany and the EU-Russia energy dialogue', in P. Aalto (ed.) *The EU-Russian Energy Dialogue*, Aldershot: Ashgate, pp. 93–118.

Westphal, K. (2011) 'The Energy Charter Treaty revisited', SWP Comment, 8, Berlin: Stiftung Wissenschaft und Politik.

Whitman, R. and Wolff, S. (2010) 'The EU as a conflict manager? The case of Georgia and its implications', *International Affairs*, 86(1): 1–21.

Wilcox, M. (2011) 'Russia and the treaty on conventional armed forces in Europe (CFE Treaty): a paradigm change?', *The Journal of Slavic Military Studies*, 24(4): 567–581.

Wilds, K. (2000) 'Identity creation and the culture of contrition: recasting "normality" in the Berlin Republic', *German Politics*, 9(1): 83–102.

Wilkinson, C. (2014) 'Putting "traditional values" into practice: the rise and contestation of anti-homopropaganda laws in Russia', *Journal of Human Rights*, 13(3): 363–379.

Wilson, A. (2014) *Ukraine Crisis: What it means for the West*, New Haven and London: Yale University Press.

Wilson, K. and Dussen, J. (ed.) (1995) *The History of the Idea of Europe*, London: Routledge.

Winkler, H. A. (1996) 'Rebuilding of a nation: the Germans before and after unification', in M. Mertes, S. Muller and H. A. Winkler (eds) *In search of Germany*, New Brunswick and London: Transaction Publishers.

Winter, J. (2006) 'Notes on the memory boom. War, remembrance and the uses of the past', in D. Bell (ed.) *Memory, Trauma and World Politics*, Basingstoke: Palgrave Macmillan, pp. 54–73.

Wittlinger, R. (2008) 'The Merkel government's politics of the past', *German Politics and Society*, 26(4): 9–27.

Wittlinger, R. (2011) *German National Identity in the Twenty-first Century: A different republic after all?*, Basingstoke: Palgrave Macmillan.

Wodak, R. (1996) *Disorder of discourses*, London and New York: Longman.

Wodak, R. (2002a) 'What CDA is about – a summary of its history, important concepts and its developments', in R. Wodak and M. Meyer (eds) *Methods of Critical Discourse Analysis*, London: Sage, pp. 1–13.

Wodak, R. (2002b) 'The discourse-historical approach', in R. Wodak and M. Meyer (eds) *Methods of Critical Discourse Analysis*, London: Sage, pp. 63–94.

Wodak, R. (2009) *The Discourse of Politics in Action: Politics as usual*, Basingstoke: Palgrave Macmillan.

WTO (2011) 'Ministerial Conference approves Russia's WTO membership', 16 December. www.wto.org/english/news_e/news11_e/acc_rus_16dec11_e.htm (accessed 11 August 2016).

WTO (2012) 'WTO membership rises to 157 with the entry of Russia and Vanuatu', 22 August. www.wto.org/english/news_e/pres12_e/pr671_e.htm (accessed 11 August 2016).

Yle (2015a) 'Finnish exports to Russia down more than 35 percent', 25 August. http://yle.fi/uutiset/finnish_exports_to_russia_down_more_than_35_percent/8251837 (accessed 25 August 2016).

Yle (2015b) 'More Finns on the fence over NATO membership', 26 October. http://yle.fi/uutiset/more_finns_on_the_fence_over_nato_membership/8408782 (accessed 25 August 2016).

Yle (2016) 'Poll: Finnish support for Nato membership still low', 1 December. https://yle.fi/uutiset/osasto/news/poll_finnish_support_for_nato_membership_still_low/9329652 (accessed on 20 November 2019).

Yle (2018a) Fortum wraps up 3.7bn-euro purchase of German power firm Uniper, 26 June. https://yle.fi/uutiset/osasto/news/fortum_wraps_up_37bn-euro_purchase_of_german_power_firm_uniper/10275079 (accessed 6 December).

Yle (2018b) Finland grants final permit for new Russia-Germany gas pipeline, but project remains uncertain, 16 April. https://yle.fi/uutiset/osasto/news/finland_grants_final_permit_for_new_russia-germany_gas_pipeline_but_project_remains_uncertain/10162191 (accessed 6 December 2019).

Yle (2019) Niinistö talks Syria, Nordstream ahead of Kultaranta summit, 16 June. https://yle.fi/uutiset/osasto/news/niinisto_talks_syria_nordstream_ahead_of_kultaranta_summit/10834732 (accessed 6 December 2019).

Youngs, R. (2017) *Europe's Eastern Crisis: The Geopolitics of Asymmetry*, Cambridge: Cambridge University Press.

Zagorski, A. (2009) 'The Russian proposal for a Treaty on European Security: from the Medvedev initiative to the Corfu Process', in *OSCE Yearbook 2009*, Hamburg: Institute for Peace Research and Security Policy, pp. 43–59.

Zarycki, T. (2004) 'Uses of Russia: the role of Russia in the modern Polish national identity', *East European Politics and Societies*, 18(4): 595–627.

Zarycki, T. (2011) 'On the contemporary Polish perception of Russian intelligentsia', in I. Novikova (ed.) *Europe-Russia: Contexts, discourses, images*, Rīga: Lu Dzsc – Levira, University of Latvia, pp. 130–141.

Zehfuss, M. (2001) 'Constructivism and identity', *European Journal of International Relations*, 7(3): 315–348.

Zehfuss, M. (2006) 'Remembering to forget, forgetting to remember', in D. Bell (ed.) *Memory, Trauma and World Politics*, Basingstoke: Palgrave Macmillan, pp. 213–230.

Zito, A. R. (2001) 'Epistemic communities, collective entrepreneurship and European integration', *Journal of European Public Policy*, 8(4): 585–603.

Zürcher, C. (2007) *The post-Soviet Wars: Rebellion, ethnic conflicts and nationhood in the Caucasus*, New York: New York University Press.

Zvyagelskaya, I. (2016) 'Russia, the New Protagonist in the Middle East', in A. Ferrari (ed.) *Putin's Russia: Really Back?* Milan: Ledizioni, pp. 73–91.

Żychlińska, M. and Fontana, E. (2016) 'Museal Games and Emotional Truths: Creating Polish National Identity at the Warsaw Rising Museum', *East European Politics, Societies and Cultures* 30(2): 235–269.

Zygar, M. (2016) *All the Kremlin's Men: Inside the Court of Vladimir Putin*, New York: Public Affairs.

Index

Page numbers in **bold** denote tables, those in *italics* denote figures.

Adenauer, K. 13, 38
Aleppo, bombing of 107, 111, 114
Anderson, B. 5–7
antimilitaristic national identity 20
anti-Russian discourses 14, 45–46, 68
anti-Soviet discourse 51
Arab Spring 1, 114; Russian attitude to
    103; to Syrian crisis 101–104; Western
    reaction to 102
Arctic Council 74, 78
argumentation 27, 75, 77
Association Agreement (AA) 57
Astana process 104, 108
Austria 29, 40, 82, 84, 87, 90, 103
authoritarian 10–11, 13–14, 36, 39, 52–53,
    74, 102, 114, 121

Baltic Sea 45, 59, 78–79, 82–83, 94
Baltic States 2, 14, 83, 85–86, 92
Barnett, M 19, 21
Belarus 41–42, 57, 110
belonging 17, 52; collective belief in 6;
    mutual recognition of 6; national 40, 46;
    neutrality 48; sense of 35; statement of
    50, 76
Berger, T. 20
bilateralism 4
Bjola, C. 20
Blaszczak, M. 109
Bolshevik revolution 12, 37–38, 53
Brandt, W. 38–39, 64, 66, 88, 122
Bush, G.W. 56–57

Campbell, D. 19–20
Chechnya 39
Christian Democratic Union 88

Civic Platform discourses in 2015 68,
    70–72, 91
civilian powers 36–37, 105
clash of civilisations 20
Cold War 13–14, 48–49, 52
collective memories 7–8, 15; inherent
    ambiguity of 9; national identity
    and 5–8
collective security 74
commercial competitiveness 83–84
communication 52, 60, 68, 71;
    fundamental role in 25
communism 24
community with shared beliefs 7–8
Conference on Security and Co-operation
    in Europe 48
conflict of interests 90
constructivist research, identity and foreign
    policy in 19–22
constructivist scholars 5
cooperative security 75, 80, 84
Crimea 32, 58; annexation of 1, 46, 56, 58,
    60–61, 63, 70, 76, 78; Russian actions in
    58; Russia's occupation of 69
critical discourse analysis 4, 25, 32, 121
crony capitalism 39
Cuban missile crisis 21
cultural heritage 7–8, 46
cultural identity 13, 46
The Culture of National Security
    (Katzenstein) 20
Czaputowicz, J. 73, 93, 111

decision makers 18, 21, 23, 31, 119–120
de Custine, A. 37
democracy 3, 34–37, 52
despotism 44

DHA *see* discourse-historical
    analysis (DHA)
discourse-historical analysis (DHA) 4, 15,
    17, 24–27
discourse-historical approach 25, 32, 121
discourses *see also specific countries*;
    analysis 4, 25–26, 30, 32, 34; contextual
    and historicist view of 25; development
    of 25; dominant 18, 23, 26–27, 41,
    53, 79, 121
discursive practices 24–25
discursive relationship 23–24
discursive strategies 27, 32, 66
dominant discourses 18, 23, 26–27, 41,
    53, 79, 121
dominant identity discourses 18, 21, 34–35
dominant media discourses 23
Donbass conflict 61–63, 65–67
Duda, A. 73, 92–94
Duma election 57

East-Central European narratives 28
East Germany 29, 106; socialism in 39
East–West conflict 48
East–West continuum 49
EEU *see* Eurasian Economic Union (EEU)
egalitarian social democracy 48
Empire of the Czar (de Custine) 37
energy policy 91; discourse 93
energy security 86
Energy Union initiative 83
epistemic communities 31
ethno-symbolists 7
EU *see* European Union (EU)
Eurasian Economic Union (EEU) 12, 57
European Council 58, 87, 104; summit of
    October 2016 111
European Council summits 95
European identity 2–3, 11; concept of 3;
    liminal case of 22; politics 11
Europeanisation 2
European Union (EU) 3, 29, 70, 82, 118;
    double-track policy of sanctions 65;
    energy policy 87; foreign policy 30;
    founding values 3; Nordic members of
    85; Nord Stream 2 project 82–87;
    Northern Dimension policy 74; policy
    debates in 87; policy of sanctions against
    Russia 60; regulatory framework 86; and
    Russia energy trade 1–2; and Russia gas
    trade 83; sectoral sanctions 65
Europe/European 11, 22; civilisation 12;
    discourse 2–3, 128–129; energy market
    90; energy policy 87, 90; energy

security 88–89; foreign policy 3, 17; gas
    demand 83–84; interests 86; Ostpolitik
    88; refugee crisis 59; security system 1,
    4; solidarity 70
Europe/European Commission 83
Europe's security system 75
EU–Russia relations 4, 57, 59, 61,
    114–115, 121
Exclusive Economic Zones 85

Finland/Finnish 29, 94, 118; diplomacy
    in 75, 115; dominant post-war
    discourses 47; economics and
    environment trump security concerns
    94–96; epistemic community 94–95;
    ethnonationalism 47, 50; Exclusive
    Economic Zone 94; foreign policy 48,
    51, 74; humanitarian consequences
    111–112; identities 121–123;
    discourses **54**; economic partner and
    security deficit 50–52; historic
    construction of 46–50; national
    identity 46; Russia's role in 25; Nord
    Stream 2 dispute 96–98; Others for 24;
    perceptions 47, 51; policy of neutrality
    48; political autonomy 123; political
    discourses 47; political identity 49–50;
    political marginality 50; pragmatic
    approach to Moscow 77; pragmatism
    and isolation of Ukraine crisis 76–79;
    relations with Russia 112; security
    74–75; self-image 47, 49; 'shielding'
    of Arctic cooperation 78
Finns Party 112
foreign policy: analysis, social
    constructivist approach to 120–121; in
    constructivist research 19–22;
    discourses 3–5, 23–29; discursive
    relationship 23–24; formulation of
    20–21, 25, 30; makers 120; narratives
    24, 31; preferences, formulation of 18;
    Wendtian conceptualisation of 22
France 2, 11, 13, 24, 28–29, 38, 42, 64,
    67–68, 84, 87, 104–107
Franco-German relations 11
Free Syrian Army (FSA) 103, 107–108
Friedrich, J. 107
FSA *see* Free Syrian Army (FSA)

Gabriel, S. 66, 89–90
Gaddafi, M. 102
GDR *see* German Democratic
    Republic (GDR)
Gellner, E. 5–7

German Democratic Republic (GDR)
35–37
German/Germany 2, 29, 40, 105, 118;
coalition government 88; commercial
project in line with European rules
87–91; compensation claims 36;
dictatorship 35; diplomacy 65;
discourses on Ukraine crisis 66;
dominant discourses on Russia 121–122;
economic instability 35; economic
interests 97; economic miracle 35;
energy policy 88; energy security 88;
foreign policy 34; foreign policy makers
29; genocide 35; industrial competitors
of 97; International Relations scholars
36–37; material and economic
reconstruction 35; narratives 88; national
identity 25, 34, 36; official discourse
60–61; Ostpolitik cooperative approach
60–65; Ostpolitik tradition 63; Others
for 24; policy of diplomatic engagement
66; protracted crisis 65–67
German identity 121–123; discourses
37–39, **54**; historic construction
of 34–37
German–Russian dialogue 73
German–Russian energy cooperation 126
globalisation 6
global politics 17
Gorbachev, M. 21, 38–39
G7 summit in Germany 65
Guibernau, M. 6–7

Halbwachs, M. 8
Havel, V. 14
Hegel, G.W.F. 19, 22
Helsinki 49, 52, 112
Helsinki Final Act 48, 74–75
Herman, R. 20–21
heroism 52
Hobsbawm, E. 5, 7–8
Hollande, F. 59–60
Hopf, T. 21–22
humanitarian crisis 1
human rights 3, 115; deterioration of 39;
primacy of 105
Hungary 86
Hussein, S. 20
Hutchinson, J. 7
Huyssen, A. 8
hybrid war 1, 73, 94, 99, 126

identity: concept of 19; conceptualisation
of 4, 17, 22; in constructivist research

19–22; discourse-historical analysis
24–27; discursive relationship 23–24;
and international relations theory 17–18;
narratives 93; politics of 17; selection of
case studies 27–30; state leaders' public
statements as primary sources 30–32
imagined communities 7
immigration 6
individual memory 8
institutional cooperation, neorealist
theorisations of 17
interdiscursivity 27
international disputes 105
international humanitarian 115
international law 74
international politics: domestic
construction of 5; static view of 18
international relations 15, 17–19, 120
international solidarity 52
intertextuality 27
Iranian nuclear programme 2
Isis terror attacks in Paris 106
Italy 2, 28–29, 84–85, 97, 103–104, 111,
116; energy security 85

Kaczynski, L. 44–46, 91, 110
Katyn massacre 44–45
Katzenstein, Peter 20
Kekkonen, U. 48
Kerch strait 60, 67
Kern, C. 90
Kertzer, D.J. 8
Kohl, H. 39
Komorowski, B. 71
Kopacz 71–72
Kornprobst, M. 20
Kremlin 87, 102, 115, 128
Kultura's foreign policy ideas 42–43
Kundera, M 13; views on Russia 13–14

Lavrov, S. 64
Lebow, R.N. 20–22
legality 64
Libya 65, 102–104, 106
Lipponen, P. 94
liquefied natural gas (LNG) 84
literary theory 19
LNG *see* liquefied natural gas (LNG)
longue durée approach 34
longue durée national identity
formation 53

Maas, H. 66–67, 88–90, 107–108
Mandelson, P. 3

marginality 12, 46–47, 50, 52, 54
martyrdom discourse 44
mass media 9, 11
material power 22
May, Theresa 85
media, privileged access to 5
Medvedev, D. 44, 102
memory 118; collective 7–8, 15; national
   see national memory; politics of 8–11;
   realms of 9; shared 8
Merkel, A. 59–61, 63–64, 67, 89–90, 93,
   105–107
Mickiewicz, A. 41
Middle East 109, 113; analysis of alliances
   in 21; developments in 1; military
   entanglements in 103
Miller, David 7–8
Minsk-2 agreement 56, 61, 63–64, 67,
   76, 125
Minsk negotiations 63–64
Mitzen, J. 20
modern philosophy 19
Molotov–Ribbentrop pact 45, 73
Morawiecki, M. 73, 93–94, 110–111
Morozov, V. 11
Moscow's energy projects 17
multilateralism 52, 64, 105
Munich Security Conference in February
   2007 56

nation 15; concepts of 5, 7; definition of 5,
   7; emergence of 8; nature of 6
national discourses 118–121
national discursive arenas, selection
   of 27–30
national foreign policy 4
national formation, process of 24
national history 9; 'usable past' in 10
national identity 3, 5, 8–9, 15, 23–24, 118,
   120, 123; and collective memory 5–8;
   conceptions of 10; concepts of 5;
   constitutive relationship among 4;
   construction 10, 28; definition of 5, 7;
   discourses 11, 47; driving factor of 10; in
   foreign policy making 18; and foreign
   policy narratives 24; formation of 8–9, 11,
   19, 25; language and discourses roles in
   18; model *23*; narratives of 10, 53; notion
   of 5; politics of 8–11; variations in 20
national interests 19
nationalism 4, 6–7; product of 7
national memory 9, 19; construction and
   diffusion of 9; discourses 10; reference
   to events 9; selected events in 9

national policy makers' discourses 30
Nazi crimes 38
neoliberalism 17
neoliberals 17–18
neorealism 17–18
Neumann, I. 11, 22, 28, 127
neutral pragmatism 30
newspapers 30
Niinistö, S. 75–76, 78, 95, 113–114
Nora, P. 9
Nordic identity 48–49
Nord Stream 2, 31–32, 98, 126; Austria
   stance on 84; cautious approach to 86;
   as commercial project 94; construction
   of 87; criticism of 93; debate 86,
   125–127; dispute 87, 96–98; Finnish
   government on 96; Finnish stance on 96;
   German defence of 90–91; German
   leaders towards 97; Poland's opposition
   to 97; project 82–89; security debate on
   95; US sanctions against 90

Obama, B. 57, 103, 113
ontological security 20
Orban, V. 86
Ostpolitik 38–39, 124; approach 39, 62;
   discourse 53, 122; framing of 88; logic
   of 66, 126; tradition with Russia 84
othering 72, 74, 129
otherness 19

Paasikivi, J. 47
perspectivation 27
policy decisions 18
policy makers' speeches 30–32
Polish discourse 71, 111–115; Civic
   Platform discourses in 2015 70–72; on
   heroism 42; law and justice and Russian
   Other 72–74; 'Russian threat' in 68;
   sanctions and security 69–70
Polish–German relations 43
Polish identity 121–123; construction of
   40; discourses **54**; historic construction
   of 40–43; nemesis 43–46
Polish/Poland 2, 29, 86, 118; attacks by
   Nazi Germany 42; complexity and
   multiplicity of 74; consequences for
   97–98; culture and language 41;
   diplomacy 111; energy security 91;
   ethnonationalism 41; focus on 'Eastern
   flank' 108–111; foreign policy 44, 102;
   foreign, security and energy policy 93;
   nationalism 41; heroism 43; identity
   discourses 43; intellectuals 40;

international self-image of 42; national
identity 24–25, 40, 52; Nord Stream 2,
91–94; official discourse 69; official
discourses on Russia 125; perceptions of
Germany and Russia 41; political
pressure from Russia 92; refugee status
in 110; relations with Russia 72;
relocation of asylum seekers 109
Polish–Russian agreement 24
Polish–Russian relations 45, 72
Polish Self 109
Polish–Soviet war of 1920 43–44
political communities 7
political elites 8, 118
political interference 89
political threat, perception of 13
positive othering 22
power relations 24–25
pragmatism 77
pragmatism in foreign policy 47
psychology 19
public education 11
Putin, V. 39, 45, 56–57, 65, 74, 86,
102, 113

radicalisation of negative discourses 50
reunification 39
Ringmar, E. 20
Risse-Kappen, T. 21
Romania 86
Russian–Georgian War 17, 57
Russian Other 34; analysis of 22;
constructions of 2, 82, 86; critical
conceptualisation of 86; European
discourse on 128–129; in German
discourses 37–39; Law and Justice
72–74; multifaceted conceptualisation of
119; negative images of 81; perceptions
of 56; in Polish discourse 108
Russian–Turkish rapprochement 114
Russian–Ukrainian disagreements 65
Russian–Ukrainian gas crises 83
Russia/Russian 1, 19, 31–32, 40; actions in
Ukraine 69; aggressive stance against
Ukraine 73; ambivalent representations
of 127; anti-terrorism cooperation with
110; authoritarian developments and
foreign policy 39; bilateral relations
with 85; bombing campaign 59–60, 101,
106; border control crisis 113;
controversial actions in Syria 108;
cooperative relationship with 63–64;
crisis in 12; dealing with European
countries 4; discourses on 11, 17;

domestic and foreign policy 26;
domestic developments 39; dominant
constructions of 123; economic
sanctions on 63; energy power 24;
energy projects 91; estrangement from
Europe 77; European approaches to 17;
European depictions of 12, European
discursive constructions of 22; European
perceptions of 13–14; European Union
(EU) and 1; exclusion 76; foreign policy
2, 45, 119; geopolitical goals 126;
German perceptions of 37; historical
interactions with 28–29; historical
involvement with 28; human rights
violations 101; identity 11–12, 82;
imperialism 70; interfering in Western
democratic processes 1; intervention in
Syria 104; MENA policy 101–102;
military intervention in Syria 1, 101,
103, 105–106; military power 123;
national discourses on 3, 24; national
foreign policy approaches to 3; national
identity 26–28, 53; negative discourses
on 38; nuclear energy 96; Ostpolitik
approach to 64; Partnership and
Cooperation Agreement 45; Polish
official discourses about 45; political
developments in 2, 118; racial
arguments against 14; radicalisation of
discourses on 119–120; relations with 4;
role as negative Other 22; sanctions on
61, 69, 110; sectoral sanctions on 58,
77; socialism in 39; subalternity and
marginality 12; threat in Polish
discourse 68; violations of international
law 61–62, 76, 119
Russification: campaigns 47; policies of 53

Schetyna, G. 70–72
Schröder, G. 39
Self/Other dichotomy 20
shared memories 8
Sikorski, R. 68–69, 91
Sipilä, J. 94–95, 112, 114
Skripal poisoning 67
Slovakia 83, 86
Smith, A.D. 5–8
Smolensk plane crash 91
social constructivism 17
social interaction, language use in 24–25
socialism 44
Soini, T. 76, 78–79, 95, 113–114
sovereignty 7; fundamental principles
of 75

Soviet foreign policy 20–21
Soviet political culture 21
Soviet Union 12–13; criticism of 51; troops on German soil 38
Spohn, W. 2
state, concepts of 6
state interests: formulation of 18; radical reconceptualisation of 21
state leaders' public statements 30–32
Steinmeier, F.W. 60–61, 63–66, 87–88, 106
strategic energy projects 86
Sweden, Northern War against 12
Syrian crisis 101, 127–128; Finnish debate on 112; German discourses 105–108; Russia and EU from Arab Spring 101–104; Russia military intervention in 1
Syria/Syrian 31–32; chemical stockpiles 103; civil war 59, 105; conflict 65, 105, 109; federalisation of 104; international negotiations on 113; Isis terrorists in 108; Russia intervention in 104; Russia military intervention in 101; Russian bombing campaign in 107; Russian campaign in 111; Russia's military intervention in 103, 106
Szydlo, B. 68, 92, 109–110
Szymanski, K. 73, 92

totalitarian 13–14
traditions 7
Trump, D. 74
Tsarist domination 43
Tsarist Empire 50
Tsarist political system 37
Tuomioja, E. 75, 78
Turkey 19
Tusk, Donald 45, 53, 68–70

Ukraine 31–32, 42, 72, 110; beginning of turmoil in 4; conflict 1, 60–61, 75, 79; conflict in 59; crisis in 12; destabilisation of 46, 58; economic and strategic interests 89; gas transit in 90; Moscow's aggressive policies in 91; Polish conceptualisation of 97; Polish empathy and criticism of 73; political and military crisis in 56; pragmatism and isolation of 76–79; protests and demonstrations in 58; Russian actions in 58, 69; Russian policies in 65; territorial integrity 68
Ukraine crisis 1–4, 60, 63, 66, 72, 74, 79, 82, 85, 112, 119, 123–125; aftermath of 101; and energy trade 73; and EU–Russia relations 56–60
UN *see* United Nations (UN)
United Kingdom 42, 85
United Nations (UN): peacekeeping force 65; peacekeeping mission 66
United Nations Security Council Resolution 1973 102
United States 87; foreign policy 19; interference in European energy policy 87; and Russian negotiations 59, 113

Vajda, M. 14
Van Dijk, T. 26
Versailles system 38
von Haxthausen, A. 37

Waever, O. 20
Warsaw 98, 110; change of leadership in 70; politics of memory 72; strategic arguments 97
Warsaw Pact 40
Warsaw Rising Museum 42
Waszczykowski, W. 68, 72–73, 92–93, 109–111
Weber, M. 6
Wendt, A. 19, 22; theoretical framework 20
Western democratic processes 1
West Germany 35; foreign policy towards Soviet Union 37; identity and foreign policy 35; Ostpolitik approach 37
Winter, J. 9
Wodak, R. 4, 25

Yalta conference in 1945 42
Yanukovych, V. 57, 68
Yeltsin, B. 44–45
Yugoslavia 1999 bombing of 102

Zehfuss, M. 22
Zelensky, V. 60

Made in the USA
Columbia, SC
27 May 2023

17375786R00098